The Failure of
South African Expansion

THE SWAZI DEPUTATION: SOBHUZA & COUNSELLORS, LONDON, JANUARY 1923
(From left to right: Benjamin Nxumalo, Mandanda Mtetwa, Amos Zwane, Sobhuza II, Loshini Hlope,
Suduka Dhlamini, [unidentified], Dr. Seme)

The Failure of
South African
Expansion
1908 – 1948

Ronald Hyam

Africana Publishing Corporation · New York

*Published
in the United States of America 1972
by Africana Publishing Corporation
101 Fifth Avenue
New York, N.Y. 10003*

© Ronald Hyam 1972

Library of Congress catalog card no. 72–88093
ISBN 0–8419–0129–5

Printed in Great Britain

TO

NICHOLAS MANSERGH

Master of St John's College, Cambridge,
and Emeritus Smuts Professor of the
History of the British Commonwealth

Contents

List of Maps and Illustrations

Thanks are due to Mr William Barnes, Mr S. B. Williams,
Mr D. R. Cowling, *The Cape Times* and Vandyk for permission
to reproduce photographic material.

Preface

My thanks are due: to Her Majesty's Government for relaxing first the fifty-year rule and then the thirty-year rule – decisions which have made available all the relevant British official documents to the end of 1946; to the Public Record Office for coping with the release of these documents; to the Cambridge History Faculty and the Master and Fellows of Magdalene College for sabbatical leave; and to the Managers of the Smuts Memorial Fund for financing my research and travel in the Republic of South Africa, Swaziland, Lesotho and Mozambique. I should also like to thank the Rector of the Usuthu Mission, together with Fr Neil Bliss, the Headmaster, staff and boys of St Christopher's High School, Swaziland, for their friendly hospitality – and Mr Derek Cowling, who introduced me to them; Professor John Blake for facilitating matters in Lesotho; and Professor Noel Garson for indispensable advice in a variety of ways. My colleague Mr Ged Martin has eased my burdens and tried to keep me up to the mark. I alone am responsible for the result.

I am conscious of the incompleteness of what follows. A more comprehensive and balanced study cannot however be made for many years yet. The subject seems to me sufficiently important to justify an interim account, and I am grateful to my publishers for supporting this view.

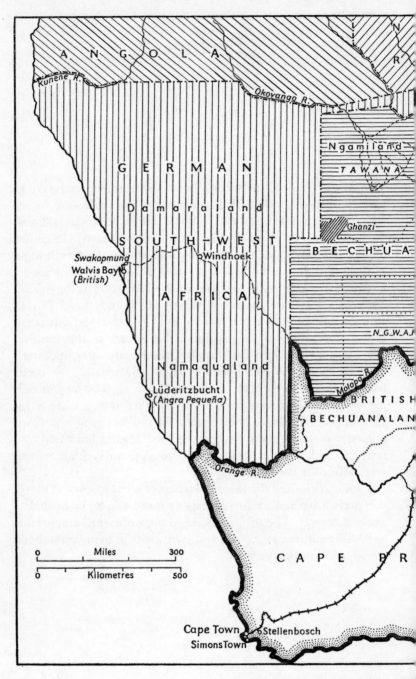

I. SOUTHE

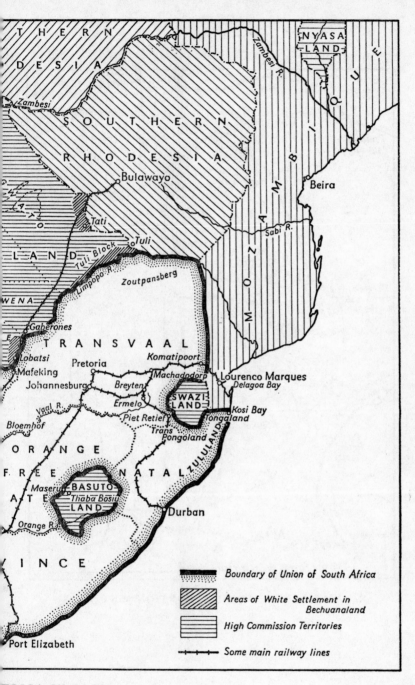

THERN
DESIA

Zambesi

SOUTHERN

RHODESIA

Bulawayo

Tati

Tuli Block
Tuli

Limpopo R.

Zoutpansberg

Zambesi R.

NYASA
LAND

M
O
Z
A
M
B
I
Q
U
E

Beira

Sabi R.

L A N D

WENA

Gaberones

Lobatsi

TRANSVAAL

Komatipoort

Mafeking   Pretoria

Johannesburg   Breyten

Machadodorp

Lourenco Marques
Delagoa Bay

Vaal R.

Bloemhof

Ermelo

Piet Retief

SWAZI-
LAND

Kosi Bay
Tongaland

ORANGE

FREE

ATE

Trans
Pongoland

NATAL

ZULULAND

Maseru
Thaba Bosiu

BASUTO
LAND

Orange R.

Durban

VINCE

Port Elizabeth

━━━━━ Boundary of Union of South Africa

▨▨▨▨ Areas of White Settlement in
         Bechuanaland

▤▤▤▤ High Commission Territories

—+—+—+— Some main railway lines

FRICA IN 1910

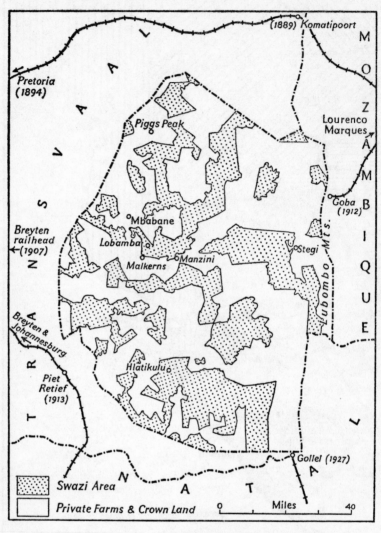

Swazi Area

Private Farms & Crown Land

0   Miles   40

2. SWAZILAND — LAND APPORTIONMENT 1907

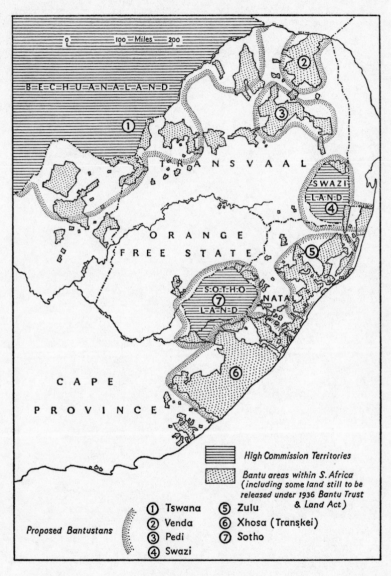

Scale: 0 — 100 — Miles — 200

BECHUANALAND

TRANSVAAL

SWAZILAND

ORANGE FREE STATE

NATAL

SOTHOLAND

CAPE PROVINCE

	High Commission Territories
	Bantu areas within S. Africa (including some land still to be released under 1936 Bantu Trust & Land Act)

Proposed Bantustans

① Tswana ⑤ Zulu
② Venda ⑥ Xhosa (Transkei)
③ Pedi ⑦ Sotho
④ Swazi

3. TOMLINSON COMMISSION'S PROPOSED CONSOLIDATION
OF BANTU AREAS, 1954

1 Prologue: to 1910

'I AM not sure', declared General Jan Smuts in 1917, '. . . whether in the distant future the South Africa Act will not be remembered as much for its appendix as for its principal contents.'[1] This book is in part an exploration of one possible implication in that forecast. The Union of South Africa established in 1910 was in effect a provisional one, bringing together Cape Colony, the Transvaal, the Orange Free State and Natal, and the Schedule appended to the Act of Union (1909) dealt with three further territories which it was hoped one day to include – Basutoland (Lesotho), the Bechuanaland Protectorate (Botswana) and Swaziland. These were known as the High Commission Territories, or 'the Protectorates' as they were often called incorrectly. At about the time when Union was established, General Louis Botha, its first prime minister, stated repeatedly his conviction that it would never be complete until Rhodesia and the High Commission Territories had been included.[2]

The expansion of South Africa thus sustained a setback from its inception. In 1931 Smuts' political lieutenant, J. H. Hofmeyr,* wrote in his book *South Africa* of a 'lack of finality in the determination of boundaries which leaves outside the Union territories, the ultimate incorporation of which the logic of facts seems to point compellingly'.[3] The British government in London likewise looked to the attainment of an old dream – a great white loyalist Dominion stretching all the way from the Cape to the Zambesi and possibly beyond. With these vague

* J. H. Hofmeyr: minister of education, etc., 1933–38, 1940–48, boy prodigy, deputy prime minister and subject of a brilliant biography by Alan Paton: *Hofmeyr* (Cape Town 1964).

hopes of a continental manifest destiny floating around, there
was provision in the Act of Union for the facultative incorporation of Southern Rhodesia, and the Schedule prescribed terms
for the transfer of the High Commission Territories. The
ultimate desirability of completing the Union in this way was
almost unquestioned in Britain in 1910: it was largely a
question of time. The Act of Union, declared Lord Crewe
(colonial secretary 1908–10), seemed to place the self-governing
Dominions of the Crown in 'something like their final form': a
great American group, a great Pacific group and a great
African group.[4] Lewis Harcourt (colonial secretary 1910–15)
found it not unreasonable to contemplate the ultimate absorption of the West Indies and Newfoundland by Canada, of the
Pacific Islands by Australia and New Zealand, and of the
Rhodesias, Basutoland, Bechuanaland, Swaziland and even
Nyasaland, by South Africa: in short, a general tidying up of the
constitutional structure of the Empire.[5] During the First
World War Britain found Smuts' local war aims by no means
incompatible with her own, and would have been quite happy
to see him realise his objectives in South-West Africa and
Mozambique.

And yet with the single partial exception of South-West
Africa, South Africa failed not only to complete its provisional
union by the officially anticipated extensions, but also its
further programme of expansion outside British controlled
areas. Within fifteen years of Union, the future of Southern
Rhodesia was decided in an alternative direction. Nearly
continuous South African pressure to take over the High
Commission Territories was frustrated. A period of thirty years
passed, and then slid into half a century. 'The great grey-green,
greasy Limpopo River' remained the boundary of the Republic
of South Africa established in 1961.

This study is an attempt to explain the failure of South
Africa to complete and extend its provisional area, to turn
widespread expectations and expansive ambitions into the
reality of a 'Greater South Africa'.

In using the word failure, it must be made clear that it is
simply South Africa's formal territorial expansion which is

under investigation. This study does not enquire into the subtler process of extending an intricate network of informal influences in the trans-Zambesi hinterland through trade and diplomacy, through the work of South African financiers, engineers and artisans on the Copperbelt, of the farmers in Kenya, the administrators in Tanganyika, the missionaries of the Dutch Reformed Church in Nyasaland, or more recently the quasi-Peace Corps efforts of Stellenbosch medical students or the financial, diplomatic and trading agreements with Malawi. South African born, or South African trained, doctors, teachers, lawyers and civil servants are today spread through half-a-dozen neighbouring countries.

And although the total planning of formal expansion throughout southern Africa has to be kept in view, the emphasis here is upon the areas of former British control: upon Southern Rhodesia and the three High Commission Territories. All these countries after 1910 came under the British high commissioner for South Africa, and in the Colonial Office they were dealt with by the Dominions Department, where they had been placed during the re-organisation of 1907. From the end of 1925 they became the responsibility of the new Dominions Office, which became the Commonwealth Relations Office in 1947.

The theme of this book is certainly not lacking in importance. Southern Rhodesia's subsequent history of Central African Federation and U.D.I. is a direct legacy of its 1922 decision not to enter the Union. The future of the High Commission Territories alone had become by the 1930s second only to Ireland as the major Dominions Office headache in Commonwealth relations, and none was more puzzling. As even *The Round Table* commentator was eventually forced to admit, the question of their possible transfer was 'one of the really intractable problems which occasionally arise in human affairs. There does not seem any adequate answer to the strong case which can be put up by each side': to South Africa's claim and Britain's refusal. The refusal was no more wilfully obstinate than the acquisitiveness wholly unwarranted. For South Africa, as Leader of the Opposition Mr J. G. N. Strauss remarked in 1954,

it was 'one of the major questions in our public life' and 'one of
the most intractable human problems that South African
statesmen have ever had to face.' He also pointed out that the
public unanimity with which all three parties – successive South
African and British governments and African leaders –
approached the problem made it one of immense difficulty,
delicacy and complexity.[6] The combined total population of the
three Territories probably did not exceed a million for most of
the period under discussion. For these people, of course, the
most fundamental political questions which face any community were involved. From the imperial point of view, owing
to their geographical position and the political interest generated
by the transfer issue, the Territories were more in the limelight
and received more attention than their intrinsic importance in
the Empire would otherwise have secured for them. In particular
there was no part of the Empire in the twentieth century which
had such a series of distinguished high commissioners.* And
since South Africa remains the chief bastion of white supremacy,
which is, in structure and ideas, the antithesis of independent
black Africa, the record of its past attempts to expand its
frontiers is of contemporary as well as of historical significance.
At a time when that supremacy seems so deeply entrenched it is
worth noting that Afrikanerdom has not had everything its
own way.

What was the history and situation of the six southern African
territories not included in the Union in 1910? It may be
sketched briefly.

* The high commissioners were as follows:
    Viscount Gladstone, 31 May 1910–17 July 1914
    Viscount Buxton, 8 Sep 1914–17 July 1920
    Prince Arthur of Connaught, 20 Nov 1920–5 Dec 1923
    Earl of Athlone, 21 Jan 1924–21 Dec 1930
    Sir Herbert Stanley, 6 Apr 1931–6 Jan 1935
    Sir William Clark, 7 Jan 1935–3 Jan 1940
    Lord Harlech, 24 May 1941–13 May 1944
    Sir Walter Huggard, 23 Jun 1944–27 Oct 1944 (also acting high com-
       missioner, 1940–41
    Sir Evelyn Baring, 27 Oct 1944–1 Oct 1951
    Sir John le Rougetel, 2 Oct 1951–2 Feb 1955
    Sir Percivale Liesching, 4 Mar 1955–1958

Broadly speaking, the whole settlement pattern of black and white in southern Africa was determined in the 1840s by the interaction between the Boer Great Trek and the even greater Bantu diaspora or *Mfecane*. The area of contact and conflict between black and white, both restless pastoral peoples, was immensely widened. The Voortrekkers outflanked the Bantu and caused a dynamically evolving African situation to solidify artificially. The abrupt crystallisation of the settlement pattern was, on the whole, decidedly to the advantages of the whites. Where it was not, the Boers expended considerable energy in the next few decades in making it so. The result was that the main two trekkers' republics, the Transvaal (or South African Republic)* and the Orange Free State, occupied fertile lands temporarily vacated by the Bantu migrations.[7] These Boer states then held at bay, or encroached upon, the African communities which were scattered around their perimeter. In some places these communities were unnaturally crowded. Looked at from the inside of the *laager*, the frontier of white settlement was shaped rather like a horseshoe.† This horseshoe, especially after the British had annexed Natal, precluded, or at least made difficult, Boer access to the sea, and it was indeed to prevent this that Natal had been put under the Union Jack.

The Boers were thus hemmed in particularly by the Tswana to the north-west, the Swazi and the Zulu to the east, the Southern Sotho and the British to the south-east. Among the African states which escaped the clutches of settler rule and became High Commission Territories under British control, Swaziland, with the largest European element, was of central significance, though paradoxically its population was, and still is the smallest of any state in southern Africa. Its history is peculiar. It has the eternal distinction of being almost the last of British African territories to achieve independence, while for thirty years if Britain had jettisoned any of the three High Commission Territories (the better to safeguard the others) it would have been Swaziland. All competent observers from the

* Throughout this chapter, for clarity I refer to the 'Transvaal', even though at some points 'South African Republic' would be more correct.

† See Map, p. xiii.

1890s onwards have seen it as the hub and microcosm of
southern African problems.[8]

Despite their uncomfortable closeness to the storm centre of
the Zulu dispersion initiated by Shaka, the Swazi held together
through the tough homogeneity of their tribal structure. From
the mid-nineteenth century however they were increasingly
subjected to an influx of Boers in search of winter grazing.
Concessions to Europeans were inaugurated by King Mswati
(1840–68). King Mbandzeni (1874–89), carried the process to
extremes. The Victorian stereotype branded him as an irresponsible ruler, seated on a gin-case, drinking champagne and
musing over his plump women and lean greyhounds. Although
he rather dolefully accepted the cash, gifts and flatteries of those
who sought concessions from him, Mbandzeni was however by
no means entirely blind to what was going on, or incapable of
double dealing when confronted with rival competitors for
concessions. Often it was he who did the fooling. He is reported
to have said in defence of his prodigality in granting concessions:
'I have white men all around me. By force they have taken the
countries of all my neighbours. If I do not give them rights here,
they will take them. Therefore I give when they pay. Why
should we not eat before we die?' He insisted upon an invariable
saving clause for the rights of his people, but he did not realise
that a concession would diminish Swazi rights to concurrent
use of conceded land, and the results were disastrous. The Swazi
came to speak of the 'documents that killed us'. Besides loss of
virtually all the land, there were concessions for mining, tanning
and minting, for collecting customs and importing machinery,
for oil and tobacco, for the right to establish everything from
glassworks to pawnbrokers', from soda-water factories to
orphanages, the right to hold auctions and sweepstakes, to take
photographs and set up billiard tables and law courts.[9]

Europeans began to settle in Swaziland in the 1880s, a fact
which increasingly made treaty guarantees of its independence
(1881, 1884) less realistic. In the middle years of the decade
Mbandzeni refused to pay the cost of a British Agent, and was
thus left to deal with the eruption of the Europeans on his own.
On the other hand, it seems he would rather have welcomed a

full British protectorate. This idea did not appeal to the British government, since they believed such a thing to be legally impossible, politically undesirable and geographically impracticable: and this because it would require the consent of the Transvaal, involve a charge on the British taxpayer, and mean responsibility for a completely inaccessible country. As Swaziland was surrounded by the Transvaal on three sides and by the Lubombo mountains bordering on Mozambique on the other, 'we should be', wrote Sir Hercules Robinson (high commissioner 1881–89, 1895–97), 'in the position of a man burdened with a property to which he had no right of way'. In 1892 Lord Ripon (the Liberal colonial secretary 1892–95) decided against annexation chiefly on the ground that owing to concessions held mainly by the Transvaal, a British administration would have 'rights of government but no power of taxation'.[10] This was doubtless a specious argument, and less real than the desire not to renew anti-British feeling in the Transvaal. The local balance of forces clearly favoured a Boer solution to the problem of Swaziland. The British did not want to fight and in any case could see no way of getting troops in. The steady penetration of Transvaal influence in Swaziland compelled Britain to give some recognition to President Kruger's claims unless she chose to oppose them by force, which was further inadvisable as South African opinion generally favoured acquisition by the Transvaal. In any case, Britain thought the Swazi would be better off under the Transvaal than under a set of seedy adventurers.[11]

A convention of 1890 provided for a species of condominium, a joint government between Britain and the Transvaal over Europeans in Swaziland. In the hopes of obtaining a road through Swaziland to the sea, Kruger surrendered all his claims beyond the Limpopo. Dual government did not work smoothly, and so a second convention was negotiated in 1893 providing for the transfer of administration to the Transvaal subject to Swazi consent. This the Swazi would not give so long as they felt there was the slightest chance of achieving a purely British protectorate. Britain then seemed to be faced with the choice of either yielding the condition of Swazi consent or

watching the country drift into anarchy. She chose the former
course, embodying it in the third convention of 1894. Ripon
agreed to it since it was still the case that the Transvaal could
legally paralyse any government but its own, and since he was
able to insert conditions maintaining Swazi interests. These
embraced security to the king for his revenue and inheritance,
to the nation for their grazing and agricultural rights, and the
exercise of their own laws and customs in matters concerning
themselves. Ripon expressly precluded incorporation of the
country in the Transvaal. This arrangement of 1894 was still
within the general principle of joint action over Swaziland.
Ripon knew full well that the Swazi would have preferred to be
annexed by Britain, but British treaty obligations to the
Transvaal precluded this. He was not disposed to take much
notice of public protest by philanthropists and chambers of
commerce in England about 'handing over the Swazis to the
Boers' knowing 'how much they are manufactured', but 'in the
case of a Swazi war they would count against us'. He feared the
Swazi might fight the Boers, but he would not support them in
such a war since he believed 'Swaziland by "manifest destiny"
must ultimately go to the Transvaal'.[12]

Ripon made sure this concession would not result in independent Transvaal access to the sea at Kosi Bay: a few months
later he annexed Trans-Pongoland and Tongaland. Kruger's
interest in Swaziland now folded up. It was nothing to him
except a way to the sea and that was now closed. It was
axiomatic for Britain to check this urge. Once the Transvaal
could enter the family of nations in the full dignity of an
independent maritime state with its own port and flying its own
flag on the ocean it would be much better placed to seek
foreign, and especially German, support in evading the imperial
design of pushing it into a South African federation. (This
policy might equally have been frustrated by the friction which
a British protectorate of Swaziland might engender.) There was
also the consideration for Britain that the east-coast Cape route
to India must be protected.[13]

The British government acquired responsibility for Swaziland
after conquest of the Transvaal in the Anglo-Boer War. From

1903 to 1906 it was placed under the British governor of the Transvaal, and thereafter under the high commissioner. Lord Elgin (colonial secretary 1905–8) steadfastly refused in 1906 to hand it back to the Transvaal, intending this stand to be 'a very effective demonstration of sympathy' for African interests and to meet the lively public demand for some recognition of them, which it was impossible to ignore.[14] Hence the declaration: 'pending any grant of representation to the natives, no territory administered by the Governor or High Commissioner will be placed under the control of the new Responsible Government of the Transvaal'.

Meanwhile Lord Milner (high commissioner 1897–1905), as governor of the Transvaal had inaugurated the 'cleaning of this Augean stable' – the disentangling of overlapping concessions which contained every prospect of friction and trouble for everyone involved. Under his successor Lord Selborne (high commissioner 1905–10), this resulted in 1907 in a decision to cut the Gordian knot and make an arbitrary and compulsory partition. One-third of the land was restored and reserved to the Swazi. The concessionaires held the rest. Their leaseholds were converted to freehold to compensate them for their partial expropriation. Selborne described the implementation of the settlement as the most 'tiresome and intricate piece of administrative work' in the history of the Empire. It was not completed until 1914. The Swazi were not consulted, and were aghast. The land reserved to them, in more than thirty areas, was no doubt technically adequate for their present and future requirements. The Colonial Office took the line that rough justice was all the Swazi deserved, having only themselves, and a drunken, greedy and gullible royal family, 'about the most worthless in all Africa', to blame. Although they felt the settlement was not substantially unjust, the apportionment could easily be criticised, and it was – by the Aborigines Protection Society. Two-thirds of Swaziland henceforth belonged to 500 concessionaires, the majority of whom were absentee landlords.[15] Although Elgin was honourably exempted, after 1907 a general distrust of Europeans was engendered, long to remain influential in Swazi policy.[16]

The creation and epic survival of Basutoland[17] owed everything to the genius of King Moshweshwe (c. 1786–1870). He possessed the singleness of purpose, and preserved a sufficiency of cattle wealth, to enable him to build a nation from many different tribes and refugees, and preserve it from destruction through many complex troubles such as internal fission and external attack from both black and white. Making the most of the advantages of his mountain stronghold, he encouraged his people to breed their own pony and convert themselves into mounted gunmen. His use of ambassadors and his personal skill in finding the right words for diplomacy were justly famed, and he sought British protection c. 1867 saying, 'My country is your blanket, O Queen, and my people the lice on it.' At this time the Sotho were at their last gasp in a war over land with Boers of the Orange Free State, the Boers having already established themselves in fertile Sotho lands west of the Caledon river. The remainder of the country was saved from annihilation by a British protectorate declared by high commissioner Sir Philip Wodehouse in 1868. Moshweshwe died in 1870, and if Britain had not been in charge at this juncture ('folded in the arms of the Queen', as Moshweshwe put it), civil war would have had full and permanent sway. Basutoland at this critical moment was saved by the British, but the basic elements in its survival had been Moshweshwe, the Maloti mountains and the missionaries. The Paris Evangelical Society was on the scene early (1833), backing and advising Moshweshwe at his invitation, sharing and consolidating the national life of the people. Wodehouse argued that wartime famine in the country might lead to raids endangering the whole of South Africa, though he also had a 'sentimental sympathy' with the Sotho in their troubles. The British government assumed the protectorate reluctantly, vaguely hoping it might contribute to containing Boer expansion seawards.

In 1871 the new self-governing regime at the Cape was made to look after Basutoland, and from 1879 it burned its fingers badly by trying to disarm the whole country. The resultant Gun War concealed internal civil war, and was sparked off by natural disasters, but there was an underlying deep sense of humiliation: 'Disarmament to us is as if we were being disgraced in our own eyes and in the eyes of all our neighbours'; and it acquired a good deal of momentum from the fact that assegais were proscribed as well as the much-loved guns.[18] The British decision in 1883 once more to rescue Basutoland, again confirmed its territorial unity, but as de Kiewiet observes, 'no measure so unquestionably beneficial and merciful was ever undertaken so glumly'. The British government expressly said it accepted 'no permanent responsibility for the affairs of this part of Africa'.[19] Britain hoped that taking Basutoland back and relieving the Cape would improve relations with the latter, which might be persuaded to show its gratitude in willingness to exercise some responsibility in southern Bechuanaland. At all events, Basutoland was lucky to secure a protectorate at a time when the government refused to sanction one for Bechuanaland or accept Australian calls for annexation in New Guinea, and at a time when British involvement in the Egyptian imbroglio was deepening.[20]

Unlike Swaziland and Basutoland, Bechuanaland was composed not of one tribe but of eight, of whom the largest was the Ngwato, occupying about one-third of the area, and it was the personality of the great Ngwato ruler, Kgama III (c. 1838–1923) which dominated the whole of Tswana history.[21] Even Lord Lugard, with his commitment to Nigerians, described him as the most enlightened and capable African chief he had ever met. Having been converted to Christianity, Kgama finally established himself as chief in 1875, though not without a difficult struggle. He abolished initiation ceremonies, rain-making and polygamy, but his proudest reform was the introduction of total prohibition. 'There are', he declared, 'three things which distress me very much – war, selling people and drink. All these things I shall find in the Boers' – and such things, he added, destroyed peoples. He saw the advantage of coming to some accommodation with European intruders while denying them mining grants, and he reckoned that it would be better to throw in his lot with the British rather than the Boers. Unlike his Ndebele neighbours he studiously avoided a passage of arms with the Europeans: 'Lobengula derided me as a fool

and a coward. He likened me to a dog licking the Great Queen's
hand. But where is Lobengula today with his mighty *impis*?'
Nevertheless the British government was extremely reluctant to
take over Tswana tribes. It tried in the early 1880s to work
within a spirit and framework defined by Gladstone's colonial
secretary Lord Derby: 'Bechuanaland is of no value to us
. . . for any Imperial purposes . . . it is of no consequence to
us whether Boers or Native Chiefs are in possession'; moreoever,
'I don't want more niggers'.[22] It might be necessary for the
imperial government to control Zulu or Sotho uprisings, or
manipulate the Swazi in a policy of conciliating the Boers, but
as yet Bechuanaland was a matter indifferent. Transvaalers
threatened to encroach on Tswana lands. If they were to be
kept out, Britain hoped the Cape would co-operate in the task.
The Cape's refusal was adamant, largely because its politicians
did not wish to upset the Transvaal. Gladstone was inclined to
think Britain could not ignore Bechuanaland in the face of the
inclination of the chiefs, and there was also a considerable public
interest in trade and mission activities in the land. But he did
not act.

The whole question of the future of Bechuanaland was
precipitated by the declaration of a German protectorate over
Damara-Namaqualand in 1884. Bechuanaland suddenly attained vital importance as the buffer between the hinterland of
German South-West Africa and the Transvaal Republic. A
Liberal government nearing the end of a stormy period of
office could not afford to take chances. It seemed possible
that colonial expansion might be shut out from the north,
imperial encirclement of the Transvaal be breached and
German influence extended far inland. Having accepted
Germany in South-West Africa, the British sought to propitiate
the Cape and strengthen British supremacy against further
German or Transvaal expansion by occupying southern
Bechuanaland, thus securing the north road for the Cape –
Cecil Rhodes' 'Suez Canal to the interior' – and checking
foreigners and filibusters. The protectorate of 1885 was
primarily a precautionary measure against a fear of Germany
which was quickly dissipated: the answer to a suspected

German–Transvaal conspiracy to establish a hegemony over South Africa.

It was intended eventually to entrust Bechuanaland to the British South Africa Company and thus link it with Rhodesia, but the Company blotted its copybook in the mid-1890s over the Jameson Raid and the Ndebele war and rebellion. Four Tswana chiefs had meanwhile visited England in 1895 to protest against transfer to Company rule. No action was therefore taken to extend Company control.[23]

In each of these countries there was a threat to British authority and African interests stemming from the moving pastoral Boer frontier. Trekking patently revived in the 1880s. All the attempts of the Pretoria Convention (1881) to restrict the Boers were unavailing. They broke out of their boundaries into Bechuanaland, Swaziland and Zululand, and President Kruger made little attempt to control his farmers as they sought fresh lands. The African reaction was uniformly to look to British protection. At the same time Kruger also wanted an outlet to the sea, which the British were determined he should have only if he agreed to enter a commercial union which might ultimately lever the Transvaal into a British-sponsored closer political union. Neither side got what they wanted. Britain became saddled with new responsibilities. There was little enthusiasm behind the British connections with Basutoland, Bechuanaland and Swaziland, which partly explains a good deal of their later history.[24] Tswana and Sotho desire for, and almost embarrassing devotion to, imperial rather than local colonial rule also make it crystal clear why subsequently they so consistently opposed transfer to the Union.

The great political importance of the British occupation of Rhodesia[25] was in part that it closed the door to further Boer trekking northwards. Towards the end of the 1880s Cecil Rhodes, inspired by a Cape-to-Cairo vision, was acquiring mineral speculations in Matabeleland, notably the Rudd concession by which Lobengula granted a monopoly of minerals in his domains, and Rhodes needed imperial protection and moral support for them. High commissioner Hercules Robinson urged that if Matabeleland were not annexed it would fall into the hands of the Transvaal. He and Rhodes shrewdly recommended a chartered company as the most effectual mode of widening the base of British prosperity in that part of South Africa without calling upon the taxpayer. The Boers would find a company more acceptable than a Crown colony. Rhodes announced his willingness to construct a railway through Bechuanaland, which helped to persuade the British government to support his empire-building. They seem to have argued that the Cape might be separatist, and South Africa by itself might be separatist, but a South Africa reaching up to the Zambesi and needing the protecting arm of Britain against Portuguese or German interference 'will lean more and more on us'. The Rhodesian enterprise would bind together the Cape, Bechuanaland and the supposedly rich north, and counterbalance the rocketing influence of the Transvaal. Having secured a Royal Charter for his British South Africa Company, in the following year (1890) Rhodes sent out his Pioneer Column, which established itself strongly in Mashonaland, and in its wake he despatched settlers, mostly recruited from Cape Colony.

Rhodes was one of those rare men who had lands called after their names, but he was bold enough also to consider buying out other people's lands too. For years he tried to purchase the Portuguese province of Mozambique south of the Zambesi, having particularly set his heart on Beira, but the Anglo-Portuguese convention of 1891 demarcated Portugal's sphere in such a way as to leave the east coast in its hands. The Anglo-German agreement of 1898 provided for a partition of Mozambique if Portuguese government collapsed – and southern Mozambique fell within the British sphere. This included Lourenço Marques.

Rhodes wanted Cape whites to take up their 'inheritance in the interior'. 'The gist of the South African question', he declared, 'lies in the extension of the Cape Colony to the Zambesi', and in his more euphoric moments he said he would stop only at Lake Tanganyika.

The establishment of a German colony in South-West Africa in 1884 was bitterly resented by South Africans, both British and Afrikaner. Hitherto the South-West had been regarded as

within the British sphere of influence, in the interests of Cape
fishermen who had settlements there. J. X. Merriman (later
prime minister of the Cape 1908–10) had called for a Monroe
Doctrine of the coasts of southern Africa. Cape public opinion
in 1884 felt, and continued to feel, that there was no room for
two European flags in South Africa.[26]

All these conceptions of interest and expansion were inherited by the Union from the partition era. As plans for a
future union or federation of the self-governing colonies began
to take shape after 1906, discussion of the future of Basutoland,
Bechuanaland, Swaziland and Rhodesia revived. Transvaal
politicians also indicated an interest in including Mozambique.

As early as 1907, at the time of the colonial conference of that
year, Botha (as prime minister of the Transvaal) discussed with
the colonial secretary the possible incorporation of Swaziland.
Elgin replied:

> We are not prepared at this early date to abandon a proposal
> which certainly was generally approved here, especially in
> view of the settlement of the concessionaires and natives
> which is in progress. I do not mean to say that the arrange-
> ment cannot be altered on cause shown, and the time may
> come when it might be possible to reconsider the matter. In
> the meantime I need scarcely assure you that it would be our
> desire to co-operate with the Transvaal Government in any
> measure for improving the general condition of the country,
> e.g. in the development of railways.[27]

Elgin found himself being 'very firm' with Botha over this,
though privately he felt it was impossible to deny that on some
points the Boers had claims which it was difficult to set aside.[28]

The so-called *Selborne Memorandum* (an over-rated document
which, while purporting to review the relations between the
South African colonies in 1907, was in fact a manifesto of
Milner's Kindergarten) had a whole section devoted to
'National Expansion', following a comparison with the United
States and Canada, whose North-West Territories were said to
be 'an exact analogy'. It suggested South Africans should look
to the north of the Zambesi and ask who was going to control

Rhodesia; they should remember the 'political unwisdom of allowing the political organisation of the northern countries to take place in utter independence of the community already established in the south'. Perhaps South Africa should acquire the Company's rights:

> The longer this problem is postponed the more difficult and the more expensive will its solution become, and if South Africa desires to emulate the destiny of the United States and Canada she cannot place herself in a position to grapple with this question too soon.
>
> British territory stretches beyond the Zambesi, far away north to Lake Tanganyika. In whatever degree this great region is a country where white men can work and thrive and multiply, by so much will the opportunity of expansion inherited by South Africans through the British Empire be increased.

In a letter to the governor of the Cape, Selborne fore-shadowed an argument which the South Africans were later to repeat endlessly:

> If one South African authority, exercising undisputed powers from the Cape of Good Hope to the Zambesi, were to carry out one consistent policy in support of the farmers, it is probable that, within a few years, not only would dread pests like the East Africa Coast fever have disappeared, but scab might become rare among South African sheep, and the scourge of locusts might have passed into the record of a bad dream.[29]

Selborne did not at this stage actually argue the case for including the High Commission Territories in the future Union, but rather seemed to assume they would automatically be included in it. The Colonial Office, with the exception of C. P. Lucas (head of the Dominions Department 1907–11), thought otherwise. Colonial secretary Crewe was inclined to withhold the Territories, but lay down future conditions for transfer. Lucas expressed grave misgivings about such a policy: it might, he wrote, 'make the position worse than at present –

and the antagonism between Colonial or Imperial policy as regards natives more marked'. The difficulty of the native question would, he feared, be increased.[30] His prediction of friction was correct.

Selborne now declared in favour of their immediate inclusion. For the Territories not to be absorbed into the new system from the beginning would be a 'grave inexpediency' causing constantly increasing friction. His opinion carried little weight. Prime minister Asquith described him as 'singularly deficient in the larger questions of policy – both in insight and in foresight'.[31] More particularly, the rejection of his advice was partly the result of his amendment to it: retain Bechuanaland until Rhodesia went in. This step would not, he argued, give rise to much friction, but the officials and politicians in London considered this change to destroy his entire argument, which must stand or fall as a whole.[32]

The imperial government decided in 1908 to accept the risks of friction inherent in exclusion.* True, it was expected that the transfer of Swaziland would become the subject of discussion within two or three years ('we are only in Swaziland as temporary tenants'), but there was no expectation that the Union would want for the immediate future to take over responsibility for Basutoland or Bechuanaland.[33]

In the perspective of imperial history, refusal to relinquish imperial control of the Territories at the time when Union was established appears to some extent as a departure from the policy which might have been expected, and was indeed expected by the African chiefs and recommended by Selborne. The normal procedure in the past had been gradually to transfer local Africans to self-governing regimes, and grants of white self-government had invariably been associated with such transfers. The Cape Colony was made to look after Basutoland in 1871, British Bechuanaland (between the Molopo and Orange rivers) had been transferred to the Cape in 1895; Zululand and Tongaland were transferred to Natal in 1897, and

---

* My article, 'African interests and the South Africa Act 1908–10' (*Historical Journal*, XIII (1970) 85–105), deals with this important decision in a more comprehensive way than is possible here.

in 1894 the British had agreed to a Transvaal protectorate over Swaziland. As far as the future was concerned, Africans in Southern Rhodesia were almost unhesitatingly handed over to the settlers in the new regime of 1923. The case of the High Commission Territories in 1909 is therefore exceptional and probably reflects a real revival of the trusteeship conscience in informed circles in Britain during the years of the Liberal government (1905–15), taking up an injunction from an earlier Liberal colonial secretary, Ripon, who in 1897 had said they should let no more Africans come under the management of South Africans 'until we have greater security than now exists as to how they would be treated'.[34] Britain held to the doctrine of 'equal rights for all civilised men' (however strictly 'civilised' was interpreted), while Afrikaners insisted there could be no equality, indeed no equalising, in Church or State.

Exclusion of the Territories was certainly not welcomed by the South Africans. We have already seen Botha's anxiety to secure the return of Swaziland. So badly did he want this that he had once mentioned possible boycott of the 1906 Transvaal constitution by his Het Volk party if its incorporation was denied,[35] and in London in 1909 he again pleaded his case fully though ineffectually. In the National Convention to prepare the Union constitution, a strong minority thought the attitude of the British government neither fair nor reasonable,[36] and its probable conditions were correctly seen to display great mistrust of the future South African government in its dealings with Africans. Merriman was so sensitive to this point that he feared the whole process of unification might be wrecked over it. Smuts always believed the case for the immediate transfer of the Territories to be unanswerable, because Zoutpansberg in the northern Transvaal had an African population equal to Basutoland's (the Territory with the largest population), and Zululand in Natal had a population which was even larger.[37] The Liberal government turned a deaf ear to Afrikaner logic. Fortunately, during the making of the Union the issue was only one among many to the South Africans, and probably not the paramount one.

Colonial secretary Crewe was, therefore, from the middle of

1b Swazi Queen Regent and Buxton

1a General Botha and Viscount Buxton

2b Young Zulu boy on ancient Ngwane rock

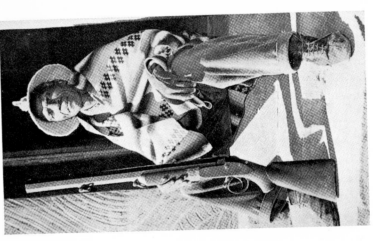

2a Guide at Thaba Bosiu with Moshweshwe's gun

1908 able to hold to four general principles of policy.[38] First, immediate transfer was out of the question; the Territories were to be kept in trust and control retained as long as possible without creating undue friction in South Africa. Second, on the other hand, they must surely be ultimately included in the Union. Third, Britain must insist upon insertion in the constitution of all reasonable specific safeguards for the Africans, without which the assent of the House of Commons could not be obtained. Finally and above all, nothing must be done to prejudice the movement for a strong Union, loyal to the Empire and no longer the weakest link in the imperial chain. Immediate transfer would be a 'leap in the dark'; once the Territories were gone 'our power of protest has practically disappeared' and if things did not go right 'a terrible responsibility will rest upon us in view of our obligations'. The marked objection of the Sotho could not simply be ignored, and House of Commons feeling was certainly a governing consideration. It would be best, Crewe thought, to seize the initiative and specify future terms: 'on the *divide et impera* principle, we are more likely to secure favourable terms for the natives while the Colonies are still separate, and Union depends on a satisfactory issue being devised for this particular problem'. At the same time, they would wait and watch developments to see how the new government thought and behaved towards Africans.

For these reasons then, Selborne was overruled, and an elaborate Schedule appended to the Act of Union, providing in the event of transfer for an independent commission of four appointed by the governor-general, and laying down five main conditions. These were: native land to be inalienable, sale of intoxicating liquor to be prohibited, Territories to receive due share of Union customs revenue, Basutoland National Council to be maintained, and legislation about the Schedule to be reserved to the Crown for approval. The Schedule was the Africans' charter, their guarantee that the principles of British trusteeship towards them would be preserved.

Thus although eventual transfer was deemed inevitable, and undoubtedly planned, it was not promised. A hope was expressed, maybe incautiously and unwisely, but that was all.

Britain was wholly uncommitted to a date, despite a hint that a
request for the transfer of Swaziland within ten years might not
be refused. Transfer was essentially conditional, and section 151
of the Act, referring to the Schedule, was purely permissive. Its
existence in fact made transfer harder. Instead of according
simple reversionary interests, it complicated and impeded the
whole possible process. During the passage of the South Africa
Act through the British parliament, important pledges (to be
much quoted in the future) were given to the effect that before
transfer could take place, parliament would be able to discuss it
(and disapprove if it wished) and the Africans themselves would
be consulted and their opinion 'most carefully considered',
although, desiring to retain the right of final decision for itself,
the imperial government did not bind itself to regard their
preference for the Empire as necessarily an absolute bar to
transfer.[39] Britain did not exactly involve herself in contradictory pledges. No pledges at all were at any stage given to the
Union. But it has been rightly observed by Professor Hancock,
that by a certain vagueness (conceivably deliberate) the
politicians in London created contradictory expectations.[40]
Strict calculation of material interests put the balance slightly
on the side of relinquishing the Territories to conciliate the
white South Africans, and so the decision to retain them,
especially in the light of geographical and economic logic,
and Afrikaner demands, reflected a humanitarian desire to
defer to African interests.[41] The first failure of South African
expansion was therefore registered even before the Union came
into being. This is a point worth emphasising.

Nor did Southern Rhodesia enter the Union in 1910. She was
represented at the National Convention as an observer. There
seemed to be no hurry, but in the long run both British parties
looked to it 'to unite South Africa on an imperial basis',[42]
regarding it as the ultimate key to effective South African unity.
To Milner the successful development of Rhodesia would mean
'that we win the South African game all round', and he defined
the ultimate goal of the Anglo-Boer War as a self-governing
white community from Cape Town to the Zambesi.[43] Winston
Churchill (Liberal under-secretary of state for the colonies

1905–8) wrote in 1906 that Rhodesia with its British population 'may ultimately be the weight which swings the balance in
South Africa decisively on the side of the British Crown'.[44]
To perform this function however it had first to acquire more
settlers, develop its own resources more fully and be able to
negotiate entry to the Union on equal terms with the other
provinces. Britain showed no disposition to press. The future
seemed foreclosed. Southern Rhodesia would fulfil its destiny in
its own good time, as inevitably as Newfoundland's entry to the
Canadian confederation. Botha and Smuts made no secret of
their desire to establish early links with it.[45]

The Union of South Africa was launched on 31 May 1910.
One day, if all went well, it would become Greater South
Africa. Its first governor-general was undoubtedly in favour of
Afrikaner expansion. He was Viscount (Herbert) Gladstone, and
his appointment was hardly flattering to the new Dominion.
There had been pressure on Asquith to rid the cabinet of this
weak home secretary (1905–10), who had incompetently handled
the controversial procession in connection with the Roman
Catholic Eucharistic Congress in London in 1908.[46] King
Edward VII thought Gladstone's appointment a bad one. It
seems Sydney Buxton's name was also put forward (he was
postmaster-general), and indeed recommended by the colonial
secretary, but the South Africans seemed to prefer W. E.
Gladstone's son.[47] Buxton's name had been canvassed even
earlier, in 1906, when there was talk of recalling Selborne. His
turn eventually came, and with great success, in 1914.

Meanwhile, after a by no means obvious process of selection,
Botha became first prime minister of the Union.[48] To the
British he appeared the French-featured farmer who wanted to
bury the hatchet and to forget that there were two white races,
and in their eyes he attained supreme greatness by suppressing
an Afrikaner rebellion in 1914.[49] Whatever the truth of this
picture, Botha was certainly a leader who saw the necessity of
lowering the temperature of Anglo-Afrikaner tension: a
persuasive and sympathetic, yet courageous and, when required,
a stern leader.[50] He remained in office until his death on 28
August 1919.

Botha's successors were, like himself, also veterans of the Anglo-Boer War. His *alter ego* Jan Smuts carried on as prime minister until June 1924, surviving a difficult election in 1920, in which the National Party (formed by General J. B. M. Hertzog in 1914) gained 44 out of the then total of 134 seats. The South African Party held 41 seats, and Smuts' ministry had only a precarious majority of four by support from Unionists and Independents. One-third of the newly elected M.P.s had never sat in the House of Assembly before. Smuts retained his position in the next election (1921) but the Nationalists were still increasing their strength and he was defeated by them in 1924. Hertzog formed a Pact government by alliance with the Labour Party, and successfully defended his position in the election of 1929. Thereafter, economic recession helped to precipitate an unpredicted coalition with Smuts at the end of March 1933. Receiving overwhelming electoral support in May 1933 this marriage of convenience was consummated as the Fusion government in 1934 (based on a United Party in which were merged the South African and National Parties), unequivocally supported by 138 out of 150 M.P.s. Dr D. F. Malan* and his followers retained their identity as a Purified National Party. Fusion lasted until the outbreak of the Second World War, and then split on the issue of neutrality. Smuts formed his own government in September 1939, declared war, won elections and held power until 1948. With his electoral defeat in that year 'The Age of the Generals' came to an end, a new phase of South African history opened.

South Africa's expansion was self-interested. Imperial Britain was concerned about trusteeship. While they discussed the future of the African Territories, social and economic realities therein remained fundamentally unchanged: soil erosion and land shortage in mountainous Basutoland, water shortage in vast Bechuanaland, over-grazing and European settlement in Swaziland. All three were heavily involved in exporting migrant labour into South Africa.

* The Rev. Dr D. F. Malan, minister of the interior, education and public health 1924–33; later prime minister, Jan 1948–Nov 1954.

2 Greater South Africa– 'Cape Town to the Equator'?: South-West Africa, Mozambique and the North, 1910–39

THE vision of a Greater South Africa was certainly not limited to Southern Rhodesia and the three High Commission Territories, although these were obvious and concrete objectives. Inheriting expansionist concepts of security and opportunity from local heroes as well as from officers of the British government – from Kruger and Rhodes as from Milner and Selborne –, the Union from the beginning had designs on German South-West Africa, and took up the legacy of the old Transvaal's urge to the sea, particularly in the direction of Delagoa Bay and its port, Lourenço Marques. Smuts, an arch-expansionist, explicitly identified himself with Rhodes, claiming in 1929 that his whole working life since the Anglo-Boer War had been continuously occupied with the same sort of questions as had governed the career of Rhodes, most notably 'the progress of European civilisation on the African continent'. From this it was but a short step to lay claim also to be the disciple of Livingstone, promoting in the area associated with Livingstone the civilising mission of Christianity and commerce.[1] Smuts looked beyond the Union to an economic and political hegemony in the north, extending far beyond the frontiers of South Africa into equatorial regions, which nature had linked to the south by what he called a 'broad backbone' of mountainous plateau.[2] The description is of course a piece of euphoric geopolitics rather than accurate geography. Nevertheless, it had enough reality to be serviceable.

Geopolitical interpretation of the map pronounced the

natural boundary to be, not the Limpopo but the Zambesi and
its extension westwards, and Delagoa Bay to be the natural port
for practically the whole of the Transvaal, in a way that
British-held Walvis Bay in the west could not be, as it was separated from the most productive parts of South Africa by great
stretches of arid and semi-arid country: Portuguese ownership
of South Africa's most convenient natural harbour represented
'a deficiency in the geographical completeness of the Union'.
Jan Hofmeyr's discussion (1931) of 'South Africa and its place
in Africa' began by quoting Rhodes' speculation in 1894 that
'five and twenty years hence you might find a gentleman
called your Prime Minister sitting in Cape Town, and controlling the whole, not only to the Zambesi, but to Lake Tanganyika'. For that policy, Hofmeyr observed, Rhodes could
find powerful backing in geography, since the chief geographical feature of southern Africa's structure was an interior
plateau which stretched almost without interruption through
the Rhodesias into East Africa and on to Ethiopia. Hofmeyr
found evidence of a marked growing interest in the North:

> certainly also there are few responsible men in the Union
> who would view otherwise than with goodwill the possibility
> of an extension of its borders to the Zambesi. . . . To the
> enterprising South African the North will always present an
> opportunity and a challenge . . . it may be anticipated that
> the bonds between South Africa and the North will be
> drawn increasingly close . . .

The Southern Rhodesia decision of 1922 had broken the possibility of organic union, but the Rhodesias might still be brought
into 'administrative continuity', and South Africa could still
exercise an informal empire, a leadership on the continent of
Africa, transmitting civilisation with the efficacy that Science
had never bestowed on the Romans, in an 'unfailing readiness
to bring its intellectual and material resources to the aid of all
who are engaged in the development of the greatest undeveloped
area of the earth's surface'.[3]

This was an extension of the best Macaulay tradition, but
Smuts was associated with much less pretty pressures as well.

One of his admirers, describing himself as a 'true Afrikaner', wrote to him at the end of 1918 to remind him that Basutoland, Bechuanaland and Swaziland and other portions of the Union devoted to Africans 'comprise some of the richest regions of South Africa'. Surely the obvious course was to hold German South-West Africa and East Africa and shunt the natives off into the captured colonies:

> Would it not be possible gradually and gently to include these regions in the Union and to make provision for the different Native races in such portions of the former German territories as are not so suitable for a white population? . . . is it possible to cherish a more beautiful image than a South Africa populated up to the Zambesi with a strong white nation, unhindered by friction with the coloured races and the bitter feelings that spring from it? . . . South Africa is still only at the beginning of things and I look forward with full confidence to the time when we shall reach the greatness and strength even of the United States of America . . . Now is the big chance for South Africa![4]

The war was indeed the big chance for South African expansion, at any rate into non-British areas, where the British government was sympathetic, on more than strategic grounds, to South African aims. The expansionist designs of the Botha–Smuts government on German and Portuguese colonies were not only well understood in England – they were approved of by the Liberal ministers of Asquith's government. To them the colonies of the 'wily, oily Portuguese', as Winston Churchill called them,[5] were 'sinks of iniquity'. The derelict condition of Mozambique in the early twentieth century hardly appealed to a commercial nation. Sir Edward Grey recognised that the Union would never rest till it had Delagoa Bay, and on every ground, 'material, moral and even Portuguese' he thought it would be best for Portugal to sell her colonies.[6]

In 1911, during the drafting of a bill to provide for the defence of the Union, Herbert Gladstone asked 'What is "South Africa"' as referred to in one of the clauses? Smuts replied: 'South Africa as used in the Bill is a geographical

expression which we advisedly do not define. It would surely
cover any part of the continent of Africa south of the equator?'
Lord Gladstone did not demur.[7]

The most interesting aspect of South African war aims
1914–19 is the extent to which these fell in with British pre-
conceptions and grand strategy. On the first full day of war in
1914 a sub-committee of the Committee of Imperial Defence
recommended an offensive attack on Dar es Salaam from India
and the capture of German South-West Africa, both for its own
sake and for the 'political effect of inviting the co-operation of
the South African government'.[8] The South African campaign
there, led by Botha, was officially undertaken at the request of
the imperial government, but it was a mission the South
African leaders devoutly wished to have entrusted to them. This
was not just from the immediate necessity of controlling the
exceptionally powerful wireless station at Windhoek which
threatened the Union's sea communications, or of forestalling
the threatened use of Australian troops. In 1908 Smuts had
written: 'From the point of view of South Africa's future the
German Empire is no desirable neighbour',[9] and in 1914 of
South-West as 'part of our Afrikaner heritage'.[10] Botha had admitted to Lloyd George several years earlier that in the event
of a German war he intended to invade South-West Africa.[11]
His actual decision created a sensation, but was not unpopular,
since Afrikaners regarded it as part of their own country.[12]

The South-West campaign rapidly grew in political significance and military cost. Even before the end of 1914 Smuts
urged that it should never be handed back to Germany:
otherwise it would yearly become 'a more threatening danger
and an expensive menace to the security and prosperity of the
Union'. High commissioner Buxton found this a quite genuine
view, 'undoubtedly founded on reasonable, and probable,
anticipation'. It was clear from many sources that German
propaganda had largely stimulated the republican movement
in the Union. Colonial secretary Lewis Harcourt naturally
entered a caveat reserving the ultimate disposition of the
captured colonies to the imperial government, but indicated to
his colleagues that it would be 'unreasonable and impossible'

to ask the South Africans to surrender it.[13] Following upon his general cabinet memorandum on the distribution of 'The Spoils' but far in advance of any formal consideration of peace terms, Harcourt enquired whether it had ever occurred to Buxton that at the end of the war, assuming German South-West was in the hands of Union, it might be possible to offer South-West to the Portuguese in exchange for Mozambique:

> By this means Britain would acquire Delagoa Bay and Beira and – if we take German East Africa and keep it – a fine continuous British territory from the Cape to Cairo (NOT with a view to the silly project of the railway of that name). I expect Portugal would not look at the 'swop', but if she would I think it would be of great advantage to us. Perhaps your Ministers have a sentimental value for German South-West on the ground of the Boer settlers there, or a less sentimental interest in the diamonds and copper which I believe it contains.

Harcourt requested Buxton to sound out the South African ministers 'very discreetly and *not as from me*'. He had no idea what they might think.[14]

Buxton had also been studying the map and the same idea had occurred to him. He was inclined to think the Union government would like the proposal: 'They hanker terribly after Delagoa Bay, and they would like to get Beira so as to hem in the Chartered Company in anticipation of Rhodesia's coming into the Union'. The scheme would, he imagined, also appeal to Botha and Smuts as Transvaal men, because of aggrandising Pretoria, and bringing the day nearer when it would be the one and only capital.* With Rhodesia and Mozambique absorbed, Pretoria would be the geographical centre of an enormous Union. The exchange would get rid of what could be foreseen as a major bone of contention if South-West was annexed to the Union, namely the construction of a railway from Walvis Bay linking up with the Transvaal railways: if passengers could be

---

* A position to which, with its statues of Kruger and Pretorius, and all the magnificence of its jacaranda trees, the outside observer can hardly say it was unfitted.

tempted into the interior by this route, instead of spending two
more days travelling via the Cape, the Cape would be put still
further into a backwater. South Africa would also be glad to
lose some 15,000 German settlers. On the other hand the
Portuguese would find great difficulty in managing these
Germans, and their willingness to accept the exchange would be
further diminished by the fact that the trade of South-West was
'not a patch on Portuguese East Africa'. However there were
diamonds and other minerals, and the Germans had spent
millions on development and made it a going concern.

When Buxton eventually sounded Smuts he discovered that
Smuts too had long been pondering the geopolitical implications
of success in German South-West. Smuts had concluded it was
unlikely that the Portuguese would consider such a deal, but
they might be tempted by a larger one. He then cunningly
revealed his desire to undertake a campaign to German
East Africa. Buxton reported:

> He said that he had another idea, and that was that if East
> Africa were conquered and annexed, that the Northern part
> might be added to British East Africa, and the Southern and
> Central part be 'swopped' with the Portuguese for the
> Southern part of Portuguese East Africa (Delagoa Bay,
> Beira, etc.) This would round off their territory, and ours,
> and he thought the Portuguese would not be disinclined to
> this proposal (personally I should doubt it) . . . No doubt the
> scheme he has in his head is one considerable reason why he is
> keen to send a contingent from here to East Africa. He said his
> plan would be contingent on Rhodesia's coming into the Union.

Buxton also saw another minister, Sir David de Villiers Graaff,
who suggested that the Union should undertake the conquest of
German East Africa, financed by Britain; if at the end of the war
Portugal took the central and southern part of German East
Africa in exchange for Mozambique, the Union government
would reimburse the imperial government for their expenditure.[15]

Hence Buxton reported to colonial secretary Bonar Law in
August 1915 that Smuts, Graaff and Botha 'would rather like to

have a finger in the German East Africa pie'.[16] And only a fortnight later Smuts was putting his special pet idea to Merriman: if they could conquer German East Africa, 'we could probably effect an exchange with Mozambique and so consolidate our territories south of the Zambesi and Kunene'. Merriman wondered whether East Africa might be a white-ruled black country, 'a sort of African India in which South Africa might play the same part that Scotland has played in British India by supplying soldiers and administrators and in becoming a field for the ambitions for our young men'.[17] The real point about sending an expedition was that it would give them a claim to some share in settling the rearrangements at the peace table. The expedition to German East Africa was despatched early in 1916. The British government hoped Smuts would take charge: it would have been 'something in the highest degree satisfactory to this country'.[18] Smuts could not be spared however. Another opportunity soon arose of offering him command and this time Smuts accepted. He then re-linquished the command in order to attend the War Cabinet in England in February 1917.

This hazy indulgence in the fascinating game of redrawing the map continued to occupy Buxton and the colonial secretary throughout 1916. Early in February 1917, Buxton had a long summarising talk with Smuts about the future. They agreed they could not be sanguine about getting Portugal to agree to any swop of Delagoa Bay and Beira. Buxton showed Smuts copies of all the letters he had written home on the subject.[19]

At a meeting of the committee of the Imperial War Cabinet in April 1917 to consider 'territorial desiderata', Smuts explained how South-West Africa and Mozambique would 'give South Africa a natural frontier and round it off as a compact block of sub-tropical territory'. But he thought Portugal would only enter a bargain if it were supplemented by financial aid which they needed for development. Lord Curzon remarked that it was 'a very big demand' to ask Portugal to surrender Delagoa Bay, which was not only of great economic value but an object of Portuguese national pride. It was also pointed out that Portugal had participated in the war primarily in order to make it impossible for Britain to permit any encroachment on her territorial or sovereign rights. Smuts in reply raised the bogey of a German *Mittelafrika* coast-to-coast across central Africa north of the Zambesi.[20]

Botha submitted to Buxton a memorandum (dated 14 March 1918) on the future of the German colonies, urging the retention of German South-West Africa. If it were returned to Germany, the Germans would be in a much stronger position than ever before to influence affairs in the Union, since the railway systems were now joined and the 'disloyal' element in the Union had grown. The German treatment of natives would lead to unrest and thus enormously add to anxiety and the cost of defending the Union. Although stating that 'incorporation in the Union is its natural destiny', Botha was careful to stress that it was not on account of military ambitions or megalomania or even of land hunger that the Union wanted to obtain control, 'but because they want to be secured in the peaceful possession and development of their own territory and secured from intrigue'. This state of affairs could not be attained with Germany as their neighbour. He claimed South Africans had proved their capacity to administer it successfully. He thought that commercially the two areas could be peacefully developed as one whole. The unspoken critical factor might well have been, however, the desire to be rid of a further European presence in the sub-continent. And the desire for land was stronger than Botha was prepared to admit. For some years Botha had been planning to settle farmers in German South-West with the deliberate objective of proving its usefulness. He proposed to organise perhaps as many as 10,000 of them into a half military and half farming class, so they would be available for defensive purposes.[21]

Buxton's own suggestions in 1919 as a basis for discussing the re-arrangement of boundaries were as follows. He would have liked to see the complete disappearance of Portugal south of the Zambesi on the east coast. Delagoa Bay would go to the Union, Beira to Southern Rhodesia. The boundary between them would be the Sabi River. This would be a suitable and acceptable reward to the Union for its war effort. The incorporation of Swaziland would incidentally thus be a natural con-

sequence of the extension of the Union to Delagoa Bay. The
time for such a transfer was in any case, he thought, ripe: but
for the war it would probably have been applied for and agreed
to. German East Africa should be split up. Portugal might have
Dar es Salaam and half of the Central Railway. The remainder
could join North-Eastern Rhodesia and Nyasaland to form the
part of a new Central African Protectorate. Since Portugal
would be confined to the south-eastern part of Tanganyika, a
Cape to Cairo route would still be possible on the eastern side of
Lake Victoria. Buxton believed the Portuguese had behaved just
as badly as they could during the war: technically Allies, they
had been mostly pro-German in sympathies, and they deserved
to lose something.[22]

As things turned out, the only concrete South African gain
from the war was German South-West Africa, the conquest of
which an exhilarated Smuts hailed as the first achievement of
the new united nation.[23] In truth it was also to be the last
victory of the expansion programme. Nor was it an unequivocal
and total victory, though press criticism harped unduly on its
shortcomings. It was *de facto* to become part of the Union, and
de jure a potential province, or so it was thought. The Mandate
allowed the territory to be administered as an integral part of the
Union, whose government had full powers of administration and
legislation subject only to the observance of safeguards for the
natives and the submission of annual reports to the Mandates
Commission of the League of Nations. Smuts chafed under the
inquisitorial supervision, and in practice treated the South-West
as if it were annexed. The Germans had left behind them some
solid achievements. They had spent huge sums in developing
Swakopmund, Luderitz and Windhoek, and in building 1,200
miles of railway approaching the Union border. Other valuable
assets included fine public buildings and the diamond output.
The South African government treated the country simply as one
suitable for white settlement. They immediately expropriated all
the land of the concessions companies and declared all un-
allocated areas to be Crown land. Their own land settlement
legislation was applied. A land rush begun. For the first 76
farms advertised there were 800 to 900 applicants. By the end of

1925, 880 holdings had been allocated to 1,106 settlers, and the white population had almost doubled since 1914 despite the repatriation of 6,000 Germans. The government spared no expense. It gave the farmers generous loan terms which it never recovered and cheerfully discounted. It granted them remissions on rent arrears, built dams, bored for water and advanced capital for stock. Land-hungry South Africans were allocated huge farms virtually for the asking and then pampered. Needless to say, nothing was done for the Africans.[24] By 1931 it seemed to Hofmeyr that the 'trend of events has been set definitely towards the incorporation of South-West Africa in the Union . . . its South Africanisation proceeds apace, and it is not likely that anything will emerge to prevent the realisation of its manifest destiny'.[25]

On the opposite side of Africa, attempts to obtain closer control over Mozambique ended in complete failure. Ironically, Smuts had been one of the initiators of the idea of mandatory control, with the idea that it might be a means of putting Portuguese colonies under international control which could be used as a pretext for intervention. Instead, it was the German colonies which were put under mandates, which Smuts had always been careful to avoid proposing. He was hoist with his own petard.

During the peace negotiations Smuts had considered the annexation of the Belgian Congo as well as Mozambique with such seriousness that strongly worded protests followed from the Belgian and Portuguese governments. Smuts had what he referred to as a 'radical interest' in the German colonies, but it hardly overtopped the attempt to 'gobble up Delagoa, etc.', as Botha put it. Peace-making seemed the best chance they would ever have for this exercise: 'Jannie, there is no doubt about it, this is a matter which we must bring up and settle in our favour. The region must be bought out and we must pay for it'.[26] At one time the Foreign Office in London seemed to think the Portuguese might possibly be prepared to make a deal with respect to Delagoa Bay, and Smuts was invited to submit a memorandum on 'Mozambique and the Union of South Africa' to the War Cabinet. In it he urged the annexation of part of Mozambique and the Belgian Congo, not least because the

Empire was 'specially poor in copper'.[27] At Paris in 1919 Smuts
and Botha made friendly contact with the Portuguese delegates
and discussed Mozambique, but the recall of the delegates to
Lisbon prevented the attainment of any real result.[28]

The 1909 convention between the Transvaal and Mozambique was due to expire on 1 April 1923. Attempts to negotiate a
new settlement or *modus vivendi* between the Union and
Portuguese governments were begun in 1921. The new convention would deal mainly with railway and harbour arrangements, but also with the recruiting of native labour for the
Witwatersrand mines, and with trade questions. Railway and
harbour facilities at Lourenço Marques were the most important question by far, and indeed became a *sine qua non*. The
need for labour was much less than it had been in 1909, but the
need for export facilities was growing every year. Smuts thought
the Union had suffered too long from the incapacity of the
Portuguese in docks and harbour management, from the chaos
at Lourenço Marques which had crippled the coal export trade
of the Transvaal. Given efficient transport and dock facilities on
the east coast, coal export from the Transvaal could easily be
increased several fold. Portuguese casual officialdom, operating
a mercurial paper currency of its own, was a genuine incon-
venience at a port full of British and South African businessmen.
Equipment was inadequate and often obsolete. The Union
wanted an autonomous commission, politically independent of
both governments, but on which the Union representatives were
to have the controlling influence. The railway and 'L.M.' might
then be able to keep pace with the growing Transvaal traffic.
They would have liked to lease a section of the harbour which
they would manage, equip and operate for themselves. The
Portuguese resisted strenuously, objecting to what they
considered a 'diminution of their sovereignty', whereupon
Smuts threatened to build an entirely new railway through
Zululand to a new port further south in Union territory. His
determination to proceed with this alternative plan seemed
quite serious at the time. He had already procured the services
of Sir George Buchanan, a well-known marine engineer, to give
expert advice on the possibility of a large-scale harbour

construction at Kosi Bay. Together with Buchanan and Mr W. Hoy, general manager of the railways, Smuts examined the prospects on the spot.[29] This may, however, have been merely to frighten the Portuguese into the *modus vivendi*. Buchanan's report was pigeon-holed, but the plan would undoubtedly have dealt the deathblow to Lourenço Marques and the existing Portuguese railway. Possibly Smuts reckoned that by thus depriving the Portuguese of British trade and financial assistance the position of affairs in Mozambique, already bad, would become so desperate that the South African government would have an excuse for intervening and taking over the administration. Smuts denounced Portuguese terms as completely unacceptable and the difficulties as utterly insurmountable.

The Portuguese felt that Smuts simply did not wish to conclude an agreement. Why else did he assume an uncompromising attitude which would not seek even a small palliative to gild the pill of 'diminishing sovereignty'? The Portuguese negotiators believed the obstacles to an agreement were sentimental rather than commercial. The Union memorandum they found aggressive in tone. Insistence on the past delinquencies of Mozambique administration was calculated to arouse Portuguese pique. The majority of Portuguese both in Portugal and Mozambique were convinced that Smuts coveted the province and was determined sooner or later to annex it, at any rate as far north as Beira. Colour was given to their impression when Smuts went almost directly from the conference table to deliver a speech at Caledon, in which he said South Africa had no definite frontier towards the north: there was no limit to northern expansion: and South Africans must not be content with their present boundaries, but must instead always be 'pushing forward the beacons'. The Portuguese understandably concluded it was useless to negotiate with the Union while its statesmen clung to these aggressive ambitions. Before negotiations could succeed they would settle for nothing less than the allaying of their suspicions by the Union government's subscribing to the existing Anglo-Portuguese treaty respecting each other's colonial possessions. A pledge from the Union not to 'violate' the territorial integrity of Mozambique would not be sufficient. The leading Portuguese delegates regarded themselves as pro-English, and the fact that they could not agree with Smuts seemed to them proof that he would not be satisfied with much less than possession of their country.[30]

As a result a new convention was not negotiated until 1928, apart from essential labour recruiting clauses renewed in 1925. The difficulty was considerable and concessions had to be made on the South African side. The agreement assured to the Portuguese the high proportion of Rand traffic which they had enjoyed under the old agreement. It cut down the number of Shangaan who might be recruited, and, to the dismay of Rand storekeepers, held over a considerable proportion of their earnings to be spent in Mozambique.[31] Only at such a price was the vital connection with Delagoa Bay maintained. A later convention in the 1930s recouped the position considerably.*

With this history of wartime encouragement from the British behind him, Smuts was never quite clear thereafter that he would not find for his expansive policies ready listeners at least among some of the imperial policy-makers. He had no reason to suppose that his idea of a chain of paternalist-run white colonies up to Kenya, expounded for example in a letter to L. S. Amery, would cause a sharp reaction:

A great White Africa along the Eastern backbone, with railway and road communications connecting North and South, will become a first-class addition to the Empire and will repay all the capital put into it. It is an expansion of the Rhodes policy.[32]

Time and time again over a long span of years Smuts recurred to these ambitions. Here was a man who wrote bitterly of the British Empire in *A Century of Wrong* (1899), yet would himself dearly have loved to build his own empire. His first lecture in Kimberley in 1895 took a 'pan-African' theme. At the beginning of the Anglo-Boer War Smuts appropriated an

* Today relations are sufficiently harmonious for white South Africans to enjoy their holidays by the Indian Ocean at 'L.M.', amid all the boulevard café tables, the little lizards and huge grasshoppers, the ubiquitous swallows and Royal Poinsiana flame trees.

old Transvaal slogan when he wrote of a great South African Republic filling up the sub-continent: in a United States of South Africa from Zambesi to Simon's Bay it would be 'Africa for the Afrikaner'. At the time of Union his vision was of 'Simonstown to the equator'. In 1915 he attempted to minimise the less attractive aspects of the war in Europe by pointing to the northern hinterland:

> There is now the prospect of the Union becoming almost double its present area. If we continue on the road to union, our northern boundaries will not be where they now are, and we shall leave to our children a huge country in which to develop a type for ourselves, and to form a people who will be a true civilising agency in this dark continent. That is the large view.[33]

Two years later he looked to the time when it would be almost a misnomer to speak of 'South' Africa because the northern limits of their civilisation would have gone so far. In 1929 he expected that a critical step in Commonwealth evolution would be the northward projection of South Africa's civilising mission. During the Second World War he propounded 'Greater South Africa' as the basis for his 'plans for a better world'. 'The Union', he wrote in 1940, 'can only realise its true destiny, even within its own borders, by keeping that larger African point of view clearly before itself . . . All Africa may be our proper market if we will but have the vision . . .'[34]

Such utterances had repercussions inside South Africa which were sometimes a little dangerous. They sounded dubious to the Afrikaner nationalist. The German South-West Africa campaign had its critics among them, and the East African campaign was even less easy to justify, though of course nothing silences criticism like success. In 1914 Hertzog thought South Africa should confine herself to defensive operations in the South-West, not it seems because he was opposed to expansion as such, but because it would be the height of folly if South Africa were unable to retain it, and he feared it would fall 'like a ripe fruit into Great Britain's lap'.[35] At the end of the war however he favoured its annexation; by 1924 he looked forward to the day when it would become 'an integral part of the Union . . . with the full and free consent of its people'. Hertzog was unenthusiastic about the possible entry of Rhodesia, fearing the additional British votes which it would bring; he certainly did not want Rhodesia forced in without consultation of the people, whom he had good grounds for supposing would be averse. By 1921 about half the European population of South-West Africa was South African, and the suspicion that Smuts was in Rhodesia seeking to call in another province to cancel in advance the accession of strength which the South-West might be expected to give to his opponents goes far, as Professor Walker suggested, to explain the vigour of opposition within the Union to his policy of incorporating Rhodesia.[36] Hertzog's major piece of vituperation against the style of Smuts' expansionist policies was, however, reserved for the election campaign of 1929, in which indeed they became a main issue. This was the 'Black Peril' election. At Ermelo on 17 January 1929 Smuts was reported to have said:

> Let us cultivate feelings of friendship over this African continent, so that one day we may have a British confederation of African states . . . a great African Dominion stretching unbroken through-out Africa. . . . That is the cardinal point in my policy.

Smuts' apologists have sometimes doubted whether his words were accurately reported, and interpretation of them has varied. Professor Hancock says Smuts was thinking rather vaguely of confederal re-arrangements of British African territories under white leadership.[37] An earlier biographer, Crafford, sees the speech as firmly in the Rhodes tradition, and, 'in itself was nothing more than one of Smuts's customary holistic, Pan-African utterances'.[38] To others, it was a far-sighted suggestion of trade and sympathetic co-operation with areas offering an enormous market for the output of South African industry. All agree, however, that the construction put upon the speech by the Hertzog–Roos*–Malan triumvirate in their devastating reply ('The Black Manifesto') was at best

* T. J. de V. Roos, minister of justice 1924–9, leader of Transvaal Nationalists.

unfair and at worst a sneering absurdity. The Manifesto denounced Smuts as 'the man who puts himself forward as the apostle of a black Kaffir state, of which South Africa is to form so subordinate a constituent part that she will know her own name no more'.[39] At stake, they contended, was

> the continued existence or the downfall of the white man and his civilisation in South Africa. It embraces the question whether the people of South Africa shall passively stand by and watch South Africa being wiped off the map, as General Smuts desires, in order to be dissolved into a huge Kaffir state stretching from the Cape to the Sudan.

It is certainly true that Smuts would not have been sorry to see the *term* South Africa dropped from the national vocabulary, but his object in trying to create a great African dominion of British states was to forge a chain of white settlement which, fashioned in a South African mould, would 'find the solution of our pressing problems an easy matter', and 'conquer and hold this dark continent for European civilisation'.[40]

The impression sometimes formed abroad was that, in direct contrast to Smuts, Hertzog and his henchmen were the incorrigible advocates of a 'little South Africa' policy, seeing the Union and nothing but the Union. In fact the term 'little South African' is about as valid as 'little Englander', which is not valid at all. Few statesmen of energetic countries are ever wholly without some admiration for or support of expansive policies, especially if presented within the context of 'civilising mission', and it seems more likely that Hertzog's declared attitude sprang more from temporary personal antagonism to Smuts than from settled ideological conviction. After all, the public which used the labels knew nothing of Hertzog's gritty determination to incorporate Swaziland and Bechuanaland. Certainly the astute Hofmeyr was not deceived.[41] He pointed out how ill the 'little South Africa' label squared either with Hertzog's support of the Kenya settlers in their opposition to the 1923 White Paper declaring African interests to be paramount, or with his finance minister's assertion in 1930 (announcing the renewal of the customs agreement with Southern Rhodesia)

that he looked to 'some measure of eventual political union or
federation of the parties to these agreements' – a declaration,
incidentally, which produced a howl of disapproval in Rhodesia.
Hertzog himself had almost certainly exempted the two
Rhodesias from his diatribes against Smuts. Moreover, in 1937
Hertzog announced that he would not surrender South-West
Africa in order to appease Germany. If Germany was to be
appeased in Africa she should have Tanganyika back instead.[42]

If Hofmeyr had been writing a little later, his observations
would have been strengthened strikingly by an analysis of
Oswald Pirow's speeches. For ten years Pirow was a pillar of
Hertzog's government, first as minister of justice 1929–33 and
then minister of railways and mines 1933–39. In October 1935
(when he was also minister of defence) he offered a plane-
load of tear-gas bombs in order to help put down riots on
the Northern Rhodesian Copper Belt,[43] thus revealing that
Smuts was not the only one to believe that defence of the Union
did not begin or end with its northern boundaries. In a paper
for the Royal African Society in 1937[44] Pirow proclaimed
South Africa to be 'almost vitally interested' in 'all the potential
white areas': that was to say in the whole of Africa south of the
equator, excluding French Equatorial Africa, but including
Kenya and Uganda. He did not, however, expect that South
African influence would ever mean much any further north
than that. Within the area described, the interest was definite
and required the closest possible harmony and co-operation
with the states involved. The Union's responsibility as the only
independent white state in the area was a grave one, 'but one
which we are capable of bearing and willing to accept.'
Outlining the 'dangerous possibility' of a concerted attack on
the white minority, it was clear that 'the white communities
south of the Sahara are and probably always will be white
islands in a vast black sea, and that we could not as a matter of
principle allow any one of these islands to be engulfed by such
black sea . . . in our very existence as white communities, we
are interdependent'. All the states referred to had recently
agreed in Johannesburg at a Southern African Transport
Conference on measures of collaboration which would

eventually establish 'a spirit of cordiality going far beyond mere neighbourliness'. There had been previous conferences on health, locusts, common postal and telegraph facilities.

Apart then from some electoral skirmishing, and perhaps some Hertzogite apprehensions that Smuts' plans fitted in too closely with British strategic interests, it seems improbable that the ideal of 'Greater South Africa' foundered on an internal division of opinion. It is much more likely that its realisation became more difficult as British support for it was withdrawn. There is a marked contrast between Britain's attitude down to the attempt to tip Southern Rhodesia into the Union in 1922 and the scepticism which emerged thereafter. The failure of South African expansion is to a large extent the story of a British change of heart. Why, in general terms, did this take place?

We may start from the assumption that British confidence in the Union was from the beginning fragile, its optimism exceedingly qualified. Hopes of a better deal for the African were never high, hopes of a resolution of the inter-white tensions always doubtful. The subsequent reluctance of Rhodesian whites and High Commission Territories' Africans to enter the Union, as well as the unwillingness of the imperial government to transfer the latter, are both reflections of the collapse of the slender hopes which the British had in 1909 entertained of the Union. Despite an original desire in Whitehall to try to keep reasonably in step with South African native policy so long as no substantial injustice was done,[45] and a hard-dying conviction that Botha could do no wrong, by 1913 controversial native policy had shown itself in the Natives Land Act. Throughout the First World War the recrudescence of bad feeling between Afrikaner and English seemed to grow worse every day. By 1915 anti-English feeling in the Union was fiercer even than during the Anglo-Boer War. In 1917 Merriman (formerly prime minister of the Cape) explained to his British political friend Lord Bryce how the old Cape policy had slipped back into the ways of the Transvaal and Orange Free State. Anti-British propaganda he found 'incredibly violent'; the British resented the Transvaal hegemony which had inexorably followed Union; the Senate, designed partly to help African interests, was 'a very inferior body quite failing to gain the respect of the public or to have any weight'. 'Our constitution', he added, 'has been a sad disappointment in many ways'. It had solved none of the real problems: 'We have since the Jameson Raid gone back in every respect and since Union at an accelerated pace'. Old sores had not been healed. Instead bitterness had revived. At the end of the war Merriman wrote to Bryce:

> Within my public life of fifty years I do not recollect such racial bitterness as that which at present interferes with every branch of our social life and accentuates the ever-present problem of our future relations with the native races. . . . The memory of the past hangs over us like a shadow and is buried but not forgotten in the tenacious Dutch nature. . . . The fathers have eaten sour grapes and the children's teeth are set on edge.[46]

Now whilst allowing for the lugubrious disenchantment of an old man in decline, a man who had always been a natural pessimist, noted for his jeremiads, Merriman was a shrewd intellectual, and his attitude was not unwarranted. Neither was it unsupported. Republican feeling *was* intensifying, and it could not be laughed off as sheer nonsense or idle dreaming. The fact that the movement had gripped the youth of even the Cape province was something which emphasised the gravity of the position to others besides Merriman.[47] Buxton himself was prone to a rather gloomy view, however much he might try to soothe it away by telling himself that the visionary optimism of 1909 was over-sanguine and therefore bound to breed a reaction, and anyway the 'balance was enormously on the right side'. It was undoubtedly disappointing to know that some South Africans would set up a republic tomorrow if they could. Buxton blamed the war itself. It had aggravated antagonisms to such a degree that peace came too late to act as the solvent of differences now deeply ingrained.[48]

Within ten years of the formation of the Union, then, real alarm was developing among British statesmen about the direction of Union politics. The result of the 1920 election seemed disastrous, even though Smuts was still able to form a government. Milner, at the time colonial secretary, wrote:

> the effect of having to put up with a Hertzog Government, after the line he has taken, would be very bad throughout the whole Empire, even if such a Government were unable *to do* anything very momentous. So I fervently pray, that we may yet escape a Hertzog ministry.[49]

When Smuts won the election of February 1921, Winston Churchill, the new colonial secretary, was so relieved that he wanted to send Smuts a congratulatory telegram. Although this step was entirely without precedent, the traditional argument that it would embarrass relations with a successor of the opposite party was admitted by officials to be irrelevant since never before in the Empire had an election been fought in which one party advocated secession, and if Hertzog ever did come to power, and the message leaked out (as it was sure to do), 'our relations with the latter will be such that knowledge of the message will make no difference'.[50]

British confidence in the future of the Union as a loyal member of the imperial circle, which was in 1909 the reason for guarded acquiescence in its expectations of expansion, barely survived a decade. Once Hertzog came to power in 1924, a whole new uncertainty developed over transfer of the High Commission Territories, an uncertainty which proved to be unexpectedly durable.

There were perhaps four major aspects of the disillusionment with the Hertzog regime. These concerned status, Africans, government policy in trade, and Afrikanerisation of the civil service. The primary symbol of independent status was, Hertzog decided, to be enshrined in a new national flag. This flag campaign was fought with exceptional bitterness. Efforts were made to eliminate the Union Jack entirely from a new flag.* The English-speaking section of the Union considered themselves in the mid-1920s to be fighting for their most

---

* There were brave British jokes about a new coat of arms which would show a cow with an Englishman grasping one horn, a Boer the other, a native hanging on to the tail, while a Jew milked the cow: undignified but not wholly unrealistic.

fundamental rights. This fact made it difficult indeed to transfer any territory to the South African government. It was generally believed that the flag controversy had set the Union back many years and certainly resulted in the postponement of all prospect of transfer of the High Commission Territories for some considerable time to come.

And then there was native policy, which assumed a more and more central place. The old theory, that Cape liberal attitudes would sweep into a hinterland purged by Union of parochial attitudes, suffered a series of set-backs, each one reducing the prospect of transfer a little more. From having been accorded quasi-reversionary interests, the South African government was put first on probation and then on a sort of indefinitely suspended sentence. By 1919 observant Africans could detect no change of heart towards them. In fact, Union administration inspired them with less confidence even than the former Cape administration. By 1926 the high commissioner (Lord Athlone) could see no more in Hertzog's native policy than 'a muddle-headed attempt to solve a problem to which insufficient thought and consideration has been given', with resort to an absurd and massive subterfuge to disguise the simple fact that the whites meant to maintain their political predominance. The native problem would not be solved, he remarked, by introducing elaborate machinery to decide who was an African and who a Coloured, or to decide who should or should not exercise the franchise. There might be a proposal to introduce more native councils to educate the Africans in the art of self-government, but 'before one can govern one must have territory in which to do it', which the Africans had not. They were simply being chased from pillar to post.[51] The 1913 Land Act started an exodus from country to towns, which the Urban Areas Act of 1923 was designed to check. Thereafter Africans were driven from the towns, and having nowhere to go, began squatting on farms to an unprecedented extent. Now this was to be legally discouraged, but still no land was to be provided, except to the mocking extent that in certain 'released' areas they would be allowed to compete with Europeans. Social conditions for the Africans were actually deteriorating.

The British government was by no means blind to the way in which economic fears lay at the root of the feeling on the native question. The incorporation of another million Africans from the High Commission Territories would hardly help to exorcise the spectre. In 1935 when Smuts tried to argue that public opinion on the native question would improve faster with such an extra responsibility, the high commissioner (Clark) replied neatly 'there is a text about being faithful in smaller things which is singularly applicable'.[52]

For some years, economic interests had seemed not only the strongest bonds of the Union, but also its most definite ties with the Empire, yet by the end of the 1920s even these seemed to be wavering. Its trade and commercial policy was reacting unfavourably on imperial interests in Bechuanaland. Worse than this, N. C. Havenga's policy as Hertzog's finance minister (1924–39) was one of encouraging industries by admitting the necessary raw materials free or at a low duty, and protecting South African manufacturers. This was thought to be anti-British. A treaty with Germany in 1928 implied a breach in the principle of imperial preference. Britain's special preferences were removed but trade with the British Empire was to be on a reciprocal basis. Havenga began a sustained effort to seek markets beyond the Empire, which led to a definite weakening of Commonwealth economic co-operation. This policy was plainly an application in the economic sphere of Hertzog's theories of constitutional equality. Hence, it has been rightly said: 'Havenga's contribution to South African independence was not so spectacular but it was fundamental'.[53] In September 1931 the United Kingdom went off the gold standard and all other 'sterling' Dominions except South Africa followed suit. Havenga and Hertzog could not be persuaded until, fifteen months later, financial hardships forced South Africa into line.[54] At the Ottawa Conference of 1932 South Africa and Ireland were the only two dissenters from a statement expressing hopes for holding future economic conferences.[55]

As Afrikanerisation was quietly adopted in administration, it was noticeable that all good posts in the civil service now tended to go to persons of non-British origin regardless of

qualifications. This, together with a deliberate attempt to ex-
pedite the process of bilingualising the public service, generated feelings of concern, uneasiness and distrust in at least
some of the English South Africans.[56] There were suggestions
that the spirit of the Union had not been perpetuated.

Thus, as relations between South Africa and the British
Empire became less close than expected in 1910, Britain felt that
it might well be asked whether South Africa could have it both
ways. If she moved away from co-operation with Britain, why
should Britain continue to be at pains to facilitate her desire for
the High Commission Territories? Britain had still not re-
linquished the ideal of a great British South Africa. Hertzog's
policy therefore tended to promote a reassertion of the imperial
factor as the shortest cut to that goal. As the British government's representative in South Africa, Bede Clifford, wrote:

> Before any partnership of continental magnitude is considered
> it is necessary to strengthen the Territories outside the Union
> so that if they ever do throw in their lot with that Dominion
> they will at least be able to hold their own, to maintain
> Empire solidarity and to redress the foreign inclinations
> which seem to inspire Union policy today.[57]

In one sense the policy of South African expansion never
really stood a chance. From 1908 it was clear that Union
would be incomplete at the outset. At the root of subsequent
failure lies this fact: that the Africans, the Rhodesians, and
ultimately the British government as well, objected to the
political power, the policies, even maybe the very existence of
Afrikanerdom. The British government were unwilling to admit
this outright – it was not pleasant to admit even to themselves
their inability to reconcile the Afrikaners; and so they fell
back on the formula that they would allow transfer one day, but
not just yet. It was the resurgence of Afrikanerdom they disliked, and of this, native policy was a prime facet. The constitution aided this resurgence. Professor Thompson believes that a
unitary constitution was the very worst for South Africa. It was
certainly not a happy choice as far as the success of expansion
was concerned. As Professor Thompson pointedly observed,

whereas a territory might be prepared to become a province of a federation, in which there were enduring safeguards for provincial autonomy in specified fields, it might be unwilling to run the risk of being completely absorbed by a union: 'Federalism had facilitated the expansion of the U.S.A. and the Dominion of Canada; its unitary constitution might prove an obstacle to the expansion of the Union of South Africa'.[58] In 1922 Southern Rhodesia strikingly demonstrated the danger.

3 Failure in
Southern Rhodesia: 1910–23

ALTHOUGH barely one-fifth of white Rhodesians spoke
Afrikaans as their native tongue, the incorporation of Southern
Rhodesia in the Union seemed at least as logical as it had
been for Natal. Apart from a similarity to South Africa in
Rhodesia's climate and circumstances, the franchise, civil service and law were all inherited from Cape Colony. In May
1909 the Legislative Council debated closer union. Everyone
was in favour of Union in principle, and some, including Charles
Coghlan, later to be first prime minister of a self-governing
Rhodesia, would have preferred to have it at once, partly in
order to escape the restrictions of imperial native policy.
Coghlan regarded incorporation as the 'absolute and inevitable
destiny' of the Rhodesias, provided only that they joined freely
and of their own goodwill on equal terms. He and his friends
quickly changed their minds as they watched the progress of the
Union. Botha seemed to make heavy weather of his premiership:
discords and schisms dashed the early hopes of white racial
unity. Hertzog's stubborn and contumacious rejection of
'conciliation' was a disillusionment for Coghlan's initial enthusiastic belief in the effective unity of the 'British' Union and
in Rhodesia's quick entry into it. The first years of the Union
were undoubtedly replete with incident and anxiety of every
kind. It proved no easy matter to bring the Act of Union into
working order. There was a Johannesburg strike in 1913 and a
General Strike in 1914. Indians posed a critical question.
Hertzog forced a division in 1912/13, and then formed his own
party. The outbreak of war saw an Afrikaner rebellion.
Hertzog's apparent attempt in 1919 to secure complete independence was to Coghlan and the Rhodesians the last straw.[1]

Such a rapid change of Rhodesian opinion was decidedly disconcerting to the Colonial Office. From the British standpoint, entry to the Union had two great advantages. Rhodesia would act as a makeweight counterbalancing Afrikaner predominance in the Union, and Union was the only way in which all responsibility for buying out the British South Africa Company could be removed from the British government. Dominant opinion in the Colonial Office in 1911 was that no one would seriously propose either to rule Rhodesia as a Crown Colony under the Colonial Office or to erect it into a responsibly governing colony outside the Union.[2] But already high commissioner Lord Gladstone diagnosed a strong undercurrent of somewhat ill-defined opinion in Rhodesia against entry: a feeling that the time was not ripe, and that the Union government was becoming dominated by 'Hertzogism'. Besides this there were more specific considerations beginning to develop:

> Many suspect the Dutch Government of the Union and fear the comparative weakness of the British population in the Union. This feeling is strengthened by the pride with which Rhodesia is held to be an essentially British possession, and the dislike of compromising its essentially British characteristics. Again, Northern Rhodesia is a difficult factor in the problem. It will not be ready for entrance into Union for an indefinite period. Why, it is asked, should Rhodesia be cut in two? Why should not Mr Rhodes' great territory form, with Nyasaland, a great British community in the heart of Africa under its own government?

Some Rhodesians, clearly, were already dreaming of a separate state straddling the Zambesi,[3] of a Central African Federation.

Lord Gladstone agreed that the time was not ripe either from the Union or the Rhodesian standpoint. In considering the terms of the Company's Charter in 1914, the Colonial Office therefore reconciled itself to 'waiting for public opinion to develop', and expected to have to postpone entry indefinitely. It was axiomatic that the white people of Rhodesia themselves must in the last resort decide their own future.

Before the war, Botha was keenly interested in bringing Rhodesia in. At the end of 1913 however he recognised that there was a distinct current against union in Rhodesia, 'a most unfortunate and unsatisfactory state of affairs'. Even if it were possible – and it was not at all certain that the Union was ready to find the large sum of money required – he too did not think it advisable without the consent of the people.[4]

The position was unclear. Colonial secretary Harcourt wrote in March 1913: 'It is obvious that they cannot have full responsible government now and though one would imagine that Union was their proper ultimate objective they do not seem to be inclined to that for the moment'.[5] The four possible choices were: Crown colony government, representative government, responsible government, or junction with the Union. The Colonial Office preferred for the time being the simplest solution, which was to continue Chartered Company administration, though with some modifications. None of the other courses seemed possible. Harcourt hoped sincerely 'it will never be the fate of the Colonial Office to have to run Southern Rhodesia with a Lyttelton [representative] or other mongrel constitution', a phrase suggested by his permanent under-secretary, John Anderson.[6] Experience with Natal discouraged the Colonial Office from setting up small responsible governments over big African populations. The Rhodesians, jealous of their British character, did not want Union, and Botha's known desire for an early consideration of the inclusion of both the Rhodesias only hardened opinion against it.[7] Moreover, as Gladstone noted at the end of 1913:

they believe Rhodes had [the] prior ideal of self-governing Rhodesia first and his work must be finished: they would get only poor Dutch settlers and Rhodesia would be made a midden heap for the human wreckage of the Union. Moderate and responsible opinion thinks renewal of Charter is unavoidable: His Majesty's Government would not give responsible government, and representative government would mean stagnation and Downing Street instead of Company.

Thus renewal of the Charter was the only possible course in 1914.[8] Though the administration was unchanged, it was felt that in the light of rapidly changing circumstances, Britain should not bind itself to the continuation of the Company administration for the full period of ten years, and so it was provided that the Charter could be modified if the Legislative Council asked for, and could provide evidence to justify, responsible government.

After five more years, by the beginning of 1919, everyone was agreed that the Company must go. But beyond this there was bewilderment. The indisposition to accept Union as an immediate solution was general. The Colonial Office set itself dead against responsible government; Lambert, the prime formulator of this opposition,* emphasised the danger of the influence which the Company could still exercise in a little state, of the lack of a leisured class to attend to politics in a community so new and small (the public men had functioned so far mainly as critics of the Company rule but had little experience of initiating policies or of actual administration). Moreover, argued Lambert,

> To give responsible government to 30,000 whites ruling a million blacks is not only without precedent, but the example of Natal . . . right up to 1910 shows how great the difficulties would be . . . Whether therefore we look to natives for whom we hold a trusteeship, or white community which is insufficiently strong politically and financially – the obstacles to early responsible government (unless it were a prelude to immediate entry into Union) appear prohibitive.

After careful study of the question, Milner (colonial secretary, January 1919 to February 1921) completely agreed with Lambert's criticism of the 'self-governing Dominion of Rhodesia' idea: 'It seems to me totally out of the question. The alternatives are absorption in the Union or to carry on a bit longer under the present system.' It was evident to him that

* H. C. M. Lambert, head of Dominions department of CO, 1907–25. His connection with southern Africa began in 1892.

3a Tshekedi Kgama (1930)

3b Smuts and Hertzog outside the House of Assembly

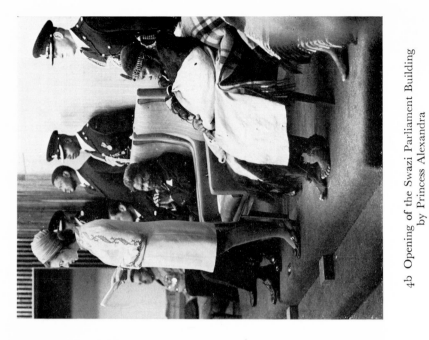

4b Opening of the Swazi Parliament Building
by Princess Alexandra

4a Sobhuza II at Swaziland Independence
Anniversary Celebrations 1969

advocates of responsible government had never seriously faced
the financial problem.[9]

In his fifth year as high commissioner, Lord Buxton complained that he was completely ignorant of the views and policy
of the imperial government with regard to Rhodesia. In
February 1919 he telegraphed for guidance. For his own part he
doubted whether Union would be generally acceptable to the
settlers either then or in the near future except perhaps as the
only attainable alternative to the continuation of Company
rule; absorption would be welcomed only by the Company and
by some of the Matabeleland settlers. Responsible government
had many advocates and would doubtless have had more but
for the fear of a heavy debt charge in respect of past administrative deficits, and the financial difficulty could not be relieved
under the present regime which held out little prospect of a
considerable influx of immigrants or capital.

Milner was not able to reply until 8 April 1919, owing to a
general state of overwork; 'the whole world was rocking', and
fundamental questions (India, Ireland, Egypt and so forth)
were mercilessly bearing in upon him simultaneously. Whilst he
himself had eventually formed an opinion, he was not aware
that any of his colleagues had any view at all on the subject, and
it would, he said, be totally useless to take a big new question
before the cabinet, since they knew nothing about it and would
have no time to think. A hasty and perfunctory decision would
be worse than useless, and so they had better reconcile themselves to having a policy statement from the secretary of state
rather than from the government as a whole. Milner's opinion
of the Rhodesians was certainly not untinged by a somewhat
weary sarcasm:

They want, of course they always did want (perhaps they are
not singular in this) a combination of things which this
imperfect world cannot provide. They want first and
foremost self-government, that universal panacea, and second,
freedom from the burdens and responsibilities which self-
government involves. The first thing to make quite clear to
them, in the most gentle and sympathetic manner possible, is

that really the two things cannot be separated. No doubt they would be very pleased if the Charter could just be kicked out, handing over to them the country, which it had created and equipped, at the expense of X-millions, for nothing. This is obviously impossible, as no doubt all sensible men in Rhodesia recognise.

Even sensible men seemed to entertain the idea, or at least have a lurking hope, that Britain would shoulder the financial burden and hand Rhodesia over free of debt. If such a plan ever was practicable, Milner continued, it was 'totally out of the question at this time of all others' when the British tax-payer was staggering under a burden which a good many people (though Milner was not one of them) reasonably thought might prove unbearable. In other words, if the Rhodesians 'want self-government *simpliciter*, they must pay for it'. A 'Dominion of Rhodesia' was not practical politics, though he tactfully proposed to let them draw this inference for themselves. As they were 'dead sick' of Chartered government and determined to have a change of some sort, Milner considered them to have two options. One was to join the Union, in which case they would have self-government indeed but with consequences which they might not altogether like. The other was to have some sort of intermediate stage of 'representative' government,

> during which they will be able to look round and muddle about for themselves, until they get sick of it and finally tumble into the Union, probably on very much worse terms than they would get today. During this interval they would undoubtedly be an unmitigated nuisance to the High Commissioner and to His Majesty's Government.

Milner thought as he had always thought, that the longer Britain kept them under Charter government the better, but whenever it became impossible to keep them there, he would decidedly prefer to see them join the Union, and he would prefer this to their having a half-way house of their own. He was equally clear however that it would be absolutely fatal for Britain to put the screw, or seem to put the screw, upon them to take this course: 'If they are to join the Union, they must not only really do so, but be unmistakably seen to do so, *by their own free choice*'. Without pressure then, the practical question was whether the Union could offer such terms as to induce her to go in with the willing consent of the majority of her white population. He believed the Union could in fact do this, by offering disproportionate representation in parliament and by paying off the Charter. Botha had assured him that he thought he could persuade parliament to act along these liberal lines. Botha might be wrong, Milner added, but he could see no earthly harm in letting him try. If he succeeded, hesitating and divided Rhodesian opinion would probably swing definitely over towards Union. This Milner regarded as much the best thing not only for Rhodesia herself, as she would fill up her land and develop more rapidly than was now possible (he dismissed the argument that *bywoners* would swamp the British), but also for imperial interests, as Rhodesian representatives would certainly strengthen the non-Republic party in the Union.[10]

Buxton agreed that they must not apply the screw, especially as Union was so obviously the simple solution of all imperial difficulties. He was particularly anxious to avoid any attempt to saddle Rhodesia with the whole financial liability of the Company, first because it would handicap her development and secondly because it would strain her loyalty if she found that while the Chartered Company had chastised her with whips, the imperial government intended to chastise her with scorpions. Rhodesians were, he wrote, now naturally really nervous as to what the political and economic future of the Union might be in consequence of the Nationalist upsurge. The prospect of his making some public utterance still perplexed him: 'I shall have to skate over *very* thin ice; and so far as I am not platitudinous I shall have to be very cautious'. Obviously it would be unfair and highly inexpedient to drive Rhodesia into the Union against her will by threatening to impose the whole financial burden on her. Apologetically he 'dragged in the natives', to mention that such African opinion as might be said to exist in Southern Rhodesia regarded entry into the Union with grave apprehension.[11]

The result of the election in the Union in April 1920 Milner thought disastrous. The whole aspect of the Rhodesian question was changed by it. He wrote to Buxton:

> I was hoping to see her join the Union at an early date. I do not think you shared my views on that subject. Now it seems to me that the possibility of her doing so has become much more remote. Smuts, with a strong majority, would have made her tempting offers. Now he is not in a position to do so, and nobody else is likely to try. Nor will the Rhodesians, unless I am greatly mistaken, ever join the Union as long as there is any danger of Separatism gaining the upper hand.[12]

The Colonial Office staff now set to work to brief Buxton for his public announcement, his 'very ticklish' engagement as he called it. Milner allowed him, somewhat against his own views, to take a more liberal view of the situation than Milner himself would have done.

Milner was anxious that people should realise what was involved in constitutional change, and asked Buxton to emphasise the twin difficulties of finance and small population. First, finance. Revenue and expenditure only just balanced, and unless reasons could be given for expecting a substantial increase of revenue in the early future, there would be no margin for interest on the loans which a responsible government would require for public works development. Imperial guarantee of loans as suggested locally was out of the question. The probable financial effect upon the status and assets of the Company of the recent judgement of the Privy Council seemed likely to involve the territory in a heavy liability whenever Chartered government came to an end.* Secondly, smallness of population,

---

* Before the First World War the Rhodesians had asserted that the Company did not own unalienated land in its private capacity, and the matter was submitted to the Judicial Committee of the Privy Council in 1914. The long-disputed legal position became clear in 1918 as the result of a judgement which maintained that the Company could sell unalienated land only as long as it administered Rhodesia on behalf of the Crown. Whilst this judgement was adverse to the Company's status, it also meant that, since it was held to be merely an agent of the Crown, when Chartered administration came to an end, a new Rhodesian government would not be able to use the unalienated lands to its own profit until the Crown's debts to the Company (i.e. administrative expenses incurred by the Company) were cleared. Lord Cave's Commission in 1920 fixed the Company's claim at £4,435,225.

both absolute and relative to the African. A white population of
just over 30,000 was significantly smaller even than the settler
population of Natal in 1893, and this would incontrovertibly be
regarded in England as a serious obstacle. Lambert wrote:

> The interests of the native population have always been a
> special concern and responsibility of the Imperial Govern-
> ment and the present system of native administration is
> excellent. Whether those interests can safely be handed over
> to the Southern Rhodesian settlers in their present state of
> political development must be a doubtful point. It is well
> known that the natives in the other South African Native
> Territories that are at present under the direct control of the
> Imperial Government, are most anxious to retain their present
> form of Government and not to be included in the Union.

Some preparation had however been made against the con-
tingency of responsible government by the settlement of the
Natives Reserves question. The findings of the Committee
appointed to investigate this matter were about to be ratified by
an Order-in-Council. [13]

Buxton believed that at least 60 per cent of the settlers in the
middle of 1919 were in favour of responsible government,
though they probably had not fully realised the financial
position. Those in favour of Union probably represented no
more than 30 per cent. Botha was now less inclined to move in
the matter as he expected South Africa for some time yet to be
pre-occupied with introducing settlers into South-West Africa,
and although Smuts was willing to try to incorporate Rhodesia,
his position on succeeding to the premiership, but to less than
his late predecessor's widespread popularity with the electorate,
was weak, and therefore not suitable for the offer of attractive
terms. Buxton was unhappy about the prospect of having to
force Rhodesians to choose between the Company and Union.
This he thought would 'greatly distress and disturb' Rhodesians,
who were one of the most loyal communities in the Empire.
Personally he would find it distasteful to tell them this was their
choice. He reported 'strong and widespread antipathy' to the
continuation of Company rule. He thought the Union would

not make any move and even if she did Rhodesia would probably reject it.[14]

The Colonial Office was therefore despairingly brought back again to the fundamental difficulty which the Union could not take off its shoulders, the financial difficulty. What was to be the burden which the government of Rhodesia was to carry? In these circumstances, Lambert was inclined to think representative government need not be ruled out:

> It presents great difficulties, but I'm not sure that in present circumstances they are not less than the other courses. Responsible government is out of the question if the full burden is to be borne. . . . Union is, I think, now out of the question. Crown Colony would not work, and though it would be most convenient that Southern Rhodesia should jog on with the British South Africa Company for a bit longer, it does not seem wise to present that as the only possible course. I should keep the door of representative government open, while indicating that we hope Southern Rhodesia will stop with the Chartered Company.[15]

On 12 August 1919 the secretary of state announced in a despatch for publication:

> . . . apart from important questions arising out of the small number of the white population as compared with the natives, I cannot regard the territory as equal in its present stage of development to the financial burden of responsible government. It would have to meet onerous charges in connection with capital and other expenditure and its finances must in addition, as a result of the findings of the Judicial Committee, be adversely affected to an extent which cannot be foreseen at present . . . There is I understand no present desire among the great body of the settlers to join the Union of South Africa, nor have any advances as yet been made to them by the Union. If such advances were made and proved attractive to the settlers I think His Majesty's Government would in no wise stand in the way.[16]

Representative government could be considered despite its

difficulty, 'if this should be the strong desire of the settlers and if they would pledge themselves to that co-operation which alone could make such an administration workable'.

The effect of this pronouncement in Rhodesia was desolating, and the apparent hopelessness of the situation seemed only aggravated by Buxton's speech on 26 August 1919. He admitted that the home government had not had time to study the question properly, a clear enough indication that they saw Rhodesia as quite overshadowed by the Union and would be thankful to see it absorbed. He said that representative government was not attractive to Britain since she did not wish to extend her responsibilities, and he hoped Rhodesia would not ask for it. 'Obviously so far as the imperial government are concerned, incorporation would be the line of least resistance, would throw upon them the least amount of responsibility, and would be a final solution of a difficult problem'. But such a solution would not be forced upon them. Buxton stressed that the white poeple of Rhodesia would themselves decide their future.[17]

Sir Charles Coghlan, a Roman Catholic settler of Irish extraction, now decided to join the Responsible Government League from which he had previously held aloof. The pressure for responsible government henceforth mounted rapidly. Whereas in 1914 Coghlan had regarded responsible government as a short cut to Union, he now saw it as the only means to keep Rhodesia out of the Union. Two main considerations had led to the intensifying demand for responsible government. In the first place, the idea of amalgamation with the Union had ceased to be attractive with Hertzog's success in the 1920 elections in South Africa. The augmentation of the 'disloyal' vote did not affect the crusted pro-Unionists, but it swayed those who put their Englishness first and created exactly the mood in which an election manifesto from the Responsible Government League could be most telling. In the second place, the administrative position of the Company had been largely prejudiced by the decision of the Judicial Committee of the Privy Council which declared the Company to be administering only as agents of the Crown. Once the Company had been reimbursed for its expenses, unalienated lands would thus be handed over to the succeeding administration as Crown property. This decision made responsible government feasible.[18] Dislike of Union was not wholly on sentimental grounds. There was a fear of the effect on Rhodesia of a protective tariff in the Union. Rhodesians also doubted whether they had enough men to provide members for the central parliament as well as their provincial legislature. On 12 May 1920 in the Legislative Council Coghlan moved that responsible government was urgently required in Rhodesia 'for the proper development of its resources and the freedom and prosperity of its people'. He believed Rhodesia could be fully self supporting. They would submit to any guarantee or safeguards for the Africans which the imperial government wanted.[19] (The Colonial Office knew this meant little: a paper formula would soon disappear.

After the lapse of a further year, Buxton looked with increasing favour on the prospects of responsible government. He was now the white Rhodesians' friend at court. Though it might be a tight squeeze, he thought responsible government was financially feasible, but only if the country did not have to undertake the heavy liability of the deficits. Incorporation might best suit the imperial government, but it was out of the question:

> Public opinion, as shown by the late election, is at present as decisive against Union as it is decisive against the continuation of Chartered rule. . . .
> If the financial position is cleared up, there seems no adequate reason why the European population of Southern Rhodesia should not manage their own affairs . . .

He did not entirely lose sight of African interests:

> It might be advisable – even if it is somewhat premature for immediate operation – to make constitutional provision forthwith, in the event of responsible government being granted, for the future creation of native councils in Southern Rhodesia, somewhat on the analogy of the Basutoland Council or of the Native Councils contemplated under the Native Affairs Act of this [Union] session.[20]

At this point, Buxton was succeeded as high commissioner by Prince Arthur of Connaught, who held office from November 1920 until December 1923. On 14 February 1921, Winston Churchill succeeded Milner as colonial secretary, not, it may be presumed, with any great enthusiasm for the idea of responsible government for Rhodesia which, as Milner had recognised, it was becoming increasingly difficult to side-step for much longer. In 1906, when he was under-secretary in the same office, he had seen Rhodesia as destined to be the 'weight which swings the balance in South Africa decisively on the side of the British Crown'* – and he was hardly the man to let the mere passage of fifteen years diminish the will to translate a good piece of rhetoric into practical politics. Nevertheless, he wanted to know – and to let the Rhodesian people know – exactly how things stood on that score. And so he appointed a committee to enquire into the question of responsible government, to suggest a date, possible limitations, and the necessary steps to be taken to devise an appropriate constitution. He asked Buxton to head the committee:

> Not only would your name command unquestioned confidence in Rhodesia, and so steady the restlessness out there, but your mastery of all the facts of the situation would enable the Committee to come to its conclusions far more rapidly than would be possible under any other chairman. . . . I am particularly anxious to get these questions settled without delay.[21]

Buxton accepted, and had his report ready by 14 May 1921. He acknowledged and favoured the demand for responsible government and suggested a referendum. He suggested a rather shorter period of interregnum than had originally been envisaged, because it had become evident to the Committee 'that the advantages of delay would be overbalanced by disadvantages', an argument to be heard frequently a generation later in other transfers of imperial power. The report put clearly before the Rhodesians what responsible government –

* See above, p. 21.

constitutionally, administratively and financially – would actually mean, the responsibilities it would entail and the limitations which must accompany it. 'If after further considera-tion', Buxton wrote privately, 'the people of Rhodesia agree to go into Union, well and good: but they should have a full opportunity of deciding for themselves, which this Committee gives them.'[22]

In the House of Commons, Col. Wedgwood* asked whether the Buxton Committee proposed to enfranchise Africans. On receiving the answer that African rights would be protected, he retorted that the Committee's report was 'one of the most reactionary documents ever to come out of South Africa'. Whereupon the Speaker intervened to say that was clearly a matter of opinion.[23] The report was well received by the Rhodesian public generally as well as by the elected members, who wished to send a deputation to London: they declared that by acting on the report the British government would take important steps towards securing the future of the territory as a prosperous and contented part of the Empire.[24]

This was not of course at all Smuts' reaction to the report, despite Buxton's personal assurances to him that it 'in no way cuts across or prejudices your ideas.'[25] Smuts had visions of the territory's slipping through his fingers. He was alarmed lest the Buxton report should imperil what he chose to regard as the 'proper decision'. A referendum on the issue raised in this way would, he thought, leave no real choice, and everybody would vote for responsible government. With an uncanny foresight he wrote to Churchill:

> I very much fear Responsible Government to Rhodesia at this stage will make of her a future problem both to Imperial Government and Union Government which it may be difficult to solve and everything should be done at this stage to help her to come to the right decision.

He suggested a referendum embracing all issues, including Union. Churchill did not feel able suddenly to propose a

* Col. Josiah Wedgwood (1872–1943), M.P. (Liberal, then Labour) 1906–42, Vice-chairman of Labour Party 1921–24, member of the pottery family.

referendum on the Union proposal, in view of the crushing
defeat of Union supporters at the last Rhodesian election. His
advisers, notably Lambert, were of opinion that entry to the
Union was so momentous, with consequences ultimately more
serious than responsible government, that no one ought to take
the responsibility of pressing a decision upon Rhodesia while she
was 'still in her nonage'. It was a question which ought to be
decided by a government and legislature fully responsible to
her people. Everyone knew the Company wanted Union (for
financial reasons), and for the secretary of state to interfere
would expose him to the suspicion of co-operating with the
hated Company. Government intervention would be inexpedient and wrong. Inexpedient because intrigue would
demolish imperial influence in Rhodesia for a long time to come
as well as effecting nothing in the short run, wrong because it
was a matter for the Rhodesians to decide: tactics and wider
considerations of justice required the imperial government to
keep the lists free and to do no more. It was even possible that
pushing Rhodesia into the Union would not help Smuts much
in the long run; not many seats could be created, and once
Rhodesia was incorporated, an Afrikaner influx might upset all
calculations.

Churchill accepted the view that the essence of the Buxton
report was as follows. The settlers were left to say 'yes' or 'no' to
a scheme of responsible government. Nothing in it really prejudiced a decision to go into the Union if they were so determined: a responsibly governing regime would have full power
to negotiate for entry if the people desired; but if responsible
government was turned down, union was likely to become a
more attractive proposition than the results of the last election
had shown it to be for the moment.[26]

Smuts' major appeal to Churchill was a private and personal
letter of 5 September 1921. Coghlan, he argued, appeared to be
the only person really strongly in favour of responsible government. Smuts did not wish to announce final terms yet, in order
to avoid the appearance of an ultimatum. In any case, he might
miss many points on which further concessions could be offered
after discussion. He would, however, give a broad indication of

the Union's readiness to concede loaded representation in parliament, to pay out the Company for their land rights and railway assets, to make special measures to foster land settlement and railway extension; they would minimise the risks of over-centralisation by ensuring Rhodesia's retention of a proper measure of local control of her administration. Under present circumstances he believed responsible government would be a 'great fiasco'. If the imperial government would make the settlers realise they could not have land and railways without paying for them, and could not look to London for assistance, 'their ardour will cool very considerably', whereas the Union would give definite terms which would satisfy the financial requirements. Now was the time to act:

> That it is advisable from the larger point of view that Rhodesia should join the Union now rather than later seems to me very clear. Today I could carry incorporation although it would mean a sensible addition to the burden which the Union taxpayer will have to carry. Could I carry such a policy later, when I shall have been politically weakened and Rhodesia will most probably have made a great financial mess of the new experiment? I doubt it. If Union is to take place, now seems the opportune time.

And Union should take place, he concluded,

> not only to carry out a great ideal and territorially to round off British South Africa; but also and especially to help in producing stability in the Union. Rhodesia will bring a very helpful contribution to the forces of order and progress and will mean a considerable setback to the disruptive influences which are and will remain at work. Besides, it must be borne in mind that the Mandated Territory of South-West Africa will within a comparatively short period probably also be incorporated as a Province into the Union; and its political influence, which will probably help the cause of disruption, will be more than neutralised by the previous incorporation of a loyal community like Rhodesia into the Union. To my mind the policy I am advocating is one of very

far-reaching Imperial significance, as you will readily understand, and I trust you will see your way to help it on in every
legitimate way.[27]

Smuts allowed himself to be convinced of a rapid change of
opinion in Rhodesia as the result of the latest Union elections
(1921) which had confirmed his position; and he believed
people were becoming more ready to admit that responsible
government without control of lands, mines, railways and
perhaps Africans, would be, as he scornfully described it, 'a
mere taxing machine', which must surely break down in bad
times. If a deputation from Rhodesia could be in London in
June or July of 1921, informal conversations could take place
between it, the Colonial Office, the Chartered Company and
himself. The beneficial result of such four-cornered conversations
might well be the shelving of responsible government.[28]

Churchill's initial reaction, guided by Lambert, was unfavourable: after the publication of the Buxton report, Rhodesian opinion must be allowed ample time to crystallise
before any further steps were taken. The great danger was of
course that the Rhodesians might suspect that a deal was
being completed with the Company behind their backs. Un-
fortunately, as Buxton wrote, 'the diplomacy of the Company
is as a rule about as delicate as an elephant dancing among
eggs'. If the Company were seen to be bestirring themselves,
any chance that pro-Union sentiment might have had would be
promptly extinguished. The British thus fervently hoped that
the Company would not, with their usual clumsiness, engineer a
press campaign in favour of entry to the Union.[29]

Union ministers did not seem willing to express publicly any
opinion about inclusion until they were approached by a
properly constituted authority empowered to deal with the
matter. Churchill wished Coghlan's deputation to see Smuts
while Smuts was in England. Coghlan did not find this convenient, and in any case felt it would not affect the object of his
mission which was to settle, in conjunction with the colonial
secretary, a Rhodesian responsible government constitution for
submission to the settler community. In the event, he was able to

see Smuts in South Africa, before leaving to accept Churchill's invitation to discuss a draft constitution with him. Meanwhile Churchill saw members of the Rhodesia Union Association (favouring inclusion) in August 1921, and simply told them it was not the moment for him to lay down a policy.[30] On 21 October 1921 Churchill telegraphed to the high commissioner:

> I have had several satisfactory talks with Responsible Government delegation, and have handed to them draft Letters Patent which they are studying and discussing with Colonial Office. I have informed them that though it by no means follows that I should recommend them to adopt it they shall go back to South Africa with a complete scheme of responsible government. . . . I now desire to elicit the terms from the Union Government on which Rhodesia would be admitted to the Union. I wish for this purpose a representative delegation from Rhodesia to meet General Smuts in the near future. This course also commends itself to him.

It was, Churchill added, his 'personal wish' to proceed in this way.[31]

Churchill took the matter to the cabinet:

> In view of the retirement of the Charter Company two courses were open: either Rhodesia might become a separate Dominion, or join the Union of South Africa. Lord Milner had offered Rhodesia responsible government subject to a waiting period; the Buxton Committee had made a similar recommendation but with a shorter postponement. In the meantime General Smuts had been returned to power and was prepared to offer substantial electoral and financial inducements to Rhodesia to join the Union. A Delegation from Rhodesia which had seen General Smuts on its way to this city, was now here discussing the details on the basis of responsible government and it has been arranged that another Delegation shall wait on General Smuts and obtain his final terms. It was then proposed that alternative solutions should be put to a Referendum.

Britain, Churchill added, could hardly compete with the inducements which were being offered by Smuts. The cabinet agreed to his continuing the discussions 'with bias a little in favour of joining the Union'.[32]

Coghlan was convinced from his interviews that Churchill was 'out to get us into the Union if he could'. At one point Churchill said 'he would give us no help financially unless Smuts refused to give fair terms'. Coghlan replied that there was a point beyond which they could not possibly go in advising the people to shoulder financial burdens which, in the case of other colonies receiving responsible government, had been discharged by the imperial government. And if that point was reached he would drop responsible government and concentrate simply on defeating Union. He saw Churchill for the last time on 21 December 1921.[33]

The revised terms offered by the Union were announced in July 1922. Southern Rhodesia would become a fifth province of the Union with, at first, ten parliamentary representatives; the Union government recognised the necessity for the construction of certain new railways, and while not pledging themselves to any schemes in particular, guaranteed a minimum development grant; they also promised special attention to developing and equipping the harbour at Portuguese Beira. There would be a separate Land Settlement Board, and sufficient funds would be available (not less than £500,000 per annum) to enable them to settle a large additional population on the land in the next ten years. Existing native reserves would be respected.

H. J. Stanley, imperial secretary and one day to become high commissioner, regarded these terms as 'generous in substance and tactfully expressed'. It would be 'unfortunate if so advantageous an offer should be rejected'. But he doubted whether the effect would suffice to turn the scale, and he feared Smuts was courting a rebuff. An impression was gaining ground in Rhodesia that the imperial government was unsympathetic to its hopes and aspirations, being mainly concerned to divest itself of financial liability and to help Smuts. Great Britain seemed to be playing the role of a stepmother who wished to be rid of them.[34].

Smuts appealed to Bonar Law, the new prime minister, on 20 November 1922. Rhodesia, he wrote,

> ought to seek relief for her financial troubles in the Union. Indeed, finance would be one of the principal causes to bring her into the Union, and the British Government should not in any way lessen the force of that cause. For the entry of Rhodesia into the Union is not only in her own interest and that of the Union but also in the interest of the British Empire. Rhodesia as a separate state struggling vainly with her impossible task is certain to become an embarrassment to the British Government in the end.[35]

The United Kingdom was bound to seek the line of least resistance. She had astronomical war debts, and huge additional mandated territories to manage. She was very worried by an almost general crisis of anti-Empire protest, centred in India, Ireland and Egypt. Milner and Churchill equally were pre-occupied by these wider issues as colonial secretaries and would gladly have handed Rhodesia over to the local statesman of pre-eminent reputation: Smuts. Smuts had been in the British War Cabinet, helped in negotiations with Ireland and the Welsh strikers, and had obtained from the League of Nations a South African Mandate for South-West Africa. The British leaders would willingly have adopted him permanently into their Establishment, finding him (as Walter Long wrote) 'quite delightful . . . he has mellowed, lost all the old angularities'.[36] Even good Liberals like C. P. Scott recognised him in 1917 as 'perhaps the most popular man in the country'.[37] For his part, Smuts was determined to bring the Rhodesians in, as his generous terms prove. 'It would be a great thing', he wrote in April 1922, 'to round off the South African state with borders far flung into the heart of the continent.' With Rhodesia secured to the Union he thought he would be able to build economic and political bridges between all territories of white settlement as far north as Kenya, and get a whip hand over recalcitrant Mozambique.[38]

In August 1922 Smuts made what seemed to him a successful tour of Rhodesia, although many Rhodesians thought he should have kept away from an issue they regarded as domestic. There was general hilarity when he asserted he had come but as a simple tourist. It made him realise however that his prospects were not good: 'They are afraid of our bilingualism, our nationalism, my views of the British Empire. In short they are little Jingoes'.[39] And so he decided to appeal to the colonial secretary for a pro-Union lead.

Clearly this could not be given without a dangerous risk, but some officials felt it might prove a sufficiently useful gamble to warrant the risk involved. A vote for responsible government was clearly not wholly improbable, advised Stanley, so any pro-Union lead would have to be worded with caution and must not involve the burning of boats which might be needed later. Nothing had been decided by October, by which time official opinion was more dubious than ever about the wisdom of an imperial intervention. If the issue was really in doubt, a judiciously worded message from the colonial secretary might turn the scale, but there was a distinct risk that an eleventh-hour message would be misinterpreted and cause bitterness rather than effect conversions.[40] Circumstances now combined to make such intervention impossible. Churchill had to have an emergency operation, and the Coalition government fell. On 19 October 1922 Churchill woke up to find himself without an appendix or a job.[41]

Smuts himself sent a message to the Rhodesians based on the theme that 'the Union is going to be for the African continent what the United States has become for the American continent. Rhodesia is but another day's march on the high road of destiny'. Rhodesia could look forward in the Union to 'rapid growth, fruitfulness and a noble destiny'. He then painted a grim picture of the futilities of responsible government. His historical parallel with the American Republic provided the anti-Union contingent (who had been dwelling on the risks of a South African republic and secession) with singularly useful ammunition.[42]

The referendum was held on 6 November 1922. The voting was 59·43 per cent against Union, 40·57 per cent in favour: 8774 votes to 5989. The polling was nearly 80 per

cent of the electorate. Such a result was decisive, even overwhelming. Smuts was cross and inclined to blame Churchill's
tactics.

Why was there such strong opposition to Union? The Unionists had money and political ability on their side, but they
lacked a sufficiently popular appeal and a leader as outstanding
as Coghlan. Railwaymen believed their wages and conditions
of work would deteriorate and Smuts did not adequately allay
their fears. Mineworkers would have nothing to do with the
man who had recently sent troops to fire on their Rand com-
rades.[43] The possibility that a flood of Afrikaner poor whites
might settle on vacant land was a bugbear and by no means an
irrational one, since Lambert at the Colonial Office shared it.
More generally there were four considerations:

First, Union was perhaps raised prematurely. Stanley
analysed the point competently as follows:

> The feeling against going into the Union as an incident in a
> bargain made by the British South Africa Company for its
> own convenience and in its own financial interests was
> overwhelmingly strong among many who might have been
> quite ready to contemplate negotiations with the Union
> Government at no very distant date, provided that in the
> meantime the Company had been eliminated from the
> Administration and they themselves had become 'masters in
> their own house.'[44]

Coghlan's attitude seems to support this analysis. He once said
to Buxton:

> I have no desire to fight Union in contrast to Responsible
> Government. Responsible Government is not necessarily
> anti-Union, as we can go into Union afterwards: but Union
> is anti-responsible government, and we can never withdraw
> from Union if we try the experiment first and it is a failure
> ... If therefore the terms of the Union are settled with Smuts
> and rejected by Rhodesia as against responsible government,
> as I am certain they will be, Smuts will have only himself to
> blame for any defeat he may suffer.[45]

On balance however this would seem to be an argument to pacify the British government. It is hard to see how Rhodesian objections to Union firmly held in 1922 were likely to be diminished within a generation.

Secondly, there were those who held the view that the existing uncertainties of the political outlook in the Union (the precariousness of Smuts' position for example) were such as to render it imprudent for Rhodesia to go in until she could do so with a strength sufficient to secure her against what Stanley described as 'absorption by the ravening maw of secessionism or ultra-capitalism, whichever the particular bogey might be'.[46] (It is of particular interest to note that the republican movement in South Africa had as disturbing an effect in Rhodesia as it did in the High Commission Territories.) In his discussions with Churchill, Coghlan stated, with a pardonable heightening of patriotic feeling, that above all:

> we in Rhodesia wished to have no part or lot [in a Union] which had apparently the constitutional right and, so far as the Dutch element was concerned, all the will, to cut us adrift from the British flag and carry us with them whether we liked it or not.

Secession was a most offensive cry to the British Rhodesians. If they had to fight to keep the British flag they would prefer to do so 'as an independent British entity', and felt they could 'do more good in that capacity'.[47]

Thirdly, there were others, probably not many at the outset, who were opposed to entry to the Union at any time and on any terms. In Stanley's analysis:

> This latter section of extremists would have been negligible had not the force of circumstances, by placing Union into immediate direct anatagonism to responsible government, brought about a temporary fusion of those who originally desired responsible government as a step on the road to Union, with those who wished to erect an insuperable barrier against Union. And in the heat of the fight, Union became the enemy which had to be attacked by all who wanted responsible government, whether they wanted it as a half-way house or as an end in itself.[48]

Presumably this is what Smuts had in mind when he complained of Churchill's tactics.

Finally, there was a widespread concern about the fact that the Union was a union and not a federation. If the South African constitution had been federal, Rhodesia would probably never have considered responsible government. 'British' provinces, like Natal and Rhodesia, were ones which preferred the federal system. As it was, many Rhodesians feared that absorption by a unified and centralised Dominion would lead to sacrifice of identity, to suffering for local interests and development, perhaps even to the checking of overseas immigration and to higher taxes. The younger civil servants and postal officials would have nothing to do with centralised rule from Pretoria which might interfere with their promotion prospects.

Smuts wanted Rhodesian votes in parliament. Coghlan found it difficult to make him see 'that the question of Rhodesia was not a matter of the ins and outs of an ordinary contested election, but the matter of a people with a soul to be saved as well as a body to be kicked'.[49] Neither of them considered saving African souls.

The result of the referendum forced the Colonial Office to set up responsible government at an early date. The cost of buying out the Company administration was shared by the United Kingdom and the new responsible government. Announcing the arrangements on 12 July 1923, the ninth Duke of Devonshire (colonial secretary 1922–24), hoped they would prove of benefit to Southern Rhodesia and to South Africa, and 'last but perhaps not least, to the British taxpayer as well'.[50] The settlement was certainly a tight-fisted one. Rhodesians asked no favours and got none.

For all that, it was a settlement of outstanding historical significance for the whole future of southern Africa. It closed an era of imperial policy in Africa since 1852: it was the last of a series of enactments placing Africans under white settler rule outside the circle of direct imperial protection.*[51] It was the last

* Embracing the imperial connection did not mean white Rhodesian endorsement of imperial principles of African policy. However, British retention of ultimate responsibility for native policy was a dead letter from the beginning.

issue upon which the British government supported South
African territorial aggrandisement. The settlement cast doubt
on the whole future of the High Commission Territories.
Bechuanaland, it had been said, should go into the Union when
Rhodesia went. The Union's terms of incorporation for
Rhodesia involved the purchase of railways through Bechuanaland and the acquisition of British South Africa Company rights
there. Acceptance must have made the transfer of Bechuanaland a matter of practical politics. The decision as taken operated to make it decidedly not a matter of practical politics. The
point was well put in a Dominions Office memorandum of July
1932: 'The chief ground for assuming that transfer to the Union
was the inevitable destiny of the Protectorate has disappeared
with the decision of Southern Rhodesia not to enter the Union'.
Rhodesia chose to remain outside:

> with aspirations of becoming the nucleus of a larger state,
> embracing Northern Rhodesia and at least a part of the
> Bechuanaland Protectorate, and counterbalancing the Union,
> with its strong Dutch influence, in the South. Whatever view
> may be taken as to the desirability and feasibility of this
> project, it is quite clear that, if and when it is decided that a
> change in the *status quo* of the Protectorate is necessary, the
> claims of Southern Rhodesia to the reversion of at least the
> northern part of it will have to be considered, and an under-
> taking to this effect has already been given in reply to a formal
> intimation on the part of the Southern Rhodesian Govern-
> ment that they regard the interests of Southern Rhodesia as
> directly concerned in its future.[52]

4 The High Commission Territories, I: The Failure of Botha and Smuts, 1910–24

THE attractiveness of the High Commission Territories to land-hungry white South Africans was obvious. Selborne forecast that many of them would deliberately and as a matter of policy seek to break them up and distribute African lands among European farmers: 'It will become a point of honour to every South African, Briton or Boer, to get control over them'. Already in 1907 they were calling the Territories a menace.[1] With only a few exceptions, even the best-disposed whites could not bear the idea of Africans' owning land. Every year some 200,000 sheep were sent to and fro between the Transvaal and Swaziland, across some of the most breathtaking hill country in the world, where line is piled upon line, ridge upon ridge, to take advantage of the winter grazing of Swaziland's green and pleasant, well watered pastures. The Union coveted the possibility of placing Afrikaner farmers, largely poor whites, permanently on Swazi Crown land. To forestall this, Buxton in 1917 urged the desirability of selling land to British farmers.[2] The Union government thought it needed more land to cope with the patently serious *bywoner* problem. It had already enacted the Natives Land Act, one of the first results of which was to direct attention to 'unoccupied' land not designated as native reserves.

Perhaps because South-West Africa from 1919 served the most pressing needs, South Africa gradually seems to have been less interested in obtaining the Territories to assuage land hunger. Emphasis shifted to other matters. Increasing alarm was felt about soil erosion caused by rivers. Would Basutoland be half washed away before they acquired it? And there was another problem: stock disease. Mr du Plessis, M.P., fulminated about Bechuanaland. 'This hothouse hatchery of disease and vermin', he called it in 1934. There was for various reasons a strong revival of interest in the Bechuanaland Protectorate in the thirties and forties. Smuts suggested to the high commissioner that Basutoland's surplus population could be directed into Ngamiland, which might take a substantial population. Public opinion focused its interest in the area as a result of various surveys. Considerable publicity was given to a scheme put forward by Professor Schwartz. Interest in the possibilities of irrigation based on the water of Ngamiland was aroused after investigations by J. L. S. Jeffares, published in 1937. It was thought there could be a big area in the north of Bechuanaland where subsoil water might be discovered in an artesian basin.[3] In the House of Assembly in 1946, Mr J. M. Conradie outlined 'very great possibilities' if they could incorporate Bechuanaland: 'We could then develop the waters of the mighty Okavango River and, as it were, create a new province of South Africa out of the desert-like Kalahari'.[4]

Thus while the basic urge to acquire land remained a fairly consistent thread among the motives, others were added to it, such as the fear of stock diseases by farmers in the border districts, the need to protect or extend the sources of the Union's water supplies, the necessity of comprehensive planning of native policy in 1913 and again after the Tomlinson Report of 1954, or the implications of railway development in the early 1920s, and the pressure of speculative mining concerns in the 1930s. At different times each of these interests was advanced to justify South African demands. Yet essentially, South African interest in the Territories was more political than economic, and more even than a desire to make the desert rejoice and blossom like a rose. Prestige loomed prominently throughout. Deep-seated within this motive there was a historical grievance. After all, as explained in the first chapter of this book, it is plain that but for Britain, all three Territories would have been under South African control. Swaziland indeed had once actually been under the Transvaal. Moshweshwe and Kgama were essentially dependent on the British presence in maintaining the

independence of their countries. But for Elgin, in 1907 Swaziland would have been returned to Transvaal control, and but
for Crewe's decision in 1908, all three would have entered the
Union in 1910. Most South Africans automatically regard
them as 'theirs' and vaguely wanted to 'own' them legally, but
it is significant that the most ardent advocates of transfer
became the National Party, also bent on the attainment of
another historic objective, a republic.[5] And getting a republic
while a British presence remained in southern Africa might be
tricky. In any case why should they have to go down on bended
knee and beg for 'their own countries'? Two important
speakers in a House of Assembly debate on the Territories
in 1936 said openly that although the Territories economically would be a burden, it was absurd for them to remain
under the control of another power in the middle of South
Africa. The 'manifest absurdity' of administration by a
country six thousand miles away was frequently remarked
upon.*[6]

Hence apart from the hopes of land settlement and water
control, and apart from Smuts' desire to remove obstacles to the
consummation of a United States of Africa, the chief consideration was negative. It became a matter of *amour propre* to oust
from South Africa any remnants of United Kingdom authority.
These enclaves, these '*kopjes* of imperial administration jut[ting]
out from the middle of the veld of a self-governing South Africa'
were, as Selborne had recognised,[7] intolerable reminders that
they were still not entirely masters in their subcontinent, and
gave the Malanite Nationalists cause and power to blaspheme.
The struggle against the intrusive role of the imperial factor did
not end in 1910. Despite our sovereign independence, our own
flag and national anthem, complained Dr Malan in 1954, 'we
are not masters in our own home'. Deep-rooted desire for incorporation of the Territories can thus be seen as an aspect of the
Afrikaner nationalist movement, and it was closely connected

* The two speakers were Dr N. J. van der Merwe, leader of the National Party
in the Orange Free State and of the Afrikaner Boy Scouts, and Mr P. G. W.
Grobler, the minister for native affairs. In 1954, Dr T. E. Donges, minister of the
interior, used the phrase 'manifest absurdity' in a debate on 12 Apr 54, and added
that they were 'desperately serious' about the question.

with the desire for a change in 'status' within the Commonwealth.[8] Eventually prestige became tied up with the question
in another form. By 1937 South African ministers were clearly
smarting under the realisation that Britain thought them
incapable of a humane native policy. High commissioner
Sir William Clark observed: 'The Territories are not a vital
concern to them except in so far as refusal to hand over becomes
part of the British attitude of reprobation on Union native
policy generally, about which they are extremely sensitive'.[9]
Lord Hailey has given his opinion that

> the opposition of the Native peoples to transfer did not in
> truth form a decisive factor in the British attitude on the
> subject, or at all events was never put forward as such. If the
> British Ministers found it convenient to lay emphasis on the
> necessity of prior 'consultation' with the African people of the
> Territories, it is clearly because they considered this to
> provide a more politic form of reply than an open condemna-
> tion of the Native policy known to be held by the majority of
> voters in the Union.

This is perhaps a shade too cynical about the British attitude to
African objections, but absolutely right about veiled condem-
nation of Union policy.[10]

As the British government steadily hardened itself against
transfer, the South African tactics shifted accordingly. At the
outset, the Union tended to assume that the British intention to
transfer was equivalent to a definite undertaking, and within
this misconception, the approaches of Botha and Smuts were
friendly enough. Hertzog however was driven to support his
case with arguments based on current relations between the
Territories and the Union, arguments which were, in Hailey's
words 'either fallacious or of very little real substance', and
which began to take the appearance of outright threats. The
dominant motive for insistent renewals of transfer requests was
caused by the implied repudiation of the native policy of the
Union, and they became a symbol of the growing ascendancy
of the extremist Afrikaner element in Union politics. Without
transfer the Territories stood as a living argument against

that policy and a reproach to the ideology which under-pinned it.

The problem was one which exercised South African ministers rather than their followers. Approaches to the British government were always made by individual ministers of the Union on their personal initiative, and never actually took the form of a formal address to the Crown by the Union Houses of Parliament, which was the procedure prescribed in the Schedule. One reason for the absence of this formal approach was the circumspect unwillingness of any South African government to risk an outright rebuff.[11] Furthermore there was probably at no stage any widespread public pressure in South Africa for transfer. In the Transvaal, Col. Collins was for many years the chief supporter of it, but the precise role even of a few interested M.P.s is uncertain, since for every farmer who wanted transfer to make doubly secure his untrammelled use of Swaziland pastures, or to combat Tswana stock diseases, there was probably another who feared the competition which would result from the unrestricted entry into Union markets of products from the transferred Territories.[12]

Another suggestion may be offered to explain why the issue interested the professional politicians more than their electors. Even more than most other Dominions, South Africa (considered as a white community) was a small country: three million people, less than half the population of London. The concerns of the 'small country politics' syndrome are mostly trivial and parochial. Ministers themselves engendered a national inferiority complex by repetition of the phrase 'we are a small country'.[13] Deneys Reitz made a typical assertion: 'We are a small people in South Africa and we play an infinitesimal part in the affairs of the Empire.'[14] A genius like Smuts could escape and hold his own on an international platform. The ordinary politician could not. The pattern of his relations with the wider world was limited to three possible objectives: status within the Empire and Commonwealth, expansion to the north, and acquisition of the High Commission Territories.[15] Of these, the first offered little scope to an Afrikaner between 1926 and 1948, the second was inchoate, and it was really only the third which offered an opportunity of parleying on equal terms (if not with equal skill) with the representatives of the British King-Emperor.

Sometimes the South African requests were accompanied by promises, sometimes by threats. Always there was the knowledge that something might be gained by the asking – if not territorial aggrandisement then the perpetuation of a suspicious grievance against the British Empire. It looks as if sometimes (for example after the passing of the Statute of Westminster) Hertzog asked for transfer without much real hope of success, simply to stir the old feelings. Of course Hertzog wanted a solution, but if he could not solve the problem, he soldiered on, with tactics which often appeared to be those of a man bent on keeping a good grievance alive. Thus one feels an atmosphere of unreality about the later negotiations. Negotiations also derived a peculiar flavour from the tendency of Afrikaner politicians to go round a difficulty rather than face it, to make a flank rather than a frontal attack, which gave an impression of vacillation. In these circumstances the British were never quite sure what to do, but always they found reasons for employing the classic doctrine of The Unripe Time. Always they fell back on the palliative declaration that of course in the long run transfer was inevitable, which removed the heat from any particular series of discussions and also tactfully reduced the temperature of African expectation. Their replies were, it is worth recording, always polite. Indeed Hertzog in the later 1930s was the only politician on either side who introduced a note of acrimonious wrangling. The unreality of the whole discussion at least while Hertzog was in this mood would be complete if we could demonstrate the hopelessness of his overtures from 1932: at present we may suspect it. With Smuts it was different. The real issues were raised by Smuts, the Good South African, in 1919 and 1939, and not by Hertzog, the Big Bad Afrikaner, in the intervening period.

If anything, Africans in the High Commission Territories were even more unwilling to enter the Union than the whites of Southern Rhodesia had been. Both were apprehensive of Afrikanerdom. African objection was manifest from the outset.

In a petition of 1910 the Ngwato stated in a perceptive if partisan way:

> We understand well the character of the Native administra-
> tion of these colonies, we know that the natives have no land
> of their own, many have no gardens to plough, nor are they
> allowed to chop wood or carry guns, nor have they any
> cattle, and a native is not regarded as a human being in those
> colonies, and we are convinced that we live under very much
> more fitting conditions of life. . . . When we submitted our-
> selves to your control it was to save our land from other
> European nations whom we feared would deprive us of our
> land. Especially did we fear this from the Dutch nation,
> who now form a part, and by far the larger part, of Your
> Majesty's white subjects in South Africa; and from this we
> find that the administration of the Union cannot be any-
> thing else but Dutch.

Not for a moment were they deceived by the idea that Union
would bring improvement in native policy: how could four
faulty administrations when united into one still be anything
but a faulty administration?[16]

The misgivings of the Sotho emerge from the deliberations of
their National Council. Nearly a hundred Sotho leaders,
resplendent on horseback and wearing their conical grass hats
and blankets (originally designed for them in the north of
England with a plethora of British heraldic symbols and
regalia), gathered among the corrugated red-roofed shacks of
dusty, sleepy Maseru* to go through the Schedule clause by
clause with the aid of the resident commissioner. The chiefs
feared the Union would not listen to them after transfer,
especially as they constituted only an advisory council.
Motsoene declared: 'for uneducated people to unite with
educated people is like inspanning a goat with an ox'. The gap
in civilisation was deferentially remarked. Abiathara said they
were still too far behind to join the Union: 'The Union will be
as if a horse had been inspanned together with a goat to pull a
waggon. The goat would be dragged and it would die'. Varying

* Its appearance in 1970 was scarcely different.

the metaphor, Malephane unconsciously appealed to the medi-
eval fable of the elephant and the whale: 'Animals living in water
cannot accept an invitation [to live with them] from animals living on land'. They were under no illusions about the constitutional duty of the British King to accept the advice of his ministers,
and this was what worried them about the Act of Union, which
the King did not initiate: 'this is a plan of those who rule this
side of the sea . . . we do not know where we are being taken to'.[17]

African awareness of current political realities was a good
deal more acute than Europeans used to think it. After all, the
Sotho had only to board a South African Railways train at
Maseru to become painfully aware of discriminatory policy.
The mere existence of the Schedule alerted them further. The
Queen Regent of Swaziland stated in 1914:

> that as Swaziland would no doubt enter the Union at some
> future date she was in sympathy with any efforts tending
> towards the betterment of the conditions under which Union
> natives live, and for this reason her son Malunge had become
> a member of the Native Congress and her people had assisted
> in contributions for the proposed delegation to England in
> connection with the Union Land Act.[18]

The Natives Land Act of 1913 was a major confirmation of
African fears. It was reactionary legislation, carried out with
harsh severity. In Bechuanaland, Baitlotle immediately
restated objection to transfer because it would involve the
application of the Act and prevent the tribes from buying land
under white occupation. Kgama trusted that controversy over
the Act would divert the Union government from designs on
Bechuanaland. In Swaziland, Malunge, able son of redoubtable
Queen Regent Labotsibeni, also expressed grave apprehension
of the Act. They decided to try to buy as much land as possible outside the reserves before the law could be applied to them. In 1915
the Swazi told their resident commissioner: 'the Swazi is in a
much better position than the native living in the Union. We
enjoy rights in the land of our fathers, whereas from our
kinsfolk in the Union such rights have been taken away by the
Natives Land Act of 1913'.[19]

At the end of the First World War another development also alarmed the Africans very much. This was the republican agitation and propaganda in the Union. If they were transferred and the agitation succeeded, all imperial connection would be severed, with, they supposed, unfortunate consequences to the Africans. The Swazi petition of 1919 stressed how their aversion to transfer 'has naturally been intensified' by the 'movement for the independence or republic among the whites within the Union, which independence from Great Britain the Swazi Nation will never consent to be associated with'.[20] The Sotho linked this distaste with disgust at the Afrikaner rebellion on the outbreak of war in 1914. How could they hope to be treated properly by people who were so treacherous to the King? 'They rebelled against the King when he was fighting his enemies'. Bernard Matete declared in the National Council (1919):

> We see in the newspapers that some men of the Union wish to get themselves released from the Government of the King. These men have been sent to Europe with General Hertzog as their leader. . . . How can we Basuto live if these Boers may be listened to by the King's government? How can these people who refuse your King govern you? . . . It is not right that we should be led into a dirty house, because the Union have not yet swept their house. . . . We Basuto are black Englishmen and not Boers. If the Boers think as we hear they do, I see no reason why we should be placed under the Union Government.

Simon Phamotse said traditional fear of the Boers had been deepened by their recent doings. 'We fear the Union because we know that . . . the Boers will one day get their independence from the British', as surely as the Americans had once got it, even though most of the American rebels were English, whereas the Boers would get it because most of the whites were Boers and some Englishmen agreed with them. Josias Mopeli added: if the Sotho were given to the Boers they feared that in the future South Africans 'may rebel against the King and compel us to help them'.

The 'anti-Native' Union was variously compared with the

hailstones which damaged African mealie crops (a powerful metaphor, considering the violence of hailstorms in this part of the world), a wolf ('sheep are never put in the same kraal with a wolf . . . if we are put together with them they will eat us up'), a lion, and most insultingly of all, a snake. The lion image proved the most durable and was perpetuated for fifty years. In the 1950s the Sotho were still saying they could never be happy when their next door neighbour was a lion, even though the beast might show no signs of an immediate intention of eating them. Britain was reminded that the Sotho had by voluntary action sought British protection from a lion and it would be most cruel if the person from whom protection was sought refused to give it and 'sent the man back to the lion'. They recalled that their original object in passing over the detested *republican* government of the Orange Free State and Transvaal in 1868 and surrendering themselves to Britain was their belief that the 'government of England was under hereditary chieftainship, which we preferred'. The distant mother country should not put them in charge of the elder brother: 'God was far away and he asked Cain to look after Abel', said one tribesman.[21]

In two petitions of 1919 the Sotho begged not to be transferred to South Africa, where 'natives have been placed under great disabilities and denied the rights and privileges of all free people'. There had been no true union that they could see between the two white sections, and there was no freedom or happiness for Africans owing to the harshness of Union native policy. Transfer, the Sotho ingeniously argued, should await the evolution of a Union policy

> which solves the difficulties already within its own borders; and until order is established out of the present chaos of Native populations bewildered and antagonised by the recent [land] legislation in the Union, Your Majesty's Government will appreciate the insistent need of not adding yet another unwilling or discontented people to the existing Native liabilities of the Union Government.

Furthermore they acknowledged their kinship with their brethren in the Union:

we see and hear their deep distress . . . The day may come
when we will wish to be united to the Union. It will come
when the sobs of the Natives in the Union have been stilled
for a generation. But as yet we hear them crying. We have
read the 1913 Land Act of the Union and we have watched
that Act in operation. Tens of thousands of Native victims of
that Act have crowded into Basutoland in the six years since
1913, and the iron has entered into the souls of the Natives in
the Free State.[22]

After a *pitso* in May 1919 Buxton assured the chiefs privately
that the question of transferring Basutoland had never yet been
raised and he did not think it would be raised 'for some
considerable time to come'. In the event of transfer, even if the
Land Act of 1913 were applied it would not have any effect
since all Sotho land was already guaranteed native land. Their
doubts remained.[23]

The history of discussions between British and South African
governments until 1948 with respect to the future of the High
Commission Territories appears to divide broadly into five main
sets of overtures: 1911–13, 1919–23, 1924–27, 1932–39, and
1939. The first was initiated mainly by Botha, the second
mainly by Smuts, the next two mainly by Hertzog, the last
by Smuts.

THE OVERTURES OF 1911–13

The earliest overtures differed from all later ones in the degree
of support they elicited from the high commissioner, weak but
well-meaning Lord Gladstone. His apparently infinite capacity
for complaisance towards Afrikaner aims was not supported by
the British government, whose colonial secretary (1910–15) was
Lewis ('Loulou') Harcourt – shrewd, capable, clever, courageous, hard-working, elegant and occasionally a trifle malicious.
Herbert Gladstone and Lewis Harcourt no more saw eye-to-eye
than their fathers had done before them.

Botha notified Lord Gladstone in April 1911 that he and his colleagues were strongly of opinion that the time had come for the 'incorporation' of Swaziland. (He should have said transfer, because incorporation was not provided for.) Smuts had calculated that altogether, between 1890 and 1899, the Transvaal must have spent nearly half a million pounds in Swaziland, hoping to secure its future incorporation. Moreover, Botha pleaded:

> a considerable portion of the land in Swaziland belongs to residents in the Transvaal, many of whom continually trek to and fro. . . . A very determined effort will now be made by the Union government to eradicate stock diseases – and in view of the constant trekking of farmers . . . this aspect of the question alone is of the greatest importance and warrants the immediate incorporation of this Territory, which is, by its relation, placed in a very different position to other territories adjoining the Union. Swaziland, too, has a fairly large white population which promises to increase rapidly, and from this point of view it also differs considerably from the other native Protectorates. [24]

Botha's proposal may have arisen out of party pressures. Personally, perhaps, he had no wish to hurry matters, since he knew he would probably be refused. A small but active section of Eastern Transvaal M.P.s, however, was possibly trying to push the Union government into objecting to the land apportionment being made in Swaziland. [25] At any rate Botha said he was most anxious for transfer. Colonial secretary Harcourt discussed the question privately with Botha during the period of the Imperial Conference in 1911, and persuaded Botha not to press the matter. The British argument was twofold. First, the settlement of land claims in Swaziland must be carried out as a prerequisite, and the completion of the complicated work ought not to be delayed further by difficulties necessarily raised by changes in the administrative machinery. Secondly, if transfer took place, the Commission contemplated by the Schedule would have to be established, which would lead to pressure to complete the transfer of the other two Territories. This would

cause a critical degree of African protest, perhaps even leading
to rebellion. Harcourt insisted Botha should drop the matter for
at least two years. Pledges had been given to parliament that
there would be no immediate transfers.[26] 'I am standing fast',
wrote Botha to Smuts, but it got him nowhere with Harcourt.[27]

Harcourt next had conversations about the Swaziland
situation with Gladstone in England in September 1912. They
agreed that they would not be indisposed in principle to
consider an application for transfer, with June 1914 as the
earliest possible date, because the land apportionment could not
be completed before then, and that meanwhile they would work
for the best possible conditions. On his return to South Africa,
Gladstone talked with Botha in November 1912, and it once
again became clear that Botha wished for the transfer of
Swaziland at the earliest possible moment. The Crown land of
Swaziland bulked large in his land policy, but he could not buy
land in Swaziland without British permission. He also said
something about pushing a railway forward. Gladstone favoured
coming quickly to some definite understanding on the whole
subject. Land sales in Swaziland to British buyers drew attention
to the question and led to 'inadvisable pinpricks'. Surely it
would be better in the circumstances to continue negotiations
rather than acquiesce in postponement until 1914? The matter
was bound to be raised next session by South African M.P.s even
if ministers did not ask for it;

> If so, any risk there may be from the course I advocate will
> equally arise and perhaps in a more difficult form if the
> subject is for the present dropped. There are sure to be
> continued demands for land from the Swaziland Government.
> If granted, the more pinpricks. If refused, we just exist as
> unimproving landlords.

He found Botha 'most friendly and reassuring' on all the Territories: transfer of Basutoland and Bechuanaland Botha put equally
in the distant future.[28] But Botha was soon to change his mind.

In the Colonial Office it was noted that Hertzog and his
supporters were full of fight, and might be expected to be
specially concerned with this matter, which attracted the

backvelder. They saw the advantage of letting Botha say discussions were afoot, with a view to an early decision, since this would enable him to dispose of criticism; if Britain refused discussion it would furnish a fine text for Hertzog, which it would be as well to avoid doing.[29] However, Harcourt preferred to drop the negotiations for the moment, in order to put off the premature discussion of the way in which the provisions of the Schedule might be expected to work: alterations to it could not in any case be discussed, since it must stand as it was.

The next, and most surprising, development was Botha's semi-official indication of an immediate interest in Bechuana-land. Gladstone, unwisely in the officials' view, asked Botha for his precise intentions. Botha's sudden interest seems related to the fact that from 1909 and especially in 1912, the British South Africa Company, believing that anticipated transfer to the Union had introduced a dubious new element into the situation, sought a definition of its preferential rights in Bechuanaland. Its aim was to have unoccupied land made over to it for settle-ment and development so that it might improve the position of Bechuanaland 'when it came into its inheritance'.* Botha referred to the Company's claim, but entered into no detailed comment, and his reference to it probably simply gave him a suitable excuse to raise the issue which he wished to do on other grounds.

In so far as Botha felt he must apply for Bechuanaland, to forestall the Company, the Colonial Office could satisfy him that it had already told the Company (June 1912) that no land would be ceded to it. The Office also believed that if Gladstone were to explain the preferential rights of the Company it was improbable that Botha would persist in asking for transfer. Officials were worried by Gladstone's apparent unawareness of the facts that 'it is the natives who really count', as well as the House of Commons, who would not be prepared to sanction the transfer of Bechuanaland for some years to come unless the Africans were really willing, and of this there was no sign. The

* See above p. 13. The Company had the right to acquire future concessions of land and minerals as a vestigial remnant of the pre-1895 plan to hand over the whole administration to them: a plan which had never been formally revoked, but vaguely held over indefinitely.

delimitation of Company rights was therefore a matter that, in the Colonial Office view, need not and should not be hurried, especially as they wished to keep white settlers out.[30]

By this time it was plain that the Territories were going to give much trouble. Within the next few months, Colonial Office disapproval of Gladstone mounted, as it emerged that Gladstone and Botha planned to utilise the Territories as dumping grounds for Union Africans. Gladstone most improperly hinted that Botha might extend his commission of enquiry on land to Bechuanaland. 'It is very disappointing to find him acting in such a cavalier fashion', one of the officials commented. Gladstone seemed to suggest that since unoccupied land in the northern Transvaal would have to be bought for Africans, it would be better to enable the Union government to provide free of cost for their Africans by handing over the High Commission Territories. The reasoning was curious, and officials thought it unwise of him to acknowledge and anticipate Union agitation for curtailment of reserves: 'It is a great pity that Lord Gladstone seems to dismiss so light-heartedly the solemn pledges given in the South Africa Act'. Gladstone's attitude was regarded in the Colonial Office as sometimes incomprehensible, sometimes impulsive. 'Lord Gladstone is by nature somewhat restless and the exact opposite of the old South African policy which was to "sit still".' 'Wise passivity' still seemed the right policy. Lambert, for example, emphasised the value of leaving Company claims unsettled. Delay suited Britain, since the earlier transfer was carried out the greater the difficulty of justifying it. Was Britain to spend money to prepare Bechuanaland for her successors? To quote the admirable Lambert:

Even if the Union comes along with solid official pressure, it is not clear that His Majesty's Government can give way. Khama and Co. cannot be treated as so many chattels to be given away, for they have never parted with land like the Swazis or lived under Boer rule; they came under the Queen with assurances of protection which will not indeed avail them for ever, but which will be hard to get round at least during Khama's lifetime – he has many good friends here who will recite us some ancient history.

His conclusion was therefore that Gladstone

> seems to me to look at the whole question from the wrong point of view – he contemplates transfer as a thing to be prepared for rather than one to be staved off, and acting on this principle he proposes to settle the Company's rights, which seem to me a useful obstacle to transfer and as such not to be interfered with. . . .

Lambert secured total agreement up to the highest level.

Gladstone, however, still failed to grasp the position, which Lambert again sharply defined as 'not what Union requires but what Parliament consents to' – this was the determining factor. The Union showed no sign of wanting to quarrel or to make the British position in the Territories impossible. The one thing likely to cause trouble with the Union would be to allow them to think they had only to cry for Bechuanaland in order to get it. Harcourt agreed with his advisers that they wanted to let sleeping dogs lie.[31]

Harcourt therefore categorically instructed the high commisioner to tell Botha that they 'could not in present circumstances' regard favourably a request for Bechuanaland. This case was quite different from Swaziland, which they were prepared to discuss quite soon, but in Bechuanaland:

> His Majesty's Government are under no obligation, legal or moral, to develop the Protectorate for white settlement. There is no reason to suppose that such development would benefit the natives, whose welfare has been, and must be, the principal concern of His Majesty's Government in Bechuanaland, while any successful policy of development would almost certainly precipitate a demand for transfer to the Union Government. Such a demand would in present circumstances be extremely embarrassing to His Majesty's Government. All existing indications point to strong opposition on the part of the Bechuana tribes and in the face of their opposition (particularly that of Khama . . .) it would be

quite impossible for His Majesty's Government to justify the transfer to the House of Commons.

Objections to early transfer were strong and would remain so.[32] Indeed this important statement was still quoted as holding good in the 1930s. It effectively stopped any further discussion of Bechuanaland while Botha and Smuts remained in power. In a private letter, Harcourt said he felt sure Gladstone would understand that so long as Kgama was alive, 'the bare suggestion of handing him over to the Union would bring the whole missionary world and others upon me at once' (a sentence he adopted from his permanent under-secretary, Anderson).[33]

How is Gladstone's divergence from the Colonial Office view to be explained? His general approach to South African problems was governed by his personal admiration for Botha and his own comfortable conviction that the Union really was working and producing a better spirit in native policy. Botha he found 'one of the most attractive men I have ever known . . . straight as a die . . . a true personal friend', and always ready in spare time to play bridge, golf and tennis. As far as prospects for the Africans under the Union were concerned, 'in every Province there is a better, higher, more informed tone'. Gladstone of course had no great opinion of the Africans: they were 'really savages' underneath, and so incompetent that although the Native Congress movement 'wants watching' he did not think it would come to much.[34]

The Union wanted more land for settlement, and Gladstone thought they might reasonably expect some assurance as to the extent of unoccupied lands which would eventually be at their disposal. This could not be given while Company claims were unsettled. Moreover:

We hold Bechuanaland in trust, and I think so far as Crown lands are concerned our policy should have regard to land settlement schemes of the Union and that within reason and within our opportunities we should work for the future. The time may soon come, if it has not arrived, when we might take the Union Government into confidence, and work out an agreed plan.[35]

Botha believed Bechuanaland could not be excluded from a general scheme of African land settlement in South Africa. Many reserves were overcrowded and the squatting problem was acute. Botha dreaded having to increase the number of small reserves and dot them about. Instead he would have liked to remove whites from the Transkei and give Africans there fuller rights. Gladstone thought this fair, and thus believed that the Commission appointed to make proposals on land segregation ought to include Bechuanaland in its possible solution:

> If, as is pretty certain, they say that Crown lands in Bechuana-land could be set apart as a vast reservoir for surplus native populations from the Union, public opinion in the Union would surely support them and perhaps in a manner not altogether to the advantage of the Bechuana tribes. The argument which would be set up seems to me irresistible. It would concern the general welfare of the whole native population of South Africa. The fear of white encroachment on the Bechuana reserves occupied by 130,000 natives would comparatively speaking be a very small consideration. We have no really solid arguments to use such as the special circumstances of Basutoland supply.

Botha did not wish to press for transfer now. But he must plan for the future. How, Gladstone asked,

> can we with justice now limit Union policy, as regards natives generally, to the Union territories and perhaps force them to make an unsatisfactory and incomplete scheme? And all this in face of the fact that transfer under the South Africa Act is only a question of date.

In a further memorandum he developed the point that if the Union government could show that the native question as a whole could not be satisfactorily taken in hand without the incorporation of the three Territories, he did not see how, in the interests of Africans generally, it could be refused. 'They will say we have no valid argument against them because they are ready to develop (we're not) and safeguard native just rights'.[36]

Botha's new interest in Bechuanaland sprang from a suspicion that Swaziland had insufficient opportunities for white settlement. But the Colonial Office responded by unequivocally ruling Basutoland and Bechuanaland to be 'black man's countries'. Harcourt sent the following despatch, based on Lambert's reasoning:

> The recent trend of legislation in the Union has I gather been such as to increase the feeling of insecurity of the native as regards his position on the land: and it is therefore all the more desirable that there should be some part of South Africa which may be considered as reserved primarily for the needs of the natives.

Hence as far as Bechuanaland was concerned the government deprecated any extensive alienation of the land, which would either disturb Africans already in occupation or would diminish the quantity of land available for those who were as yet insufficiently provided for.[37]

By contrast Gladstone so far missed the significance of the 1913 Land Act that he actually thought it would not cause any great hardship to Africans and suggested it would be desirable to adopt its principles, 'that natives should be prohibited from holding land in territories under white occupation and vice-versa', in British Africa. The Colonial Office unanimously agreed that the government of their own motion could not possibly be committed to the policies of segregation and an increasing divorce of the Africans from the land.[38]

The Colonial Office successfully blocked Gladstone's desire for precipitate action in both Swaziland and Bechuanaland. Further discussion of Bechuanaland it prohibited. Swaziland was more of an open question, yet Gladstone accepted the decision even to postpone further discussion for a year or two with 'much regret': to do nothing, he complained, was 'neither dignified nor satisfactory'. Gladstone entirely underestimated the difficulty of transfer. But for the 1909 pledges, or 'entanglements' as he dared to call them, he could see no reason why Swaziland should not have been transferred in 1913; these were the sole difficulty.[39]

The outbreak of war in 1914 precluded early resumption of discussions about Swaziland.

THE OVERTURES OF 1919–23

By 1919 Viscount Buxton was an already highly experienced high commissioner. Helped by a wife who was sympathetic to Africans, he was a more effective holder of the office (September 1914 to July 1920) than either of his two predecessors or his successor. This is true whether effectiveness is measured in terms of social charm or administrative ability. Buxton knew the importance of a little imperial swagger, unlike Selborne, who, for all his zeal and vigour of body and mind, had never realised how poor his credibility as the King's representative was in African eyes simply because he always wore a shabby coat and a soft hat. Nor can one imagine Lord Gladstone buttering up the notorious old Queen Regent of Swaziland, as proud as she was shrewd, with the gift of a huge cloak, the colour of crushed strawberry, and trimmed with yellow satin and a gold fringe. This Ndlovukazi, widow of Mbandzeni, kept dignified if ramshackle state in the royal kraal at Lobamba in the shadow of the imposing Mdimba Mountain. Buxton visited her there. At Government House, protocol was waived, to the consternation of the secretary, Mr H. J. Stanley, and Africans were invited to immense teas of mutton pies and stodgy sweet cakes. Buxton bore his responsibilities lightly, and achieved considerable mitigation for African interests even in the Union itself. 'The Governor-General', he wrote, 'should strive to acquire two useful accomplishments – how to ride on the snaffle and how to skate over thin ice'. With Botha he felt his relations to be frank, close, friendly and elastic.[40]

Buxton took much interest in the High Commission Territories, which had first interested him in the 1890s when he was under-secretary at the Colonial Office and concerned with the Swazi crisis of that time. During the 1914–18 war he easily dissuaded Botha from asking for Swaziland, on the reasonable ground that it would be taking an unnecessary risk to raise such an acute native question during war. Harcourt in May 1915 reaffirmed the desire to postpone the contemplation of transfer 'as long as possible'.[41]

Some weeks before he died, Botha wrote to colonial secretary Milner in July 1919 to press strongly once again for the transfer of Swaziland. He could see no reason whatever why its transfer should not be immediately effected, and he supported his carefully reasoned claim with three justifications. First, calling the Schedule into operation in Swaziland would give the Union valuable experience to guide her in the eventual administration of other territories both within and without the Union: 'It would be an experiment on a small scale with a native population already living among whites and well affected towards them, and therefore likely to be fruitful of suggestion for the future'. Secondly, it would enable the Swaziland whites to obtain better political representation, instead of being in a somewhat anomalous situation. Finally, the Union could spend money on development, which was badly needed, especially a railway from the Transvaal highveld through Swaziland to open up the mines of both countries and provide additional communication to the coast, 'but the Union government would not move in this matter, however useful and urgent it may be, while Swaziland is still an administration independent of it'. Botha implied that there was no special urgency as far as Bechuanaland was concerned, but as soon as the inclusion of Rhodesia in the Union became a practical question, its transfer would have to be dealt with too.[42]

The high commissioner let it be known that the moment was not in his opinion expedient for raising the question, nor indeed propitious for carrying out the incorporation of any African territory, since it would accentuate the alarm and unrest arising out of the special suspicion engendered by the Natives Land Act. Afrikaner Nationalist agitation for independence had also disturbed the Africans as possibly foreshadowing the withdrawal of imperial protection altogether. African protest at transfer would damage Union prestige and embarrass the British government. Furthermore, ample time for whites and Africans to state their views must be allowed: the British

government would be in a false position and open to the charge
of bad faith if transfer was not preceded by preliminary discussions with the Africans. Such was his reply. What he could
not say to the Union was that in reality 'the ingrained suspicion
and fear of a Dutch government among natives in the Protectorates as well as the Union is the fundamental difficulty'.

Both Botha and Smuts spoke to Milner several times while
in London and revealed themselves eager for action. Milner
understood Buxton's objections, but as they would in effect have
ruled out transfer at any time, he telegraphed him some
considerations on the other side:

> Basutoland I hope may remain autonomous native state
> always. In Swaziland, external conditions and native
> capacity far less favourable for self-government. White
> settlement is important and is bound to grow, and country is
> inseparable economically from adjoining districts of Trans-
> vaal. Assuming as I do that ultimately Scheduled Territories
> will come under Union, by far the best to begin with is
> Swaziland. Botha tells me he has no intention at present of
> asking for transfer of Basutoland or Bechuanaland and I think
> he understands perfectly that unless Union Government can
> make a success of handling of native question in Swaziland,
> the transfer even of Bechuanaland to Union will be deferred
> indefinitely. His own ideas as to treatment of natives, in which
> I believe he is sincere, seem to me liberal and quite on right
> lines. Of course you will have to satisfy yourself that he is
> likely to be able to carry them out. If he is, the present is, I
> believe, as good an opportunity as we are likely ever to have
> for making a start with transference of Native Territories
> under really good conditions.

While these were his general (and indulgent) views, he quite
agreed with Buxton that even if transfer was decided upon, every
care must be taken not to proceed in a precipitate manner
alarming to the Africans. The drafting of this telegram was
Milner's own.[43] Lambert for once had been overruled: he had
simply recommended approval of Buxton's stalling tactics.

Buxton himself could hardly contradict so imperious a chief.

In reply he claimed not to dissent from Milner's views in any way:

> My only desire was that question of incorporation should not be sprung upon the Swazis suddenly but that opportunity to allow them to digest the idea before incorporation was carried out should be given and that there could be no grounds for any allegation of breach of faith which if believed would have a bad effect in Basutoland and elsewhere as well as in Swaziland.

His observation that the European settlers, including the Afrikaners, were opposed to incorporation, drew from Lambert the tart remark that 'nobody wants Union in Swaziland'.[44]

Shortly before his death, Botha in private conversation spoke about 'restitution to the Transvaal of what had been wrongfully taken away by the imperial government'. He hinted that another reason for wanting Swaziland was that he could reassure the Africans in South Africa generally by providing an object lesson in Swaziland of Union government administration on the lines of a new native policy which he hoped to introduce there.[45]

Much intrigued, Buxton got Smuts to sharpen this rather vague language with his usual striking precision. There were, Smuts explained, two currents of thought about the transfer of Swaziland: status and native policy. 'Status' reflected the South African grievance of not being in control of all Europeans in the geographical area, their feeling that though they had achieved improved status in external affairs, they had not yet done so within South Africa itself. This approach naturally left Buxton completely unmoved. But Smuts' second point impressed him greatly. Smuts confessed how he and Botha agreed they must cease drifting in African affairs and find a solution. Perhaps this could be found by setting up a Native Commission as defined in the Schedule. It was because the incorporation of Swaziland would automatically put Commission machinery into motion that they were anxious to carry it, and the policy could be subsequently extended with comparative ease to other parts of the Union. It would give Africans some form of representation. This was an objective Buxton felt he could whole-

heartedly support, and if it really was the purpose of asking
for Swaziland, and if it would 'automatically start the ball
rolling' for a fresh native policy, his objections (though indeed he
did not really have any in principle) would be removed and the
transfer would be adequately justified. His only proviso was
against sudden or high-handed action. A new native policy, he
warned, could hardly be inaugurated by methods which
aroused African suspicions. Smuts spoke of setting up Native
Councils where they did not exist, and generally created
expectations of excessive liberality. He even mentioned the
possibility that one of the commissioners might be an African,
which was probably more even than Buxton could stomach.[46]

After Botha's death on 28 August 1919, Smuts succeeded him
as prime minister, and, robbed of his tactful old comrade, was
left to face alone elections and all the tricky post-war problems
in a more acute form. In consequence Smuts did not expect
Swaziland to be pressed forward so rapidly as it otherwise
would have been, and on 12 September he told Buxton he
definitely did not propose to tackle the matter at present: 'I have
too many stiles to get over'.[47]

Towards the end of 1920 the Native Affairs Act, on lines
outlined by Botha, provided for the establishment of a Commission of the same kind as that envisaged in the Schedule. Its
enactment afforded an opportunity for re-opening the question of transfer.

Meanwhile there were British moves to set up an Advisory
Council for Europeans in Swaziland. Buxton was reluctant to
sanction this without informing the Union government, but
feared that if he did so, it might prematurely re-open the
question of transfer. It could not be postponed however as it was
needed to sweeten the pill of raising European taxes.[48] The
mere mention of the proposal to Smuts had exactly the result
predicted. It drew from him (24 August 1920) an intimation of
his intention to move for the transfer of Swaziland at an early
date.[49]

Smuts did not like the idea of a European Advisory Council.
It might make people think the transfer had been shelved. On
the other hand, he did not wish to obstruct the raising of

necessary additional revenue, particularly in view of the financial difficulties of the Territory. By April 1921 he said he would, subject to transfer, provide for a Swaziland railway line as soon as any considerable programme for new construction became practicable, and he hoped to arrange for representation of settlers in the Union parliament without altering the Schedule.[50]

The Europeans of Swaziland were still averse to going into Union, but they were open to persuasion in two directions. First, a definite undertaking that a railway would be built within a comparatively short time, which Smuts thought possible, would be an irresistible inducement to a fairly large majority. Second, when represented in the Union Parliament, they wished this to be on the basis of one M.P. to every 800 voters, instead of the electorate's being split between and merged in three neighbouring Transvaal constituencies.[51]

A railway survey had been conducted by the Transvaal from Pretoria to Delagoa Bay through Swaziland in 1879. Milner as high commissioner in 1902 had promised support for a railway from Johannesburg through Swaziland to join a Portuguese line from Lourenço Marques at the Swazi border. It was an 'honourable agreement', and although no formal undertaking was given, the Portuguese built their section 1906–12. British governments refused to acknowledge the arrangement and would not build a railway, partly because of its uncertain freight potential. In September 1917 Buxton declared that in view of the 'inevitable transfer of Swaziland at some future, and possibly early, date to the Union Government, the last word as to the construction of the railway rests with them'.[52] The Union undoubtedly had a special interest, since a line from the Breyten railhead to connect with the Portuguese railway would relieve congestion and be a much shorter route from the Transvaal to Delagoa Bay than the existing Machadodorp–Komatipoort–Lourenço Marques line. The Union conducted four surveys: in 1918, 1921, 1922, and 1924. Local interests involved in the older line were strenuously opposed to so formidable a rival, and as an actual investment, apart from the development of the country, the Swaziland line was not likely to pay for several years to come. In January 1922 transfer was regarded as imminent enough for Smuts to meet the new Advisory Council informally. He listened sympathetically to their attitude towards possible incorporation and their yearning for a railway. Incorporation was in some ways tied up with his troubles over Portuguese management of the Lourenço Marques docks, and it might 'soon become necessary owing to the necessity of building new railways from the Eastern Transvaal to the Indian Ocean and possibly through Swaziland'. Railways were required for the 'prospective probable' development of the coal industry of Eastern Transvaal, which made incorporation 'a matter of urgency'.[53] Smuts seemed impressed by the possibility of strong resistance to transfer, from the European residents, if the desired railway line could not be promised.[54]

At this point Smuts notified the high commissioner that the question of transfer would probably be discussed during the next parliamentary session, although he had not yet come to a decision:

> The future of Swaziland is largely bound up in the decision that must be taken concerning the extension of the railway through the Eastern Transvaal coalfields to the coast, which again depends upon the route selected. . . .
>
> Until the engineering problems have been solved and until some definite decision has arrived at in regard to Delagoa Bay, the Union government are not in a position to lay any concrete proposals. . . .[55]

Smuts' failure to realise his aims in negotiations between the Union and the Portuguese government of Mozambique partly caused the abandonment of the idea of a railway through Swaziland,[56]* which in turn set back proposals for transfer. Other reasons for the Union government's waning interest were the failure of the attempt to incorporate Rhodesia and the beginnings of the economic depression. Smuts decided to await

---

* See above, pp. 33–4 Swaziland had to wait until 1964 for the opening of a transterritorial railway, freight only, an extension of the Portuguese line from Goba to Lourenço Marques.

more favourable circumstances. Then in the general election of 1924 he was defeated by Hertzog.

In the meantime a Swazi deputation had been received in London.[57] In December 1919 and January 1920 the Swazi had been promised permission to send a deputation whenever the question of transfer was formally raised. Knowing that the Union government was likely to raise it soon, the Swazi wished to act at once before it was too late for an effective protest. The newly installed paramount chief, the Ngwenyama, Sobhuza II,* had two objectives: to be told officially the reasons for government action during his minority and to protest against transfer. A claim to Swazi independence was put forward in petitions of May 1922 as an argument against the powers used in the land apportionment and especially against the right of the British government to transfer Swaziland to the Union. Permission for the deputation was reluctantly granted solely in the light of the admitted imminence of the question of transfer, since nearly all the other and more specific issues the Swazi wished to raise had already been debated *ad infinitum*. The Swazi were told that since there was 'some intention of raising' the question in the 'next few years' they should say what they wished about it while they had this opportunity.

Finding the sea an alarming phenomenon, Sobhuza and his party took little exercise on board ship during their journey to Europe.† In London they stayed in Maida Vale. The press gave them a good reception. Visits for them were arranged (as was traditional for African chiefs) to the Coliseum, the Hippodrome, the Zoo, and a Native Students' Club. They were entertained to several teas, including one with the former high commissioner, Buxton. The King received them on 29 January 1923. They saw the colonial secretary, the Duke of Devonshire, on 10 and 31 January. The secretary of state admitted the question of transfer had been under consideration for some time but it was not known when the Union government would approach His Majesty's Government formally. He reaffirmed the safeguards of

* Sobhuza II, b. July 1899; his father Bunu died Dec. 1899; Sobhuza installed at the full moon of 31 Dec. 1921. The Regency of his grandmother was now over.
† A photograph of the deputation, the chiefs dressed in stiff morning clothes, was still displayed in 1970 in the store at Malkerns in Swaziland: see *frontispiece*.

the Schedule as adequate; the 1909 pledge to the House of Commons that it should have a say in the matter still stood. Moreover, a further point of reassurance was rather optimistically put forward:

> The Native Affairs Commission for the Union, which as you know has been established by an Act of the Union Parliament, has not yet been very long in existence, but I have reason to believe that it has done excellent work for the natives of the Union even during that relatively short period and that its advice carries very great weight with the Union Government and Parliament. This circumstance if fairly and reasonably considered ought to go far towards reassuring you that the rights and interests of the natives of Swaziland would be protected as adequately under the Union Government of South Africa as they are now.[58]

The resident commissioner, Mr D. Honey, who accompanied the deputation, made the following scout-masterly report after the return journey:

> The behaviour of the Chiefs was excellent throughout, with one exception. The Paramount Chief informed me in London that he was drinking no spirits. I had reason subsequently to doubt this, as, on the return journey he secretly brought aboard several bottles of spirits in his baggage and after some days (after his liquor ration had been suspended), developed an attack of *delirium tremens*. This attack lasted some days during which he had to be guarded by a European sailor, two of whom were placed at my disposal for the purpose, by the Commander.

This passage of the report was marked by a Colonial Office official, disapprovingly, one suspects, rather than gleefully.[59] However, Buxton believed Sobhuza had brains and would make good.

Back in Swaziland, Sobhuza was organising a legal test case (for which he needed to raise a good deal of money) concerning the validity of the 1907 land apportionment. By implication this would challenge the whole validity of British jurisdiction in

Swaziland.[60] He claimed the title 'King', and the inherent rival
sovereignty which went with it. For the British there could only
be one King in the Empire.[61] Sobhuza appears to have wanted
for his country the same kind of privileged treaty relationship
as that enjoyed by Barotseland in North-Western Rhodesia.
The test case went against him, but in 1924 he obtained leave
to appeal to the Privy Council. The British government was
confident it would win against him, but if Sobhuza had
succeeded, the financial consequences for it could have been
serious, since the basis of the grants of Crown land in Swaziland
since 1907 would be upset, and the government would be faced
with claims for compensation.[62] Needless to say, Sobhuza's
appeal was unsuccessful. The Swazi did not take at all
kindly to the judgement of the Privy Council. They protested
strongly.

Nevertheless, Sobhuza's reputation improved as he gained
maturity. By the 1930s the British accepted him as the most
distinguished Swazi, a chief of excellent though not outstanding
qualities. Some high commissioners continued to murmur that
he was basically weak of purpose: although recognising the
need for change he was apt to be pulled in an opposite direction
by his reactionary uncles.[63] In the 1940s, Lord Harlech as high
commissioner found it difficult to be enthusiastic about him,
disliking his habit of consulting Johannesburg lawyers, and
(rather humourlessly) finding him 'sensual, suspicious and
intensely superstitious'.[64] Sobhuza's relations with Christian
missionaries were seldom smooth. By the 1960s, however, the
British generally regarded him as a rather lovable ardent
traditionalist who had shown good sense and determination, and
if it was true that he admired General de Gaulle, well, that was
not wholly reprehensible. But a transfer of power in 1968 to a
ruler with an estimated 117 wives was without parallel in the
history of British decolonisation. By 1972, H.M. King Sobhuza
II completed fifty years as the active head of his people, and
even the Emperor of Ethiopia could not beat that. The Lion of
Ngwane outstripped the Lion of Judah.

5 The High Commission Territories, II: The Failure of Hertzog, 1924–27

GENERAL J. B. M. Hertzog was prime minister and minister of Native Affairs from 1924 to 1929 in a Pact Government which joined his National Party with the Labour Party. Unlike his predecessors Botha and Smuts, Hertzog enjoyed no sort of admiration in London. British politicians deeply appreciated Botha, who was in many ways a sort of Sir Edward Grey on horseback, with all his 'old world courtesy', chivalry and common sense, honesty, practical straightforwardness, strength, simplicity, sense of duty and of spiritual values. They also had the greatest respect for Smuts on account of his Cambridge-educated intelligence, his philosophy, his international stature and his constructive contributions to the Commonwealth. By contrast Hertzog seemed dissident, headstrong, obstinate, petulant, blunt, intransigent, and in some ways petty.[1] In Fabian circles he was spoken of as a 'hysterical dunderhead'.[2] The enmity between Hertzog and smooth, subtle Smuts was legendary, and did not help to endear the former to the British. His politics were thought to have proceeded from personal hatred of Botha. As long ago as 1910 his inclusion in the first Union ministry had been lamented in the Colonial Office.[3] (Rather nervously, Botha had made this former controversial minister of education in the Orange Free State his minister of justice, but dropped him with much publicity after Hertzog announced in 1912 his principles of 'South Africa first' and Empire second.) In 1914 Hertzog formed his own National Party, which had a remarkably speedy rise to power. Botha and Smuts, in his view, had always acted not as ministers of a free country, but as agents of Great Britain. British adulation of Botha and Smuts had weakened their internal position. And Hertzog was, as Deneys Reitz described him, 'a fierce hater'.[4]

In November 1924, L. S. Amery became colonial secretary, to which office he added the newly established Dominions secretaryship in July 1925. He held the two together until June 1929. Amery was one of the two or three best informed right-wing colonial secretaries Britain has ever had. To his admirers, he was a man of imaginative vision and fearless determination, alive to the demands of a new time, a dynamo of energy and a passionate believer in England's imperial mission. He never quite carried sufficient weight among his cabinet colleagues to secure easy implementation of his policies. Perhaps he talked too much: it is always fatal. In deference to supposed strategic realities and imperial solidarity, some critics thought him unduly inclined to sympathise with settlers and to humour the Afrikaners.

The governor-general and high commissioner on extended tenure from January 1924 to December 1930 was the Earl of Athlone, son of the Duke and Duchess of Teck and brother-in-law of King George V. Court circles, Eton, Sandhurst, campaigns against the Ndebele and the Boers, and long chairmanship of the Middlesex Hospital (since 1910) had moulded an unassuming approachable figure of great kindness. Smuts had been impressed by him in the First World War, and welcomed him as a 'jewel of a governor-general'. Although it was his first major non-military assignment, Athlone discharged his duties admirably, his sincerity and shrewd common sense gaining the confidence and respect of both white groups, although an excessively paternalist speech in Bechuanaland was long remembered against him there. The main event of his term was the controversy over the flag, which brought South Africa to the verge of civil war.[5] Trouble began in May 1926 with a proposal to omit the Union Jack from the new national flag. (Malan advised Hertzog it would be simpler as well as more striking to attack the flag rather than stamps or coins.) Although in the end a diminutive Union Jack appeared on the new flag (first flown on 31 May 1928), the struggle had been marked by extreme hostility to the Union Jack, culminating in an incident at Bloemhof on 3 September 1927 when some Nationalists tore up the British flag. To the English this was a grave act indeed, since the flag was 'the outward and visible sign of the white man's ascendancy', and what sort of example was this to set to the blacks?[6]

Even despite such alarming demonstrations, it was extremely difficult for Britain to give a flat refusal to South African requests for the transfer of Swaziland. The Union had stood by Britain in the First World War, at the real risk of openly dividing its own European population. South Africa was to Britain even after 1924 still the country of Botha and Smuts, and even Hertzog proved friendly and amenable in manner, charming outside controversy, and showing fitting respect for the Royal family. Some said his anti-Britishness was a political pose.

Moreover by the beginning of 1924 it seemed probable that the Swaziland Europeans would turn increasingly to the Union, for financial reasons. The British government refused a grant-in-aid recommended by the high commissioner, who had been anxious to prevent a collision between Swazi perhaps aggressively opposed to transfer and Europeans clamouring for it. There was no alternative way of raising revenue. Crown lands could hardly be sold without consulting the Union, who would not approve the assets of its future inheritance being taken away.[7]

Hertzog became prime minister on 30 June 1924. Less than four months later he was asking for the transfer of Swaziland and Bechuanaland. The speed with which he acted is extraordinary, especially for a man apparently sceptical of Smuts' 'United States of British South Africa'. He does not seem to have consulted Smuts on the state of the question at the time he took over, or to have sought to exploit a bi-partisan approach. Nor does he appear to have taken any civil service advice. And so he plunged into a major imperial issue in apparent ignorance of how far Smuts had gone towards obtaining agreement over Swaziland. If he had known this, he might have realised what a bad tactical error it was to raise the more difficult Bechuanaland issue simultaneously with Swaziland. His lieutenant and biographer, Oswald Pirow, betrayed a Nationalist irritation with Smuts' failure to effect a transfer which they thought he could easily have persuaded the British into if he had really wanted to, but 'for some reason or another he was not sufficiently interested in this expansion of the Union's frontiers'. Out of office Smuts not only did not support Hertzog (to whom, according to Pirow, 'incorporation' was of primary importance) but did his best to make Hertzog's native policy suspect in the eyes of Whitehall. According to Pirow, Hertzog had a special reason for wanting the High Commission Territories. This was the 'dangerous native policy of the Colonial Office', which, while maintaining a theory of black supremacy, allowed whites to become part of their population, and he foresaw that the Territories would become a jumping-off place for countless agitators whose main object in life would be to make trouble for the Union.[8]

Pirow's emotive interpretation is difficult to evaluate, though patently moves over the Territories were in one aspect masked discussions of native policy. Whatever the motive, the intriguing thing is the speed with which Hertzog moved. Inexperience may have led him to rush all his fences, but presumably he could not have acted so fast unless the action fitted plainly into a basic pattern of fundamentally agreed ministerial policy. The key to that pattern was the enhancement of the Union's international status with the fullest internal self-determination, leading to an entrenchment of white supremacy. It is probable, therefore, that his object was as much to get rid of the imperial presence in the Territories, so irritating to South African susceptibilities about sovereignty, as to get hold of them for its own sake. This, rather than a sheer expansionist policy, seems at this stage to have governed his approach. The difficulty experienced in securing transfer came to be quoted as typical of the kind of treatment which might be accorded to a Dominion which, while it might in most respects seem to enjoy a full measure of self-rule, had so far been denied recognition of complete sovereign status. At the same time of course, the agreed policy of white supremacy meant segregation, which could not work without more land, which caused eyes to turn towards the High Commission Territories.

Nevertheless, it is as well to bear in mind that throughout these early overtures, Hertzog was offering status improvements to his followers and above all had objectives concerned to demonstrate to the outside world that South Africa was 'no longer subject to British sovereignty, i.e. a subordinate of Great Britain'. How it rankled to learn the publicly proclaimed ministerial opinion of the wretched Portuguese on South African status: 'a Colony with large autonomy but dependent on British sovereignty'. In international matters, Hertzog argued, it was only the really independent state that counted, and for South Africa to act with full international effect there must be a formal declaration of constitutional rights communicated to the whole world. At Stellenbosch in May 1926 he announced his desire for

> the recognition of the personal bond of a common King with Great Britain, without any other legal ties, but strengthened by such further ties as historical contact, common interests and mutual agreements, as the will of the people of each separate Dominion might have been prepared to approve of.[9]

The famous Imperial Conference of 1926 proved to be a triumph for Hertzog, and it is arguable that the Balfour Report, which encapsulated its deliberations, gave him what he wanted on the main issue. To him, its central conception was the notion of 'freely associated' Dominions. South Africa's freedom had thus been proclaimed to the world; the Empire need no longer be feared as a domineering super-state. Rather in the manner of the Society of St. Peter and St. Paul, who held that in the 1530s the Church of Rome seceded from the Church of England, Hertzog persuaded himself that the old Empire he disliked had seceded from South Africa, and that accordingly he could give up his own secessionist and republican policy. As a result his government did not venture far along lines which Britain had feared it would follow. It is however also arguable that his success over the theory of status stiffened imperial resistance to conceding anything over the specific issue of the transfer of the High Commission Territories. Upon this, all he extracted from Amery in 1926 was a promise that the secretary of state would study the problem on the spot. Thus the desire not only to be an independent nation but in all respects to be seen to be one remained unsatisfied. Here was the rub: non-possession of the High Commission Territories weakened South African international prestige, affronting people with minds as tidy as Nationalist emotions were strong. By a curious irony, South Africa's achievement of an improved status created a fresh constitutional distance from the Territories, and a constitutional problem of some magnitude.

Hertzog's 1924 overture asked for serious consideration to be given to the transfer of both Swaziland and Bechuanaland. He put forward three main arguments.[10] His first was in essence a tactless threat to deprive Africans of a market for their cattle if imperial consent to transfer was withheld. A recent agreement with Rhodesia prevented the importation of cattle into the Union, and this, it was argued, would necessitate similar restrictions for Bechuanaland and Swaziland. His second point was the impossibility of internally developing the Territories owing to their limited resources and geographical relationship to the Union, and so 'incorporation with the latter has become essential to their own development and, as it seems to me, is fast becoming essential to the development, through railways and irrigation, of the Union itself'. Any further development of irrigation from the north was effectively prevented until incorporation was achieved – hardly a fair point and in any case one which was surely too remote to be cited as a reason for immediate transfer. Hertzog's third argument was based on a claim to have received petitions from Swaziland chiefs as well as whites asking for incorporation. This incredible assertion the high commissioner found 'almost too absurd to deserve refutation', since, if there was anything in it at all, it represented merely petty chiefs wishing to escape the authority of the principal chiefs, who were firmly opposed to Union.

Such unconvincing arguments were hardly likely to persuade the British government to abandon its past extreme reluctance to consider the transfer of Bechuanaland. The high commissioner was 'most emphatically opposed' to it. Gone were the days when the high commissioner had been complaisant, as Gladstone

had been to Botha. Athlone upheld trusteeship in no uncertain
terms; he realised that Hertzog's segregationalist motive was to
provide 'non-Union' land for Union Africans who had been
retrenched from industry or to whom he was not prepared to
allot Crown land in the Union. Athlone was not taken in as
Gladstone had been eleven years earlier:

> I think therefore that in the interests of the natives it would be
> advisable to withhold Bechuanaland in order to force the
> Government to set aside adequate reserves in those parts of
> the Union where they are now urgently needed and where
> the demand will become even greater as segregation proceeds.

A movement of Africans into Bechuanaland could be extremely
damaging unless done gradually and with careful supervision.[11]

In December 1924 there were South African press reports
that negotiations for Bechuanaland's transfer had been started.
This premature announcement constituted a premeditated
attempt to force the hand of the imperial government, who
remonstrated with Hertzog for a 'culpable breach of confidence'.
Amery's reaction was to describe the situation as 'very materially
altered'.[12] Athlone told Hertzog that he had unnecessarily
disclosed ambitions which for at any rate some time to come he
might not be able to realise. Hertzog protested that he was not
actually asking for the Territories but only saying the time was
ripe for consideration.[13]

The British did not agree with this proposition. Indeed they
forcefully rejected it, invoking once more the classic doctrine of
The Unripe Time. Athlone did not wish to give the impression
that he was opposed absolutely to the transfer. On the contrary:

> . . . amalgamation with the Union Administration system is
> inevitable sooner or later. That this is their ultimate destiny I
> do not wish for one moment to dispute. The only point to be
> decided is when the psychological moment for effecting the
> transfer of the Territories arrives and whether they are to be
> transferred individually and at intervals or simultaneously
> *en masse*.

Since however the whole native policy of the Union was in
a state of flux, and making Africans apprehensive and restive,
this was not the suitable time to consider even the transfer of

Swaziland, which ought to precede that of Bechuanaland by at least two or three years.[14] Favourable conditions simply did not exist. Hertzog's native policy contemplated a fundamental departure. Its basic principle was segregation. South African administration was abnormally subject to political influences, and the jury system was unfair in trials involving whites and Africans. Athlone poured scorn on the idea that a commission similar to that of the Native Affairs Commission could satisfactorily discharge the functions demanded by the Schedule: it was subject to political pressure and split between Afrikaner and British members with fundamentally different attitudes. He did not think the Union would be anxious for Swaziland without Bechuanaland because the Europeans would oppose transfer without a definite promise of a railway, and a railway would involve the Union in serious financial commitments in addition to the existing deficit. The attractions of Swaziland were also seriously diminished by the fact that nearly all the land had been disposed of already. Why did Hertzog want Bechuanaland? None of his professed arguments really gave the answer. Athlone wrote:

> Personally I am inclined to attribute it to the Dutchman's insatiable appetite for land and to his constitutional inability to see why natives should be allowed to occupy more than is needed to maintain them in labour colonies for the benefit of white employers. This rather than the system of individual tenure contemplated under the Glen Grey Act is what they understand by segregation. Reports of fine land in Batawana reserve may explain desire to have it in preference to Swaziland.

The South Africans were searching for cheap land as a step towards the solution of the poor white problem, and Ngamiland offered the additional attraction of placing these people at a comfortable distance from the Union heartlands. If settlement were once established on the confines of the reserve, it would soon be difficult to resist a demand for the exploitation of the 'very beautiful and well-watered country' inside the reserve.[15] Athlone's extremely able despatches were matched by his success in February 1925 in persuading Hertzog to drop the question of Bechuanaland, although he thought Hertzog's desire for its early incorporation was unabated because of the pressure of the Transvaalers in his cabinet. Instead Hertzog resorted to 'peaceful penetration', sending teams to survey locust and irrigation problems, in order to strengthen Union claims. Not only did Athlone induce Hertzog to accept indefinite postponement of the transfer of Bechuanaland, but he also secured his agreement to the temporary deferment of the transfer of Swaziland.[16] In the former case Hertzog was given no indication of the period which might have to elapse. Swaziland could not be discussed while Sobhuza's appeal to the Privy Council was being heard.* Amery pointed out (19 January 1925) that

> no decision will be taken until all sections of the population have had an opportunity of expressing their views and until such representations have been considered by His Majesty's Government . . . and it would certainly be embarrassing to His Majesty's Government to submit such a proposal to Parliament when native affairs may be [the] subject of contention in South Africa.[17]

The high commissioner informed Hertzog that in coming to his decision the secretary of state had been influenced by

> historical considerations, solemn obligations to certain Chiefs, various agreements with the British South Africa Company and other bodies, as well as by political complications, including pledges which were given to the House of Commons by a former Government when the South Africa Act was before the Imperial Parliament.[18]

In March 1925 Hertzog made a most important admission which he must surely have come to regret. At any rate, the British were quick to seize upon its significance. Hertzog declared South Africa would not insist on transfer of the Territories 'unless the people are prepared and desire to come in', and the people meant Africans as well as Europeans. (He

* See above, p. 100.

had, of course, the fullest hopes that in Swaziland they would soon want to.) The Colonial Office imagined that if Hertzog really meant this the question would not come up again as soon as had been suspected. One of the officials summed up the situation at the end of 1924:

> If General Smuts were still in power and put forward a definite request for the transfer of the Territory it is unlikely that we should suggest further delay. But the position from the point of view of His Majesty's Government is necessarily affected to some extent by the coming into power of the Hertzog Government who have still to declare their native policy.[19]

In view of the financial position in Swaziland and, if Britain retained control, of the pressure likely to be brought to bear on Britain to render some practical assistance in the development of cotton-growing, the Colonial Office thought it would 'be convenient to be relieved of the responsibility of administering the Territory', but it would be awkward to deal with transfer pending the appeal of Sobhuza to the Privy Council and during the confused state of native affairs in the Union. Lambert thought the high commissioner had made a most convincing case for delay, but he considered that the proposal to ask Hertzog about his native policy and its possible effect on transfer and about the schemes of development he had in mind 'puts the case on the wrong ground, i.e. more or less as one for a bargain – But there are much more important questions involved and questions of principle'.[20]

The difficulty about development in Swaziland was partly the British lack of money and partly the uncertainty about its future. In December 1925 Amery noted that the

> present state of uncertainty, consequent on the various statements made during recent years, indicating that an application for the transfer of the Territory must be regarded as imminent, is very embarrassing to His Majesty's Government, and makes it impossible to administer the Territory except in a purely hand-to-mouth manner.[21]

At the beginning of 1926 the new Dominions Office became responsible for the High Commission Territories. By this time certain firm points of policy had been decided. The guiding principle was still to regard Union as the ultimate destination. Change was to be gradual. Swaziland was to be the first Territory to be transferred – as an experiment and a test of South African ability to discharge obligations to the Africans. The principles of the Schedule were held to be sacrosanct, except that where the Schedule had contemplated simultaneous transfer of all three Territories this was to be replaced by transfer *seriatim*. It had long been recognised that Swaziland was not in quite the same situation as the others – the conditions were 'less unfavourable' to transfer – owing to its European settlers. There were now a number of problems being forced into prominence by the pressure of these white interests. Amery was however most anxious to discourage Hertzog from making any official application for the transfer of any of the Territories. Since the Union was about to be subjected to radical revision of native policy, this was not, he felt, an opportune moment for transfer. The greatest prudence was required both in selecting the moment to consult Europeans and Africans and in framing proposals since, as he warned Hertzog, if the reception accorded them 'were such as to render it necessary to withdraw the application it would hardly be possible to revive the question for some years to come'. In Swaziland the main concern of Britain would, he claimed, be the Swazi, who might be presumed not to favour it. In the present circumstances, no application for Basutoland or Bechuanaland could be entertained. The whole question of transfer was governed by pledges to parliament and to the inhabitants about consultation, by the conditions of the Schedule and by the wishes of the inhabitants both European and African.[22]

The pattern of Hertzog's native policy became clearer during the course of 1926. When Athlone heard of the proposal to abolish the Cape native franchise, he commented:

I am inclined therefore to predict that, if the prime minister adheres to his resolution to postpone asking for the transfer of Swaziland until his Native Bill becomes law (now not so likely as Smuts will probably oppose), the Imperial Government may expect to have control of the Territory for some years to come. H. M. Taberer, general manager of the Witwatersrand Native Labour Association is a very reliable authority on native opinion and says unrest and discontent is far more serious among natives than generally supposed and that Protectorates natives would not give even sullen acquiescence to transfer.[23]

Hertzog said Britain could reckon on retaining control at least until 31 March 1928. Athlone was content with this assurance, but thought that in the meantime the European community in Swaziland must be helped with small annual advances for development.

In August 1926 Lords Buxton, Selborne and Gladstone encouraged Amery to refuse to consider the transfer question if Hertzog tried to raise it during the Imperial Conference. African nervousness (induced by colour bar legislation and the flag incident) would make any transfer at present 'especially delicate and difficult', while Hertzog's five bills for 'dealing radically and exhaustively' with native policy in the Union could not, without much fuller information, be judged either as a whole or with regard to the possible extent of conflict with the conditions of the Schedule.[24]

Meanwhile, although agreeing that the present was not opportune, Hertzog mentioned nine proposed conditions of transfer for Swaziland.[25] And the British government went so far as to formulate the terms on which it would be prepared to discuss it with him: the necessity of consultations, the maintenance of the Schedule and the acceptance by the Union of all financial liability for its obligations. The most contentious point of difference was Hertzog's wish to confine the application of the Schedule to administering the areas designated for exclusive Swazi occupation. In the face of Swazi sensitivity to changes of plan, Athlone impressed on Hertzog

that if there is any attempt to restrict the *application* of the Schedule to a specific area or to amend its terms we will be accused of bad faith and of having repudiated our pledges. We will encounter strenuous opposition, which it would be difficult to override if we mean to observe our promise to consult the wishes of the Natives before transferring the Territory. Under your scheme the form of government prevailing outside the Reserves will be very different from that which was promised.

A considerable number of Swazi labouring as residents on European farms or employed in industries would be affected – the colour bar and Land Act could be applied to them. Since it was a fundamental principle of imperial rule that Africans should have equal opportunity with other races to compete for jobs for which they were eligible by intelligence and education, Britain could hardly accept a scheme of administration 'which might involve any curtailment of the privileges at present enjoyed by the Swazis or which did not safeguard certain fundamental principles which have become characteristic of Imperial rule in all Native Dependencies'.

As you are aware, [he proceeded] the Swazis are opposed to the transfer of their Territory to the Union, and although it may be argued that their objections are not founded on any substantial reasons, His Majesty's Government is anxious to avoid all appearance of coercion and to do everything possible before consulting the Swazis to make the change appear as attractive as possible to them. . . . The Commission is in fact the very soul of the system of government which has been promised to the Natives, and the personnel, terms of appointment, functions and security of office of the Commission, represent fundamental requirements demanded by His Majesty's Government as a condition of transfer and constitute the understanding upon which the reversionary claims of the Union Government were accepted when the South Africa Act was passed by the House of Commons.

The Schedule and the Commission were two aspects of the issue to which Britain attached outstanding importance. Britain had always been emphatic and explicit about maintaining the Schedule which had been designed to protect Africans against the foreseeable dangers.[26] Athlone told Hertzog most plainly that any parliamentary allegation of a breach of faith would be certain to receive powerful support from 'Aboriginal Societies, Missions, international socialists and advocates of universal brotherhood';[27] the Schedule was by gentleman's agreement passed as an agreed measure: 'a gentleman's agreement which should not be subjected to political pressure, and if the Schedule went the Union's reversionary interests went with it'.[28]

To this illuminating and firm stand upon the Schedule Hertzog replied that he was looking to the interests of the Europeans. Athlone reminded him bluntly that these did not want Union for Union's sake but for money for development and if they could get it from Britain they would prefer not to be transferred.

Athlone thought it most important to insist on three points: first, no official request for transfer to be made until the new native policy had been enacted by both houses of the South African parliament; second, transfer to be under the Schedule; and third, the non-political character of the Commission to be maintained. Under pressure, Hertzog was prepared to accept all these principles. Acceptance of the first point particularly involved a crucial stipulation, and the British had no intention of losing the advantage it conferred by letting discussions be carried too far meanwhile, lest they became so involved as to make it difficult to withdraw from negotiations should it ever become expedient to do so. Athlone did not trust Hertzog: 'I do not think Hertzog means for a moment longer than necessary – to impart a show of sincerity to giving trial to its suitability – to apply the Schedule to European areas'. Hertzog perceived the fundamental difference between them to be that Britain stuck to the Schedule as universally applicable, while he thought a dual system of administration would give Swaziland more advantages.[29]

Railway problems demonstrated vividly the argument that the logical place for Swaziland was in the Union, but Athlone remained 'somewhat puzzled to understand why they are so keen to get control of the Territory'. Economically Swaziland could, he was satisfied, with advantage be entrusted to the Union at some future date, but he was just as convinced as ever in October 1926 that the present was not an appropriate moment to consider transfer. He wished the European Advisory Council to understand that European and African wishes would be considered and if they differed it must not be assumed that the wishes of the Swazi would be necessarily disregarded or subordinated.[30]

At this stage in the analysis it is necessary to examine in detail the origins of Amery's reappraisal of policy, the first radical rethinking of the entire problem since 1909. From 1926 two ideas began slowly to crystallise: that development need not necessarily be held up pending transfer, and that perhaps the Territories had a more positive role to play in the general structure of imperial interests in southern Africa than had hitherto been supposed.

To take the development idea first. Amery hoped to 'push ahead rather more with developments in Swaziland'.[31] His reasoning would seem to have been that of Capt. Bede Clifford (imperial secretary and representative of the British government in South Africa, 1924–31): that there was a community of settlers in Swaziland, demanding money for the development of a country which would evidently respond more quickly to a development programme than most parts of southern Africa; uncertainty of political future need not be an obstacle to a development loan, since if Britain remained in control she must do something, and if she handed it over, the Union would have to assume all financial obligations, while Britain would get all the credit for initiating a forward policy and at the same time set an example which the Union would feel obliged to follow.[32]

Subject to the reception which might be accorded to Hertzog's native legislation in the Union parliament, an application for the transfer of Swaziland was to be expected in 1928. It would be difficult for the British government to undertake development if they were to remain in control for only another year or two. But if as a result of Amery's forthcoming discussions with Hertzog in September 1927 the question of transfer was postponed for a considerable period, Amery wanted to have in his possession definite information as to the measures required, while Swaziland remained under imperial control, to meet its reasonable needs. It would be convenient, he added, if he could have this information before his discussion with Hertzog. The settlers' case for a railway was, he believed, a strong one and whatever the outcome of discussions he hoped that at all events they would have the effect of hastening its construction.[33] By May 1927 reports suggested that opinion in the European Advisory Council was hardening against transfer if there was a possibility of financial aid from Britain. Thus it was plain that, thanks to the flag furore in the Union, if financial equilibrium in Swaziland could be restored and some money found for communications, not many British settlers in Swaziland would remain favourably disposed to transfer in the near future, although of course the opinion of the poor Afrikaners in the Hlatikulu district was unlikely to change.[34]

To come now to the point that there was emerging a more positive evaluation of the role of the Territories in the total structure of British southern African interests. One of the first persons to expound this view also was Capt. Clifford, who elaborated his theme for some years after 1926. Briefly the argument was as follows. Britain's hold on South Africa was weakening. The Simonstown naval station was of the greatest importance, and he thought it a grave mistake to have given the South African government control of the shore garrison. Tielman Roos (leader of Transvaal Nationalists) continued to insist that 'independence' was still the cherished goal of the National Party, and while ministers preached such doctrines, Britain should dig her heels into every foothold and nurse all 'the meagre "interests" we still possess'. Of these, the Africans were important: 'one of our biggest allies in the country'. Everything possible should be done to retain their loyalty and confidence 'as a buffer against the process of secession by attrition which is going on now . . .' When the Territories went, 'direct Imperial interest in [South Africa] ceases', and 'an important bridgehead is lost, and with it our influence upon the Natives which we maintain through our position as trustee for their reserves and welfare'. In the eyes of the Africans the Territories were 'something in the nature of a sanctuary'.[35]

Working on this theme, Amery saw in the Territories a

potential means of influencing Union native policy. By the
time he was ready to visit South Africa he had decided that
if Swaziland was not to be haneed over, 'we must lay out our
plans for something like a ten years' policy and include a
settlement as well as one of development'.[36]

Amery's South African tour took place in August and
September 1927. Looking back later, he recalled in a notable
passage of his memoirs:

> My brief visit to the three territories and my talks with the
> Administrators was sufficient to convince me that any early
> transfer to the Union was out of the question. It was not so
> much the apprehension of the natives themselves at the idea
> of the change that weighed with me, though naturally I made
> the most of the point with Hertzog. What I felt most was that
> we had done so little for the Protectorates ourselves; that
> instead of spending money and thought on developing their
> resources and, still more important, raising the general
> standard of their peoples, we had been content to protect
> them from outside interference, leaving them to carry on
> under a very unprogressive form of indirect tribal rule as
> museum pieces, human Whipsnades, in an Africa that was
> being transformed at a breathless pace. Our first duty, it
> seemed to me, was to bring forward the peoples for whom we
> were still responsible till they were more fit to stand up to the
> impact of transfer.[37]

In his actual discussion with Hertzog on 6 September he
placed House of Commons opposition to transfer first and
foremost as the 'governing consideration'. (Politicians usually
use parliamentary and public opinion as sticks to beat their
overseas opponents with.) His visit convinced him that African
feeling was 'if anything more opposed than at any recent time
to transfer'. Paramount chiefs in Swaziland and Bechuanaland
had insisted this was so. Hertzog ruefully remarked that the
Africans were never likely to be eager for transfer. Amery
replied almost too tactfully:

> there was all the difference between a situation in which the

natives are vehemently opposed and the House of Commons critical, or at any rate, uncertain as to the native policy of the Union, and the situation in which the policy of the Union had been proved in actual working to be such as to satisfy the House of Commons that the natives would in effect not be substantially worse off. In such circumstances the House of Commons might well be prepared to disregard the comparatively mild objection and agree to the Administration using its influence to persuade the natives into acceptance of the transfer.[38]

After this remarkable observation, Amery stressed that it was not enough to have the legislation simply passed; Britain required actually to see it in working order for some little time. He touched lightly upon the feeling that South Africa generally was passing through a critical and controversial period, which increased British dislike of the idea of transferring any of the Territories. Their discussion ended with Hertzog's saying he had no wish to hasten the matter against the wishes of the populations affected. Accepting this view, Amery suggested that the best policy was a gradual closer approximation on both sides in development for the white areas, and in 'education, etc.' for the Africans 'so that incorporation when it came would come most naturally and easily'. Meantime he hoped that the two administrations could work together as closely and intimately as possible in every direction.[39] Clearly foreshadowed here are the germs of a policy which was later to give rise equally to hopes of a solution and to misunderstandings which destroyed the possibility. Amery found that Hertzog accepted his conclusions cordially and without demur. Throughout he felt Hertzog had dealt with the question in 'a reasonable spirit.'*

The immediate effect of Amery's visit to southern Africa was

* Hertzog's personal relations with the British leaders remained friendly and cordial. Cromer once described him as 'the perfect gentleman', and he was perhaps never so much anti-British as anti-imperial. But plainly his followers did not always approve of his attitude and it was by no means certain that he could control and vanquish the sinister spirits he had conjured from the bigoted backveld in his rise to power.

that the transfer of Swaziland, hitherto regarded as an imminent problem, was postponed for at least five to six years, an interval which was to be filled with constructive action. No transfer for the other two countries was to be contemplated for a 'long time to come'. The high commissioner was instructed to proceed on the general basis that nothing would be done until Hertzog's native legislation was on the Statute book.[40]

What was the root cause of this decision? Amery himself admitted it was not pure response to African objection. The answer lies, therefore, in dislike of the upsurge of Afrikanerdom, together with the belated sense of shame at British inactivity which was referred to above. Several weeks before his discussion with Hertzog, Amery was inclined to think that the passage of the Flag Bill alone would prevent the British parliament from agreeing to any transfer.

Essentially the Union was holding together on the basis of rapid economic expansion, which more than compensated for the divisive forces: the existence of jealous capitals, the over-powerful provincial administrations in the Transvaal and Orange Free State, a rather vicious form of exaggerated bilingual practice, recurrent outbursts of Anglo-Afrikaner racial feeling, and policies concerning the flag and the Africans which did not appeal to Britain. In this context the establishment of responsible government in Southern Rhodesia and the delay in deciding the destiny of the High Commission Territories were slowly being seen as useful facts which together, it was believed, supplied the necessary corrective to the deteriorating Union situation. In a policy of continuing to dangle the prospect of a Greater South Africa before the eyes of both white sections of South Africa it was thought lay perhaps the best opportunity of securing national unity without too severely impeding economic expansion. The whole future of South Africa seemed to be at stake. The fact is, wrote Amery,

that the future position of the Empire in South Africa is going to depend very largely on the Protectorates and Rhodesia, both as regards native development, and on a smaller scale, as regards British white development. From this point of view the Protectorates are an undeveloped asset of the first importance. Swaziland is an extraordinarily rich little country with the best rainfall in South Africa and capable within the area alienated to white occupation, of supporting quite a considerable number of settlers. If we can get those out from England in the next four or five years, we shall have carried the British settlement beyond Natal right to the eastern border of the Union and made its position secure against swamping by the policy of giving all the land to poor Dutch whites when transfer takes place. . . . The more we do for the development of the Protectorates the greater the prize that is dangled before the eyes of the Union and the greater the influence in keeping the Union straight.[41]

The key to the whole policy was making Swaziland 'effectively British before it goes into the Union'. Transfer before a prosperous and contented British community was established there was held to be undesirable and even dangerous. The essential assumption remained that the ultimate destiny of the Territories was Union. Indeed Amery considered that the modern conception of Dominion status, accepting the Dominions as qualified to exercise such imperial functions as the administration of Mandates, had made it more than ever an anomaly for Whitehall to govern indefinitely African enclaves within the confines of a Dominion. For the time being however 'for reasons of native policy' among others, they could not comply with a demand for transfer. Whereas the intimate geographical and economic association with the Union had always been regarded as complicating British responsibility, Amery now discovered in it 'a by no means negligible opportunity for influencing the future political development of South Africa as a whole'. In the general interests of the Empire, his object was to make sure that when the time for transfer came, any areas available for European settlement were 'definitely British in sentiment'. In a cogent memorandum Amery wrote:

In the present close balance of forces making for Imperial unity in South Africa, and those which would keep South Africa in sentiment and action, if not formally, outside the

Empire, it would be difficult to over-emphasise the importance of this point. Nothing during my visit has impressed me more than the powerful influence which a progressive and intensely British Southern Rhodesia may yet exercise – is, indeed, already exercising – upon the Union. To create similar centres of progress and British sentiment east and west of the Transvaal in Swaziland and in such parts of Bechuanaland as may be available for white settlement, instead of leaving the areas in question unused, till, after transfer, they are filled up with unprogressive Dutch of the 'poor white' class, is something that may still make a very valuable contribution to the whole future of South Africa.

Such a policy would suit the European Advisory Council, which wanted an increase of whites by all available means, because really successful irrigation and co-operative schemes were impossible without more good British settlers. But as Amery repeated, 'Not only will closer settlement greatly increase the chances of success for the whole community; it will, if the settlers are of the right sort and of British stock, build up a prosperous British community which may exert an influence on the Union out of all proportion to its numerical strength'.[42] Athlone agreed that Swaziland was pre-eminently suitable for a comparatively close white settlement.[43]

As for the Africans, 'who are our primary concern', much was demanded of the British government: no less than raising them to such a level of general civilisation that they might be in a position, when transfer took place, 'to hold their own and to justify, in the eyes of the South African public, the retention of their privileged position'. At present Amery thought the Africans lagged behind in their capacity to 'hold their own under modern conditions'. Britain was at the same time responsible for affording South Africa such an example of what the African could achieve, 'if he is given reasonable opportunity', as might exercise 'a potent influence in shaping South African native policy on sounder lines', thereby enabling Britain to 'give a lead to the whole of South Africa as well as help to keep the British uppermost'.[44]

Amery was therefore determined to bring to an end a policy under which the Territories were backwaters in danger of becoming a real disgrace to the imperial government, with conditions which led to continual unrest among the white settlers and to a demand on their part for transfer. What practical steps did he propose? The first need was to infuse new blood into the administrations. Part of the trouble had been that the Territories had been 'officially little stagnant pools, the same people staying on in the same jobs for twenty years on end', so that administration became hopelessly unprogressive; twenty years in the same small country with no policy from above except that of marking time was, he remarked, ruinous to any man's initiative. Amery accordingly wanted to find really good new men, 'keen both on making the most of the native, and on development generally'. There was, he said, an immense amount to be done and a real field for youth and ability. It was essential from the personnel angle to treat them in future as to all intents and purposes part of the Colonial Service, and so to secure reasonable rotation of offices and prevent stagnation.[45] The question of assimilating the administrative services was a tricky one, not solved until 1935.

The second desideratum was to find money to initiate development, desirable in the interests of the Africans and essential in justice to the Europeans. The actual amounts Amery required were really quite small and could, he felt, be more than met by economies he would effect on the Middle East and other colonial estimates. Living from hand to mouth must stop: Britain must justify the Territories' separate existence and 'make them centres of progress and development'.[46] It was extremely difficult to persuade the Treasury to take the same view. By April 1928 Amery was still trying to 'make them see sense'. 'The futile irrelevance of their letters is appalling': such was his melancholy grouse. The Treasury's awkwardness was a severe worry to Amery since he had entered into something approaching a definite commitment to the Swaziland settlers, having satisfied himself on the spot as to the urgency of demands he thought very moderate: 'I am committed up to the hilt to the Swaziland settlers and the money must be found somehow'.

Eventually however Winston Churchill as chancellor of the exchequer closed the squabble by authorising loans which met Amery's requirements quite satisfactorily: an immediate loan for administrative expenses of £12,500, a loan in total of £36,000 for capital development, and £40,000 to start a fund to provide advances to settlers, to be increased later up to £80,000 if necessary.[47]

Amery's third step was to try to promote a comprehensive scheme of British settlement, hardly an uncongenial task for a man with pro-Delamere sympathies in the Kenya settler issue,[48] but none the less a tough objective. He had several discussions with various people, including Sir Ernest Oppenheimer, hoping to interest them in Swaziland. He also approached Sir Abe Bailey, suggesting he would 'have a really great chance there of doing something that will help the future stability of South Africa'. The Dominions Office negotiated with the Mushroom Land Settlement Company to provide for 35 settlers on Mushroom Valley Land, and tried to arrange for other schemes under the Empire Settlement Act of 1922. Lord Lovat, as Dominions under-secretary and also as chairman of the Overseas Settlement Committee, aimed at the settlement of 200 families in Swaziland.[49] Things were slow to move however, and November 1928 still found Amery minuting, 'I am very anxious to get a move on with this'.[50]

Finally communications had to be improved. As we have already seen, Amery had seriously considered the promotion of a railway, but he was relieved of the necessity of pursuing this by the decision in the summer of 1927 by the Railway Board of South African Railways and Harbours to introduce motor-bus road services to connect Manzini (Bremersdorp) and Mbabane to the railhead at Breyten, and also Manzini to the Pongola rail terminus at Gollel and Hlatikulu to Piet Retief. This was a stroke of luck, making a real difference to the whole development of Swaziland, enabling the Swazi to go in a day by the railway bus and train to Johannesburg and the Rand mines instead of spending ten or twelve debilitating days walking there. Regular mails and supplies could also now be brought in and out. Amery had to fight hard to get the small sum of money necessary to put the dirt roads into reasonable order, but he knew it 'would mean everything to the little country.'*[51]

Amery's contribution to the history of High Commission Territories was a significant one, even if results did not match his vision. To him goes the credit of producing the longest single interruption of discussions in the whole period from 1909 to 1939. The tough line taken is all the more remarkable in view of the otherwise marked progress of Dominion status in the 1920s. Whether the question would have remained closed so long if Smuts had won the 1929 election is of course open to speculation; the Colonial Office continued to believe 'it might not be very easy to resist a strong demand from him'.[52] With Hertzog in control however it was different, and no more was heard of transfer proposals from September 1927 until August 1932, a full five years later. In 1929 Tshekedi Kgama, regent of the Ngwato, wanted to state his case in London but was told there was no point.[53] In England in 1930 Hertzog showed no disposition to press anything, merely asking the secretary of state, J. H. Thomas, to keep an open mind. By 1931, on the other hand, it was expected that Hertzog would take advantage of any favourable opportunity to re-open the question.[54] When he eventually did so, the whole issue could never quite be on the same footing as previously. Maybe the decisive point of no return had already been reached by the British government. Certainly the discussions of the thirties never seemed quite to have the air of reality which they possessed until the mid-twenties.

Two decades had elapsed since Union and the Union was still incomplete. For the small progress in the matter of transfer, wrote Hofmeyr, 'the small progress which the Union has made in the solution of its own native problems would, doubtless, be advanced as a good and sufficient reason'.[55] Just so. As Agar-Hamilton observed in 1929, Union native policy was but a 'welter of greed, panic and faint glimmerings of a sense of responsibility'.[56]

* The Breyten railway bus is still, more than forty years later, the principal artery of communication with the wider world (if the Republic of South Africa can be so called). The railway bus is strictly segregated, and the climb from the middle veld to the high veld is desperately slow and tortured, but the daily scores of Swazi passengers seem to enjoy the trip.

6 The High Commission Territories, III: The Failure of Hertzog, 1932–39

By the time discussions were renewed in 1932, the situation had changed in several ways. The office of governor-general of the Union was separated from that of high commissioner for the Territories as from January 1931, to the lively satisfaction of the Africans. Their delight in having an officer no longer connected with the Union government is indicative of their attitude to the latter. The high commissioner for the first four years of the new dispensation was Sir Herbert Stanley,* but the main brunt of the negotiations in the thirties fell upon Sir William Clark (January 1935 to January 1940). Clark was a man with over thirty years' administrative experience, particularly of Indian economic affairs, and he had just been high commissioner in Canada.

The situation was altered in other ways too, each of them tending to operate against transfer. African assent was further away than ever. Some observers considered that if the Swazi were transferred the Sotho might put up a fight to defer their own transfer. The death of Kgama the Great made no difference in Bechuanaland: his successor Sekgoma II (1923–25) and his youngest son, Tshekedi Kgama, regent from 1925, more than maintained traditional opposition.[1] European opposition was actually growing. In 1925 the Swaziland whites were on the whole in favour of transfer. By 1932 they would probably have opposed it, apart from a number of poor Afrikaner settlers in the south. This change of opinion was partly due to the programme of development which had for the

* H. J. Stanley: secretary to governor-general of S. Africa 1913–15; imperial secretary 1918–24; governor of Northern Rhodesia 1924–7 and of Ceylon 1927–31; high commissioner 1930–4; reputed to have been very wise.

past few years been initiated and financed by the British government and partly to the pronounced inter-white racial bias of Union politics. It was unlikely that the Union could now build a railway.*[2] The only explicit grumbling the high commissioner heard among Europeans in 1932 was directed against the unfriendly attitude of the Union government as shown in the import restrictions on the free access of Swaziland cattle to the Johannesburg market. As in Bechuanaland this restrictive fiscal policy had estranged many settlers who might otherwise have looked to transfer as a step towards wider openings in political and economic matters. The settlers in Manzini seemed to regard the possibility of transfer as a menace; the Colonial Development Fund had assisted the improvement of their water supply and the building of a new butter factory. Substantial grants and loans had been made since Amery's visit and this was appreciated.[3]

The passing of the Statute of Westminster in 1931 and of the Status of the Union Act in 1934 made inoperative all clauses of the Schedule providing for the reservation of bills for imperial consideration. This was the conclusion of a parliamentary committee chaired by Selborne. Britain therefore sought to make transfer conditional on the substitution of some alternative security equivalent to that hitherto afforded. The general scheme of the Schedule it wished to maintain notwithstanding. Though it had lost its legal force as a safeguard for African interests, Britain regarded it as still, in a moral sense, binding on South Africa. There was also the question of what the Union might propose to substitute for the provision relating to the power of disallowance of proclamations made by the governor-general in council. In both cases of constitutional re-examination it was left to the Union to suggest viable alternatives.[4] The Schedule remained South Africa's paper guarantee of possible transfer, and there was not really much reason to suppose that the Union would not respect its expressed regard for fundamental law. But the technical impossibility of relying on the

* Instead of constructing rural branch railway lines as approved in 1925, the question in the Union (by 1932) had become one rather of which existing lines should be pulled up and replaced by roads.

Schedule in future as an absolute safeguard intensified the
interest of educated chiefs, as well as British politicians, in the
permanent and deliberately adopted native policy of the
Union, since the relevance of this to the Territories was
considerably increased. The things done in the Union were
frequently found shocking by the British. And in view of what
was said and done, the attitude of Africans to transfer could
'hardly be deemed unreasonable or disentitled to sympathy'
wrote high commissioner Stanley.[5]

Generally speaking, of course, the passage of time had
created a different atmosphere regarding standards of trusteeship and the rights of self-determination from that which had
prevailed in 1909. In the thirties the body of opinion in England
opposed to transfer grew steadily.

The secretary of state for Dominion affairs from June 1930
until November 1935 was J. H. Thomas. A leading Labour
politician, former errand-boy and trade unionist, he was found
to be sensible, practical and genial. An inveterate dropper of
aspirates, the newspapers once reported him as having spoken of
'the islands of Kenya'. He had undoubtedly a careless streak in
him, and some Conservatives found him vulgar. His free and
easy ways did not preclude good relations with the throne, and
won him some popularity in the South African backveld. He
once addressed a meeting of Orange Free State farmers for
nearly an hour without ever taking his pipe from his mouth, a
feat which evoked considerable admiration from that hard-
smoking community.[6]

J. H. Thomas rarely committed himself to paper, but he
went on record in a cabinet memorandum as believing that the
Union's general attitude to Africans, 'to say the least, does not
induce to confidence here that we could properly hand over our
trusteeship in respect of the Territories'. Like the good trade
unionist he was, he seemed ready to defend his hard-pressed
clients against greedy Dominions.[7]

Preliminary overtures were made at the Ottawa Conference in
August 1932, when a discussion took place between J. H.
Thomas and Hertzog's minister of finance, N. C. Havenga.

According to Havenga's statement, Thomas had raised no fundamental objection to transfer and agreed that the present was opportune for settling the whole matter. Thomas retorted that this account was 'seriously misleading'. He was annoyed to be thought to have committed himself, and forced Havenga into an admission that in fact he, Thomas, had merely listened and said he would consider carefully what had been said to him. Thomas swore to his officials that he had not said anything which could possibly support any idea of immediate transfer; the talk was quite general, though he had mentioned a possible visit to South Africa. Even this admission made the officials uneasy, as they did not want anything to be done which might suggest that transfer was within practical politics at this stage. He could reasonably refuse the subsequent invitation to visit the Union on the ground of the economic situation at home and his personal responsibility in the unfortunate controversy with the Irish Free State, and he did so.[8]

In the spring of 1933 Hertzog was joined by Smuts (desperately anxious for a return to power) in a coalition government which won electoral approval and in 1934 became the Fusion government. Their two parties were merged into the United South African National Party under the leadership of Hertzog. Smuts' party entered Fusion with misgivings, and difficulties were constant.[9]

British officials were worried by this development, as it might mean pressure for transfer would be more difficult to resist. If Smuts became a negotiator it would be harder to say no to him as a representative of a united nation than it had been to Hertzog's National government. Smuts personally was believed to be at least as anxious as Hertzog for the earliest possible transfer. He wanted to seem as good an Afrikaner as any of them. Success in negotiation would ensure his reinstatement in the confidence of South Africa. Smuts was minister of justice. He certainly kept in touch with the transfer issue, but Hertzog insisted on keeping the threads in his own hands and co-ordination with Smuts was decidedly imperfect.[10]

After 1933 there was nearly continuous negotiation, though the temperature of debate rose and fell; it was at its peaks in

1935 and 1937. The problem for Britain became really difficult. By 1937 references to the cabinet were frequent. For J. H. Thomas the problem became second only to Ireland in magnitude and worry. His aim was to administer the Territories without constant regard to the possibility of early transfer. The best course, he decided, was to 'backpedal a bit'.[11] He was inclined to be influenced chiefly by the hatred of the Africans for the Union; whereas Amery had placed uppermost British distaste for Afrikanerdom. Thomas also had less conviction in the desirability of white settlement.

In the light of this background the Dominions Office was compelled to work out a revision of policy for the mid-thirties. As this evolved, it had three basic objectives: postponement of transfer, finding a compensating political gesture, and diminishing through co-operation the risk of South African economic pressure. A fourth objective was tentatively explored, namely moving Bechuanaland out of the South African orbit.

As to postponement: until the mid-twenties the official view was – transfer by stages, beginning with Swaziland, probably quite soon, since a virtual promise had been made to Smuts. Since 1925 however the prospects of even an early transfer of Swaziland had receded, and from 1930 policy was redesigned to secure a long postponement of the whole question until conditions were more favourable. This object was achieved by agreement between Hertzog and Thomas in 1935; thereafter it was considered most undesirable to disturb the settlement then reached.[12] The question was not considered purely from the point of view of the Africans. Had it been, the answer would have been simple. Instead of postponement Britain would have said transfer was impossible. It had to be assumed however that Britain might one day be forced by political and economic considerations to meet the Union government.[13]

As to gesture: if there was to be long postponement, it clearly would have been foolish to repel all pressure with a plain 'no'. The advantages in a conciliatory gesture were obvious. The problem was to find one which would both have substance and yet not cause trouble or give the appearance of committing the British government beyond her pledges. Accepting transfer

as ultimately inevitable, the Dominions Office, under the
guidance of Sir Edward Harding (permanent under-secretary
1930–39) set itself the statesmanlike task of finding a way of
overcoming the difficulties: and thus the Thomas – Hertzog
concordat of 1935 was the culmination of its efforts.[14] To the
Office, the only good reason for resisting the Union's desire for
Swaziland and Basutoland was the aversion of their inhabitants.
If African opposition (shown with unqualified emphasis and
consistency) were withdrawn (which was all but inconceivable
in the case of Basutoland and exceedingly improbable in the
case of Swaziland) the objections of Britain would disappear,
though they would remain for Bechuanaland whose position
had repercussions on the future of central Africa. Since Britain
would not object if the Africans did not, the only possibility of a
real solution seemed to be the creation of an atmosphere in
which difficulties in the way of transfer would cease to exist.
To gain time, there must be an agreed delay, but not an
unqualified delay. The risk of open breach with South Africa
had to be counteracted by agreement on a long-term programme. As Thomas said on 15 November 1934 to a deputation
led by Selborne, with Lothian, Lugard and Amery (who seem
independently to have come to pretty much the same conclusions):

> I do not disguise from you my absolute horror of handing over
> any natives to the Union unless there is a radical change in
> the South African policy towards the native . . . but . . . it
> is no good blinding ourselves to the political difficulties that
> may arise. . . .

An economic boycott would be very awkward, embarrassing
to Britain and fatal to the Africans themselves. Then there was a
further point:

> In this troubled world today, I am more convinced every
> hour that I am in office, that the British Empire as a whole
> must play a dominant part in the future, and anything that
> would widen the breach in South Africa, when so much has
> been done to heal it, would be bad statesmanship. I am

balancing the whole situation as it were, and I do not want
to allow even this discussion to embitter our relationship, but
to try and keep it on an even keel. Remember this, whatever
may be the future, except with the goodwill and co-operation
of South Africa we shall never make a success of it. Therefore
it is to our interest, as well in the best interests of native
policy, that we should carry them with us rather than
antagonise them.

For this reason he was anxious not to send Hertzog away with a
grievance. It would be fatal to slam the door in his face.[15] An
offer of co-operation would be a valuable political gesture, but
also valuable in its own right.

As to the third new direction: this was therefore towards
economic co-operation, mainly to reduce the threat to the
Territories, but also positively to give them the benefit of
overdue development. The Union's economic power was
already being exercised adversely to a greater degree than
most people realised, through restrictions on cattle importation, with results which were lamentable in Bechuanaland
and nearly as serious in Swaziland. Internally in the Union,
too, the Transkei suffered from a 'veterinary embargo'. In the
Union, commented high commissioner Stanley, 'veterinary
science waits upon economic and political exigencies'. Veterinary embargoes were just as effective as economic ones and they
would not be affected by pledges given for the removal of
economic barriers. If therefore a policy of co-operation could be
devised, it might help to divert the Union from recourse to
economic and veterinary pressures which were inconsistent with
it. There would be the bonus benefit that the Territories might
through it be brought to the development level of other
African dependencies.[16]

It should be emphasised that Stanley would have preferred a
categorical rejection of transfer requests, and that the Dominions
Office wanted ideally a firm agreement on a long period during
which the transfer question should be dropped. A period of
twenty-five years was mentioned. Each recognised however
that such policies were impracticable. In the existing unstable

political conditions of South Africa the only course was to temporise and refuse to be pushed. As Thomas expressed it, 'the real solution was to be found in the accommodation on both sides of their obligations and commitments'.[17] Instructions to Sir William Clark when he took over from Stanley as high commissioner emphasised his duty to examine what could be done in economic co-operation as upon this would largely depend the chance of converting African opinion to acquiescence.[18]

As to a possible fourth objective: the future of Bechuanaland in particular was no longer straightforward, having become associated with planning for the future of central Africa. Stanley directed special attention to this:

> Whatever might happen in regard to the other two Territories, it seems to me quite essential, on grounds of high policy, that we should hold on to the Bechuanaland Protectorate. The Protectorate may very likely become the key to a satisfactory solution of the problem of building up a strong British state or group of states in Central Africa, and in the meantime we shall have quite a good chance, if we are reasonably lucky in the matter of mineral development, of doing something effective for the advancement of the local natives and of showing that the principle of trusteeship, of which we hear so much, can, even in Southern Africa, be applied successfully in practice. I hope with all my heart that we shall not cast off either of the other two Territories, but I put in a special plea for the retention of the Bechuanaland Protectorate, no matter how severe might be the pressure for its transfer.[19]

Although tentatively mooted since 1926 or earlier, the idea that Bechuanaland's destiny lay with Rhodesia rather than the Union was not one requiring an immediate firm decision. Hence the Dominions Office attitude in 1929–30 was to regard it as a policy towards which it might be possible to work gradually.

There were certain settler districts of Bechuanaland which bordered on Rhodesia or the Union: Tati, and the Lobatsi, Gaborone (Gaberones) and Tuli blocks. The Tati settlers had long looked to Rhodesia, and Bulawayo being their nearest urban centre, they naturally turned there for social, educational and commercial amenities. The other three blocks of land were vested in the British South Africa Company and their settlers wanted transfer to the Union. Many of the farmers were bound to the Union by ties of blood and marriage, and their law was based on the old Cape system. In the Tati and Lobatsi cases, however, there was a serious administrative difficulty as the railway ran through them, and new cold storage works, whose whole object was the development of the cattle industry of Bechuanaland, were on the railway line. To separate the Bechuanaland Protectorate from the railway and the cold storage works would upset the entire administrative and development policy envisaged by Britain. In any case European desire for transfer was waning as there seemed to be increasingly good prospects of reasonable development under British rule, although the settlers would gladly have been out of an area governed primarily in the African interest. The British objection to transferring the Tuli block was simply that it was north of the Limpopo, which boundary the Dominions Office wished to retain as a natural barrier to the absorptive power of the Union over the rest of Bechuanaland. This argument had not carried much weight with Amery, who held unnatural (but carefully surveyed) boundaries to be quite common in the modern world and seldom the cause of difficulty. As he saw it, the real objection to transferring Tuli was the fact that while the flag question remained as it did in 1927 it would be difficult to obtain parliamentary consent to it. If this had not been so, however, Amery would rather have liked to let the blocks go, as a means of strengthening the British grip on the remainder of the Protectorate. [20]

Precisely for this reason of course, Hertzog did not want them, though he had no objection to the handing over of Tati to Rhodesia. [21] By September 1927 Amery had decided to effect this. It then occurred to him that it might embarrass Hertzog if Britain showed herself willing to make a transfer to Rhodesia but not to the Union. Hertzog took the point. He ought to have thought of it himself. He agreed that political capital would

probably be made out of it, and so Amery dropped the idea. He
explained to the Rhodesian prime minister, H. U. Moffat, that
this by no means meant that the question was finally disposed of,
and he hoped that Rhodesia could afford Tati residents facilities
for obtaining such expert advice as might help to place them on
the same level as their neighbours across the boundary; there
were other directions too, such as education, in which perhaps
they might be able to assimilate administration in the block to
that in Rhodesia.[22]

From this moment British official opinion began to harden
against the separate transfer of Tati district, as the indisputable
claim of Rhodesia to this area might one day be needed to
strengthen a request for at least the whole of the northern half
of Bechuanaland. Amery by February 1929 certainly approved
the notion of all or part of Bechuanaland's going into Rhodesia,
and if Rhodesia broke with the Customs Union, Bechuanaland
might, he thought, follow suit: 'The Union could not treat
Bechuanaland much worse than it does'. (The effect of tighten-
ing veterinary restrictions on the entry of Tswana cattle to the
Union was at times extremely onerous and led to big smuggling
rackets.)[23]

It began to seem most unfortunate that Bechuanaland had
been 'linked' to the South by the South Africa Act, when her
true destiny might be to the north. Union commercial policy by
no means suited her, and she marketed increasing numbers of
cattle in the Rhodesias and the Belgian Congo. For development
she needed the cheapest possible supply of commodities of every
kind, including tools, food and utensils. The scale of Union
duties was already burdensome and restrictive in several ways.
There was, for example, an absurd duty of 1s. per lb. on
cotton blankets and goods imposed in 1925, causing a 50 per
cent drop in imports of them in one year, and obviously pressing
hard on the Africans.

There were therefore some leading British policy advisers who
recommended clearing the path towards associating Bechuanaland with Southern Rhodesia, and perhaps with a big Central
African Territory also embracing Northern Rhodesia, South-
West Africa north of Walvis Bay, and Nyasaland. Sever the

fetters which bound Bechuanaland to the South, they said, and allow a real freedom of choice when the time came to decide whether Bechuanaland should throw in her lot with the Union or Rhodesia, or be divided between the two.[24]

The case presented by Hertzog in 1932, with some reinforcement from Smuts after 1933, essentially hinged on threats of economic pressure. For some years, they said, the question of transfer had been engaging more and more attention in South Africa, until, 'owing more particularly to economic considerations in connection with Union markets and questions of stock disease, it is very generally felt that the time has come for the Union to assume responsibility in connection with these Territories and to take them over'.[25] Economic facts, they said, made the Territories 'entirely dependent on the Union' – there was practically no other market for their produce or outlet for their labour supplies. Most banking and other business was controlled from the Union, and the Territories were already being dealt with as one entity with the Union for customs and excise purposes. Separation by 'purely artificial boundaries', they said, had many disadvantages for the Union: she could not control the administration of customs laws, could not prevent the entry of prohibited immigrants from abroad, could not deal with the erosion caused by rivers rising in Basutoland, or with animal diseases, originating in the Territories, which vitally concerned her. Coming to details, Hertzog said it was becoming more difficult to resist the daily pressure of his people for measures to restrict competition from the Territories in Union markets. The Depression had much accentuated the demand to ban Bechuanaland or Swaziland livestock and dairy produce, Swaziland tobacco and maize, and Basutoland wheat, since the countries of origin were politically as distinct from the Union as if they were on a different continent. A further main consideration, he said, was the question of reserving jobs in the Union for Union Africans as far as possible, with the consequent exclusion of Africans from outside the Union. Unless the Territories were handed over he did not see how they could avoid making such an unfortunate distinction, as a large number of Sotho and Swazi got work while Union Africans were unemployed.[26] In a summarising (and threatening) memorandum (July 1933) Smuts wrote:

> There can be no doubt that the Union bears the brunt of the economic maintenance of the Territories and it is felt that if the Territories are to be maintained by the Union and to form part of the Union economically, they must also form part of it politically. The Union may find it difficult to continue the economic maintenance of the Territories, to its own disadvantage, unless they form part and parcel of the Union.[27]

It is by no means clear why Hertzog re-opened the question in 1932. Was it an attempt to take advantage of Britain's economic plight? Was it perhaps that the Statute of Westminster had removed much of the basis for the suspicion of Britain which was necessary for the successful resurgence of Afrikanerdom? Was he simply stirring old feelings, knowing he had no real hope of success? At any rate, some of these reasons put forward by Hertzog and Havenga in their initial moves were decidedly odd, and they were easy to refute, particularly the alleged need for 'reserving as much as possible fields of labour within the Union for the Union natives, with the consequential exclusion of natives from outside the Union'. As late as 1930 an Inter-departmental Committee on Labour Resources had emphasised that, except for a brief period in 1924, there had not for many years been an adequate labour supply in the Union. How, therefore, could it be true that African labour coming in from the Territories had ousted Union labour, forcing up the bill for unemployment assistance? As Lord Hailey observes in his best magisterial manner: if these arguments merit any place in a record of transfer discussions, it is 'only because they were a tacit admission that the Union now felt it needed some substantive reason for urging the case for transfer, other than the natural sense of disappointment that the British government had so far delayed carrying out its avowed intention of handing over the Territories to its administration'.[28]

The Dominions Office was not disposed to take too seriously the threat of stopping the recruitment of labour from the

Territories. They thought Hertzog probably wanted a pretext for raising the Swazi cattle weight restriction from 800 lb. to 1000 lb. in order to bring it into conformity with the Bechuanaland embargo. They were perhaps a little irritated by the way in which the South Africans seemed to harp mainly on the administrative and economic aspects of the question instead of facing the vital consultative and constitutional ones, but this bias was in fact extremely valuable in enabling Britain to deflect the whole problem into the channel of economic co-operation. The South Africans had unwittingly made a case for administrative co-operation rather than political control.

The cabinet agreed that it was impossible even to consider the question of transfer without taking steps to ascertain the opinion of the populations, for which the present was not a suitable time.[29] In informing Hertzog of this, somewhat peremptorily, Thomas added that he hoped still to have his friendly co-operation in dealing with various economic and other problems facing the Territories, since the difficulties referred to in Smuts' memorandum were surely not insuperable.[30]

Hertzog's reaction to this decision was petulant, and he wrote a rather blustering reply, underlining his disappointment:

> I had confidently hoped for a more reassuring response. . . . The matter is almost daily becoming more pressing and acute . . . creating a very unfavourable state of feeling in this country. . . . The position today, with respect to these Territories, is very unsatisfactory . . . [leading to] feelings of hostility which may permanently affect their relationship, to the detriment of all concerned.
>
> Quite frankly, the position of the Union with respect to these Territories, whether viewed from the economic, administrative or judicial aspects, is . . . fast becoming intolerable . . .[31]

Old arguments were reiterated, and he seemed to imply that the red locust invasion had originated in the Territories. The Dominions Office was able gleefully to chide him on that score, since the locust came from north of the Zambesi. Hertzog, in

laying such stress on the ravages of the locust, had confused two
different types, the red locust and the desert locust. Moreover,
in the campaign conducted against the red locust, Union
authorities had by agreement taken charge of operations in
Bechuanaland and expressed themselves fully satisfied with the
co-operation they received. Equally effective retort was given
to the alleged legal difficulty in dealing with foot-and-mouth
and similar diseases, since twelve months before the receipt of
Hertzog's letter, awkwardnesses in getting witnesses to Court
had been adjusted, to the apparent satisfaction of Union
authorities. As for the argument of labour competition: the
amount of labour going into the Union from the Territories was
much less than that recruited from other external sources under
arrangements directly negotiated by the government to fill a
known deficiency. Once again Lord Hailey's commentary on
these matters is masterly:

> Those who intend to cite arguments of a technical character
> in order to support their case in a political controversy need
> to make certain of their facts before stepping into the arena,
> for failure in this respect may gravely weaken their approach
> to their main objective. General Hertzog had unfortunately
> neglected this precaution. . . .
> Every Government has in its employment services those
> whose duty it is to provide Ministers with ammunition with-
> out which many would prove to be ineffectual either in
> attack or defence. On the present occasion Mr Thomas
> could certainly congratulate himself that he had been better
> served than General Hertzog. But the major issue, so far
> from having been decided, had not even been debated.[32]

The solution to disease control and the labour problem, the
secretary of state replied (16 July 1934),[33] 'lies in close co-
operation and the joint working out of a policy' which would
take into account all the complex considerations involved. But
he could not see how it would be furthered by transfer which in
itself would merely mean that under the Schedule the Union
would be debarred from imposing any discriminatory restriction
whatever upon the entry of Africans from the Territories into

the Union. The permanent solution to future relations and
present difficulties seemed to be the closest association and
co-operation between the Union government and the British
administrations. All the information went to show that the
result of consultation with the Africans would not be such as to
make transfer feasible, if Hertzog stuck to his declarations about
not pressing unwilling peoples and if Britain honoured her
pledges. Consultation would be for the moment 'embarrassing
and undesirable from every point of view'.

In effect Thomas associated himself with Amery's reply of
1927.[34] Romney Sedgwick, better known for his edition of
George III's letters to Bute, had a large hand in drafting
Thomas' reply.*

On the whole Britain took a firm stand in 1933 and 1934 in
the face of Afrikaner threats. After all, the British position was
not quite so weak as it might at first sight appear. The Territories imported about a million pounds' worth of merchandise
annually, most of it manufactured in the Union. If Britain
instituted tariff rates of her own which no longer protected
Union manufacturers against overseas trade, South Africans
would lose a valuable trade. Those who, like the Harrismith
blanket-makers, manufactured specially for the Territories,
would be hard hit. If South Africa applied economic sanctions,
Britain could produce a counter-threat of considerable importance in the case of Bechuanaland and one by no means
negligible in the case of the other two. A South African economic
boycott of the Territories would be unpleasant and uncomfortable, but it could be combatted. It might be possible to divert
Swaziland's trade to Lourenço Marques; and Basutoland
might be assisted to draw its imports from Britain in bond and
export its wheat and wool to the United Kingdom direct. In
any case, a boycott would be so unfriendly an act that Britain
would certainly have been justified in definitely severing all
links between Bechuanaland and the south. The final and

* R. R. Sedgwick, principal clerk in the Dominions Office 1930–8, editor of
Letters from George III to Lord Bute, 1756–66 (1939); deputy U.K. high commissioner
in the Union of South Africa 1946–9; under-secretary of state in Commonwealth
Relations Office from 1949.

permanent loss of Bechuanaland would never compensate Hertzog for acquiring Swaziland and Basutoland even if it could be effected. Threats regarding migrant labour could be simply dismissed. Would the Orange Free State, Nationalist centre though it was, actively support a policy which would withdraw all Sotho labour from its farms? Or Transvaal mine-owners a policy which would force them to employ more Portuguese Shangaan who had to be paid in gold?[35]

Having arrived at this advanced stage in the account, it may be as well to pause for a moment to allay the impatience of those readers who will, quite understandably, be wondering why public opinion has been so little mentioned. The reason is simple. At a time when public interest in all colonial affairs was apathetic, and press and parliament mostly inattentive, public concern for the Territories remained dormant between 1910 and 1933. It revived in 1933 and never wholly disappeared again. The Anti-Slavery and Aborigines Protection Society, the only radical pressure group in Britain which concerned itself with South African affairs, had nothing to offer towards the formulation of policy. Sir John Harris, its parliamentary secretary, lamely admitted in May 1934 that it had not occurred to his organisation to take the line that Britain was fully entitled to refuse assent to transfer till native policy in the Union was clearly defined; mostly they had assumed Hertzog would be met by a request to declare his native policy for the High Commission Territories, but they were all for the larger issue 'if those interested think it is the best line to take'.[36]

The issue first came prominently to notice in Britain in 1933 from a combination of circumstances, not all of them particularly relevant. The proximate cause was probably excitement over the action of Vice-Admiral Edward Evans, acting high commissioner, backed by Union marines and field guns, in deposing Tshekedi Kgama for supposedly exceeding his powers. Details of this episode, with its quarter-deck swagger, do not concern us, and Tshekedi was fairly promptly reinstated, but the incident attracted widespread press comment and Bechuanaland was propelled into the limelight. Revival of interest was encouraged by an increase of information. Sir Alan Pim's report on the economic and financial condition of Swaziland was published in 1932, followed by similar surveys of Bechuanaland in 1933 and Basutoland in 1935.[37] The reports sharply focused the extent to which the government had until recently neglected their economic and social development. News of the coalition United South African National Party also obviously suggested a renewed South African initiative for transfer; one London newspaper even speculated with the idea that a campaign for transfer would furnish a rallying point for the new Fusion government, as it would appeal on the one hand to Afrikaners anxious to see the end of imperial rule and on the other hand to cosmopolitan Rand interests eager to develop the minerals of Bechuanaland and to draw upon labour even more freely than they did already. Johannesburgers certainly began strongly to favour transfer now that limited prospecting for minerals had at last been permitted in African areas. Stimulated by Pim's reports, the House of Lords considered the condition of the Territories on 26 July 1933 and again on 13 December, with Lords Lugard, Selborne, Buxton, Olivier and Snell taking leading parts. They concentrated on the need for financial aid and improved administration as well as on the unsatisfactory nature of Hertzog's native bills.[38]

The Round Table published its first articles about the transfer question in September 1934 and March 1935, setting forth first the factual background, then urging the case for transfer. It particularly criticised the British requirement that the Union first produce an acceptable native policy. This was not, it claimed, a reasonable contribution to the solution of the problem, as no policy statement could adequately lay down the lines on which so complicated a development could proceed, nor any formula have the efficacy of a medical prescription. In any case, it maintained, such a requirement invited the retort: define your own policy for the three countries. Could Britain in fact look for anything, the journal asked, except 'the day to day adjustment of certain principles to changing circumstances'?[39] The Economist carried an opposing commentary on 5 May 1934.

Margery Perham however had beaten *The Round Table* into print with an article in *The Times* on 28 September 1933. It was largely historical, but presented with the warmth of an on-the-spot observation of the Sotho in their gorgeous blankets with their heads held high in the pride of their freedom under the Union Jack. Her statement of the difficulty and undesirability of transfer impressed the Dominions Office. As pressure from Hertzog mounted, Miss Perham, with support from Selborne and Lugard, Col. Josiah Wedgwood and Sir John Harris, did what she could to inform public opinion. This was the reason for two further articles in *The Times* on 5 and 6 July 1934. If Britain hesitated in 1909, she wrote, there was even stronger reason for doing so in the thirties. Then in mid-May 1935 *The Times* published three articles by Lionel Curtis which urged prompt acceptance of South African demands in accordance with the old notions of benevolence generated by trusting colonials with responsibilities. Miss Perham was not disposed to let these 'authoritative and uncompromising' articles go unanswered. Her reply appeared on 16 May 1935. To gain still wider publicity, she proposed to Curtis that their articles should be reprinted within the same covers. He agreed, and generously allowed her in the arrangement of the book to have both the first and the last word.[40] The Dominions Office was amused by this co-operative venture: it was, as one wag had it, 'truly a case of the lion lying down with the lamb'.[41] In this volume, *The Protectorates of South Africa: the question of their transfer to the Union**, Miss Perham restated her argument that the excluded Territories were not a limitation on South African status or a serious check on its freedom of action; it was a geographical exclusion, not a constitutional restriction; and they should be retained until it was possible to transfer them at some later date in a state in which they would be a credit to Britain (which they were not yet) and an asset to the Union. Curtis, maintaining a wooden adherence to the doctrines of 1909, replied that Britain could only refuse transfer on the ground that South Africa could not be trusted, which not only

---

* Oxford, 1935. See especially pp. 16–22 (Perham), 36–7 and 74–80 (Curtis), 3–6 (Perham).

united 'a whole people in anger' but checked the growth of a more liberal opinion; and since people unconsciously acted as they thought others expected them to act, one of the possible results of not trusting the friendly, strong, broad-minded and co-operative Fusion government would be the return to power of the Afrikaner National Party implementing a more un-compromising policy for a long period of office, and the blasting of the nascent liberal outlook of the younger generation which he detected in the South African universities. In the end the Africans would be 'starved into asking for admission'. There were many who agreed with his prophecy.[42]

In January 1935 acting chief Tshekedi Kgama submitted a petition which attracted considerable attention in the British press. A few months later he published an article in the *News Chronicle* issuing a challenge to any white man to deny that Tswana fears were not justified by the whole history of South African treat-ment of Africans. Miss Perham said the historical and legal arguments of such a man – probably the most intelligent and enlightened chief in Africa – could not just be brushed aside. Lugard wrote two pieces in the *Manchester Guardian*, advocating more development and commending as 'brief and temperate' Tshekedi's pamphlet *Reply to the Propaganda for the incorporation of Bechuanaland in the Union* published by the Anti-Slavery Society. Tshekedi played a larger part than any other African leader in anti-transfer publicity. This hard-headed, stocky and indomitable figure, favourite son of Kgama the Great, had a remarkable library of Africana and parliamentary blue books, together with items such as *How to play Association Football* and Kingsley's *Water Babies*. He found the opposition to transfer beginning to be expressed in Britain highly gratifying.[43]

Professor Arthur Berriedale Keith (the noted expert on im-perial constitutional history), in a letter to the *Morning Post* (18 March 1935), stressed Britain's moral obligation to obtain the consent of the peoples, mentioning changes in the constitutional position and Hertzog's commitment to white racial paramountcy as influential considerations on the side of the case for delay.[44]

By 1935 too the pattern of Hertzog's plans for the total restructuring of the South African political framework was much clearer. After five years' deliberation, the joint select committee considering his five native bills reported. Two main bills emerged: the Representation of Natives Bill, by which no more Africans were to be admitted to the parliamentary roll and a Natives Representative Council was set up; and a Native Trust and Land Bill, by which segregation was supposed to be made more practicable and justifiable through the purchase of more land for reserves. These were subsequently followed by a third bill, the Natives Laws Amendment Bill restricting movement of Africans into and within the towns. The British generally regarded this proposed legislation as retrogressive and thus a new obstacle to transfer was created.

Hertzog's campaign moved into a more determined phase from March 1935 in anticipation of his visit to England for George V's Silver Jubilee celebrations. The high commissioner Sir William Clark had separate conversations with Hertzog and Smuts. Hertzog said he was about to demand the transfer of Bechuanaland within a year; if refused, he would prohibit the entry of a single African from Bechuanaland. He did not consistently maintain this surprising position and Clark was not much bothered: 'the prime minister's utterances are, as you know, growing increasingly irresponsible about matters which move him and he is causing considerable anxiety to his colleagues in that respect'. He did not think Hertzog would take drastic action, but he was always liable to be carried away and say something injudicious. Clark discovered that Smuts thought Britain 'somewhat unyielding', and wished 'something' to be said to indicate 'some relaxation of what he regards as a certain rigidity in the United Kingdom government's attitude on the question'. Smuts wished the question had not been raised, but since Hertzog had said so much in answer to a parliamentary question in April 1934, and since it had in fact been brought forward, his principal (and perhaps genuine) anxiety was about pressure from their supporters and especially from the farmers who were, he said, a powerful political influence. Clark thought both Hertzog and Smuts were rather embarrassed by the situation which they had helped to create; they realised that it would not be sensible to press the matter unduly. It seemed improbable that Hertzog would in further discussions with the secretary of state wish to limit himself to the possibilities of closer co-operation unless it could be shown that such co-operation would represent an advance towards transfer. Clark felt that the explicitly mentioned South African administrative difficulties were not in fact the real source of trouble: the government was exposed to political pressure about the Territories from diverse quarters and was anxious to anticipate it before it became acute. He sensed that Hertzog's 'whole position and attitude suggested that while he wanted something done as soon as possible he would be content with comparatively little' – for example, an undertaking to make a transfer within a specified period.[45]

Hertzog and Thomas met again on 14 May 1935. Thomas reported to Clark what he himself had said:

> it seemed to me that, if transfer were ever to take place, and whether it took place by stages or not, the essential preliminary was that the goodwill of the natives towards the Union Government and towards Union policy should be won, so that, if possible, the natives should be got to look upon transfer as being in their own interests. It seemed to me that the best method of achieving this end would be to work out methods of co-operation, the closer the better, between the Union Government and the Administrations of the Territories over as wide a field as possible, and in particular in all matters relating to the economic welfare and development of the Territories.

He added – and in the light of later controversy, the wording should be studied carefully – that he was sure

> that the right policy, especially in dealing with chiefs and their followers, was to discourage agitation against joining the Union and to concentrate on getting everyone, natives and Europeans alike, to work for the success of such co-operative measures as might be found possible. It seemed to me that this was the best way of creating the right atmosphere. General Hertzog concurred.[46]

After their discussion, Thomas handed to Hertzog an important *aide mémoire*. The draftsmanship was perhaps not good. Was
the vagueness deliberate? In its critical portion, which certainly
gave little away, it was worded as follows:

> the policy of both Governments for the next few years should
> be directed to bringing about a situation in which, if transfer
> were to become a matter of practical politics, it could be
> effected with the full acquiescence of the populations
> concerned. With this end in view we felt it important that the
> closest possible co-operation should be established between
> the Union Government and the Administrations of the
> Territories. We realise, of course, that some measure of
> co-operation already exists; but we feel that there are many
> directions in which it could be fruitfully extended. In
> particular it appears to us to be an essential condition of the
> success of such a policy that the native population should feel
> that the Union Government are working in concert with the
> local Administrations with a real and generous desire to
> develop and improve conditions in the Territories.
>
> We would very gladly consider sympathetically any pro-
> posals which the Union Government may feel able to make
> as to further practical steps which could be taken for pro-
> moting co-operation on these lines. . . .[47]

Announcing this agreement, Hertzog said that before
transfer could take place there were certain prerequisites which
had to be complied with:

> We have consequently agreed that we shall, in a spirit of
> mutual helpfulness and friendly co-operation, assist in
> bringing about the conditions and circumstances under which
> effect can be given to the Schedule subject to such revision as
> may be mutually agreed upon.[48]

The 1935 Thomas–Hertzog concordat was a Dominions
Office plan. It enabled Margery Perham and Lionel Curtis to
find some common ground, and they wrote a joint letter to
The Times agreeing that the new policy would offer the best

solution and hoping that public interest would not die down. Like them, *The Round Table* commentator was relieved that Hertzog had not received a bare negative: both sides had made a 'constructive effort to bridge the gulf' between the existing state of native opinion and all the forces making early transfer advisable. The same journal made further reports on the situation in 1937 and 1939.[49]

In July and August 1935 the high commissioner had various conversations designed to work out areas of co-operation. Since the special object was to impress Africans in the Territories with Union goodwill, in compiling a list of suggestions it was necessary, he thought, to include proposals for the removal of certain grievances under which they laboured. He made it quite clear to the South Africans that Britain could not guarantee results: the policy of co-operation in development was merely one element in acquiring African goodwill – other things, such as restrictions on cattle and the policy of the current native bills, militated against it.

A member of the Native Affairs Commission, Mr G. Heaton Nicholls, made a 'not very fruitful trip' to Basutoland to assess for the Union the possibilities of co-ordinating policy: he saw the country was happy as it was.[50]

At a cabinet meeting in October the Union government agreed to go as far as possible to meet British requirements. Next, Hertzog told Clark he did not wish to seem to be rushing things, but when would incorporation take place? Clark replied, 'we could none of us foretell when the time would in fact be ripe for transfer'. Hertzog nevertheless felt an important step had been taken: for the first time the British government had admitted that his request for transfer was reasonable and had not held back as previously.[51] His belief was not without some justification.

The immediate future was dominated by various matters arising out of the interpretation of the *aide mémoire*.

It was soon decided that the Union's co-operation would extend to financial contribution. Clark thought that South Africa would expect a definite and quick return for the money: she was trying to buy the Territories and wanted to commit

Britain to a guaranteed early delivery. The sum proposed would be quite large. Clark commented:

> Hertzog has always given me the impression of not personally being in any great hurry about transfer, but I confess to looking forward with some anxiety to the pressure which may be exercised in the future if the Union Government maintain the proposed lavish scale of expenditure. I am not opposed to transfer – indeed, I believe it to be essential eventually to the well-being of the Territories – but we must have a reasonable measure of native acquiescence, and I doubt very much whether two or three years of developmental expenditure by the Union is going to have much influence on the Chiefs.

'Fear the Greeks even when they bring gifts' was much more likely to be their attitude.[52] Thomas agreed that any action of the Union which seemed unduly precipitate or impairing of British administrative responsibility would be adversely criticised. This being so, their contribution should be limited to a fifty-fifty basis.[53] In March 1936 it was announced that the Union would contribute £35,000. This decision was denounced by Dr Malan in the House of Assembly as, without a date agreed for transfer, 'purely and simply a gift to the British government'. Hertzog had aroused great expectations. But what, asked Malan, had the negotiations actually achieved? Their result was exactly nil. Behind his rhetoric, there lay perhaps an acute perception: the policy of co-operation was, he said, a polite cloak for an indefinite postponement of transfer.[54]

Some months later, in a heated debate on the subject in June 1936,[55] Hertzog was much attacked over the £35,000, which probably explains why he then alleged, contrary to the facts, that an actual timetable for transfer had been fixed. In 1935, he said, it had been mentioned by the British that transfer of Swaziland could be expected to take place 'in two years' time', and that after a further interval of a year or two, the next Territory would follow. Since last year they had been in the position that England was holding the Territories only until they were quiet and the shouting had died down. He claimed it was a special mark of honesty and goodwill on

Britain's part to say:—let us co-operate to facilitate transfer. Hertzog repudiated the suggestion that he was doing anything so stupid as trying to buy the Territories for £35,000: advancing this sum was doing nothing more than they would have to do ultimately when the Territories were handed over.

In the end parliament voted him the money, but it was a pyrrhic victory at best, and in the end availed him nothing.

The initial reaction of the chiefs was certainly adverse. They suspected that the Union contribution was part of a bargain which had been concluded for transfer. Professor Eric Walker* talked with Sobhuza who said it would be 'ungentlemanly' to accept money and then oppose transfer.[56] The Sotho eventually accepted the proposal, after an assurance that acceptance would not commit the paramount chief to transfer. The other Territories might have followed suit, but for the statement by Hertzog which caused the British government itself to prevent payment of the contribution, as once it became linked with the suggestion of an early transfer it would only have the effect of hardening African attitudes and alarming the House of Commons.

Hertzog's statement of his belief that Thomas in 1935 had mentioned a definite timetable for transfer, beginning with Swaziland 'in two years' time' was as unexpected as it was awkward. British official comment described it as 'a serious misunderstanding': Hertzog was certainly mistaken.[57] Alarmed that Africans would doubt British good faith, Britain extracted from Hertzog an admission that Thomas did not state a definite number of years, but there was, he insisted, in the discussion during November 1935 a definite presumption that a beginning would be made 'within a few years'. Hertzog apologised for creating embarrassment. In his defence it was said that the statement was impulsive, made without preparation and when he was tired. The secretary of state refused to make allowances. The damage had been done and Hertzog must pay for it. The statement must set back both the prospects of

* E. A. Walker, author of *A history of Southern Africa*; King George V Professor of History in University of Cape Town 1911-36; Vere Harmsworth Professor of Imperial & Naval History, Cambridge 1936-51, and Fellow of St John's College.

transfer and the policy of co-operation which had started well. It was altogether premature to speculate about dates before the policy of co-operation had a fair and unhurried trial. Union financial contribution must now be suspended. Hertzog agreed. He also accepted the point that there was no agreement or understanding between the two governments except the *aide mémoire* of 1935, while he continued to believe it implied that if co-operation was a success, transfer would begin within a few years, i.e. about two years thence.[58]

By the beginning of 1937 it was obvious that the policy of co-operation as a means of influencing the Africans was probably dead, and that the manner of its dying had enhanced African suspicions. Prospects of transfer were thus less favourable than they had been two years earlier. Hertzog could not see that Britain was prevented from taking overt action to smooth the way for transfer because this would be equivalent to championing the Union cause. In his frustration, Hertzog began openly to accuse Britain of not carrying out what he believed to have been a central part of the 1935 agreement. In December 1937 he most forcefully stated his conviction: Thomas had clearly stipulated that local officials should exert influence to bring transfer closer.[59] The *aide mémoire* definitely does not suggest that this was so, and Hertzog's contention, if it rested on anything at all, depended on something not written into the record of their meeting in May 1935. A supplementary *aide mémoire* (July 1935) drawn up by the high commissioner is thought by some commentators to give probable support to Hertzog's view:

> It will then be the duty of officials in the Territories to expound to the Chiefs and peoples the extent of the benefits which they may be receiving through the goodwill of the Union . . . it would seem that the most substantial contribution to the growing sense of co-operation which could be made by the Administration of the Territories would be by instructing their officers to bring home to the Chiefs and peoples, as and when assistance is afforded or grievances removed . . . the extent of their debt to the Union.

Despite the fact that this passage does not mention transfer, Mr J. E. Spence[60] feels that in the light of it, Hertzog's contention – that Thomas had undertaken to instruct officials to 'inculcate in the inhabitants ideas favourable towards transfer' [though this was Hertzog's phrase] – was not unreasonable, and that 'perhaps the kindest interpretation from Thomas's point of view would be to say that in the discussions that took place between Hertzog and Thomas, something was said which Hertzog took to be a firm undertaking; having done so, he read all the subsequent official documents and correspondence with them at the back of his mind'. Spence also wonders whether it would be possible for officials to discourage agitation against joining the Union without substantially inculcating in the inhabitants ideas favourable to transfer. As he says, the distinction is a fine one. But it is surely one which the British government was quite capable of making.

The copy of the *aide mémoire* in the South African official published account (1952) of the discussions reproduces a ministerial covering note:

Saw Mr Thomas, Dominions Office, in company with Mr Duncan. Discuss with him the matter of the transfer of the Protectorates. He hands me this typed document after having agreed with me that the Territories should be transferred and that the necessary steps should be taken by the British Government to instruct their officialst hat the necessary spirit should be fostered with the inhabitants of the Territories preparing them for transfer.[61]

'The necessary spirit' is at best a vague phrase and less than Hertzog subsequently alleged.

One has to balance the chances of an indiscretion by Thomas against those of misconception, inaccurate remembering or sheer imagining by Hertzog. The repeated evidence for Hertzog's mistakes and passionate overstatement are cumulatively strong presumptive evidence that he was wrong once again. Hertzog had ample capacity for believing what he wanted to believe. Indeed he was a past master at the art of self-deception. He had already in March indicated his belief that the result of African consultation might be favourable, especially if Britain were prepared to instruct her officers to use their influence.[62]

On the other hand, almost equally, one cannot feel absolute confidence that Jimmy Thomas might not have accidentally overstepped his official brief. The verbal solecisms, the jocular *bonhomies* the meet-you-half-way style of bargaining characteristic of the former trade unionist – all these became more suspect with the rather pathetic decline of his mental vitality, his growing resort in speeches to bluster and woolliness. His minutes were seldom more than ten words long and not usually cast into sentence form. He had not been a notable success as Dominions secretary; he had become a favourite target for the Opposition; and only a year later his career was shattered by the allegation that he had leaked the gist of budget secrets while in his cups. Still, he was not finished in 1935 and could occasionally rise effectively and judiciously to the challenge of the moment.[63]

Knowledge of Thomas's discredit over the budget may of course have subsequently tempted Hertzog to discredit him (from the British point of view) over the *aide mémoire* and so extract advantage for his own cause. For it does seem unlikely that Hertzog was right. The memorandum which Thomas himself made the day after his meeting gives no suggestion that instructions to officials of the kind which would meet Hertzog's views were contemplated: and there is no reason why he should have omitted to make a full record of the discussion.[64] Instructions to the high commissioner in 1935 were shown to Hertzog and he concurred in their terms. They were silent on the matter. One further possible shaft of light comes from the presence at the meeting of Mr Duncan (minister of mines 1933–36). He was the only other person present. After it, he told the Dominions Office staff that they had had a very good talk but had not got much out of Mr Thomas.[65] This hardly suggests that Thomas had made so valuable a concession to the South African side. Notes of a meeting between the high commissioner and the minister for native affairs on 11 February 1936 also give some possible clarification:

Sir William Clark thought it unlikely that anyone would expect acquiescence to be unanimous. The Chiefs could exert great influence if persuaded of the advantages of transfer. He agreed that Basutoland would be difficult to influence and it could not be taken for granted that matters would be easy as regards Swaziland and some of the Chiefs in the Bechuanaland Protectorate, e.g. Tshekedi and Bathoen. This was, however, looking very far ahead as the first step was co-operation towards securing goodwill: as regards this he was prepared to undertake that officials would be instructed to give the fullest publicity in respect of any assistance rendered by the Union.[66]

The instruction here was in an area sharply distinguished from that of persuading chiefs to favour transfer, which was put as something far in the future.

In raising this whole issue in a rather sinister way, Hertzog was doubtless determined to find a justification for the difficulties in which he had placed himself by accepting the *aide mémoire* and especially by committing himself to the stipulation about full acquiescence of the inhabitants, which made transfer more difficult, especially as he must have known that British officers were as a matter of fact required not to influence opinion about transfer either one way or the other. Hertzog seemed to think of Britain as administering the Territories as a trustee for the Union, and if after Union efforts to help, the Africans still refused transfer then it must be regarded as Britain's fault and the Union would be justified in enforcing compliance by using economic pressure. His attitude to transfer was marked by increasing overtones of assurance and self-confidence. He would not admit as practicable 'anything which carries the semblance of an admission that they are not completely competent to fulfil the trust which rests upon them'. As for his native policy, that must 'remain a matter of purely domestic concern'.[67]

Hertzog's next visit to England was in June 1937, when he had two long conversations with Mr Malcom MacDonald (secretary of state for Dominion affairs, November 1935 to January 1939, with one brief interval). MacDonald was young, and the son of former premier James Ramsay MacDonald. He achieved a much closer personal grip upon the problem than his predecessor Thomas had done, doing much of his own drafting and conducting a considerable number of interviews, all of which were assiduously recorded. MacDonald's view was as follows. Britain could not agree to transfer in the face of strongly expressed African opinion and parliamentary disapproval; but if he did not satisfy the Union that he had done all he properly could to obtain African acquiescence he would be charged with what amounted to a breach of faith and serious friction with South Africa would arise, probably with undesirable consequences to the Africans concerned. South African opinion was apt to be 'particularly sensitive and impatient'. In his opinion, transfer ultimately ('indeed in some cases sooner rather than later') was in fact likely to be in the best interests of the inhabitants, for geographical and economic reasons. Though it might not be possible for a long time, it was inevitable in the long run. He believed the Union would be anxious to show they could make a success of administration: they would be put on their mettle and might be expected to devote considerable sums of money to development. He saw no reason to suppose the Africans would not be properly governed: the Transkei did not compare unfavourably with much of British colonial administration. The Schedule meant Africans would never get the franchise anyway, and so the native legislation of the Union was not strictly relevant. Europeans in Bechuanaland and most of those in Swaziland were in favour of transfer on economic grounds, as nothing could be worse than the present uncertainty. But, and it was a big but, getting African acquiescence was difficult, if it was possible at all. The only feasible course was to watch for a lessening of African objections. Transfer by stages would be the best procedure, Swaziland first.

Professor Hancock detected 'a slackening of purpose' in British policy on this matter in the 1930s and a resultant relaxation of tension. Be that as it may, it undoubtedly does not say much for Hertzog's political skill that he was able to extract so little advantage from so diplomatic and sympathetic a Dominions secretary. MacDonald found Hertzog overzealous and felt that his periodic outbursts prejudiced the whole process of quiet consideration.[68]

In one of his long talks with Hertzog in 1937, MacDonald dealt with the possible contention that there were two sets of British pledges in conflict. In certain circumstances, he admitted, they might well prove to be contradictory; the problem was how to reconcile them. Three or four years ago they had reached the conclusion that they could be reconciled only if the Africans were persuaded of Union government goodwill. He explained that House of Commons concern was not confined to the Opposition or 'negrophils' but included a good many of the younger supporters of the government who were not connected with propagandist organisations. MacDonald said he had been surprised at the strength of African opposition to the proposed Union financial contribution.[69]

Hertzog pressed for early transfer, but was told, to his deep disappointment, that African opinion was too strongly opposed and the two governments must therefore pursue the policy of co-operation laid down in the Thomas–Hertzog agreement. In addition to this unpalatable reply, Hertzog was further angered by a House of Lords debate on 'Native policy in the Empire' on 9 June, in which Lord Noel-Buxton and the Marquis of Lothian expressed anxieties about the divergence of South African and imperial policies (supremacy and segregation as opposed to trusteeship) and Lord Lloyd referred to the High Commission Territories, the future of which he thought had been 'bandied about rather lightly' in the last year or two in parliament.[70]

Nevertheless Hertzog obtained a clear understanding that the next step was for Britain to draft a statement of policy which might be issued as a joint statement. MacDonald assumed that until this was accomplished, no public statements would be made on either side, but before departing from England Hertzog gave a press interview on 18 June growling that 'unless a different attitude is taken, consequences are going to be of a most unpleasant character'. MacDonald learned that Havenga was disturbed by this threatening utterance, and the high commissioner reported that Smuts deplored it – 'he hoped and thought it had no special significance but was merely another instance of Hertzog's unfortunate habit of thinking aloud'. Hertzog also privately charged the British government with deliberate dilatoriness in carrying out transfer. Back in South Africa, he complained publicly that in Britain the question was played with and misrepresented for political purposes; there had been a 'serious departure' from the 1935 policy, and he alleged that nothing had been done about instructing officials to establish 'a disposition towards the Union' which would facilitate transfer. He also said that in 1926 he had been told the time was unpropitious because a British general election was imminent – an assertion for which there is no warrant in British records for 1926.[71]

MacDonald now prepared his public statements in reply. Life was becoming difficult for him, though Hertzog seemed sublimely unconscious of the extent of his own responsibility for these embarrassments. MacDonald affirmed that he had not been guilty of a breach of faith with the Africans. He did his best to pour oil on troubled waters, to restore the confidence of Hertzog and to re-establish constructive co-operation. In his submissions to the cabinet he analysed the fundamental difficulty as the difference between the native policy of Britain and the Union, which was however 'probably not so serious as it was sometimes represented to be' and was shared to some extent by Southern Rhodesia and the whites of the central African colonies. The crux of the problem was how to reconcile the transfer intentions of 1909 and the claims of the Union, with the pledges given to the local populations and to parliament. Hertzog's unfortunate statements he described as full of inaccuracies. 'It was somewhat difficult to understand the reasons, but this was not the first occasion on which General Hertzog had been betrayed by his bad memory or taken impulsive action in this matter'.[72]

A whole barrage of parliamentary Questions descended upon MacDonald during the course of July 1937.[73] He made a lengthy reply to one from Capt. Peter MacDonald on 9 July and C. R. Attlee (among numerous supplementary questioners) complained that it was not good enough to say that consultation meant consultation. (Within ten years, Mr Attlee as prime minister was to be equally evasive when questioned on the same point.) On 13 July, MacDonald dealt with six questions and five supplementaries. A week later, Creech Jones returned to the 'consultation' issue. Another week after that, on 27 July, in a further reply, this time to a Question about administrative personnel, MacDonald stated that many officers in the Territories were recruited in the Union. Dominion affairs were debated in the House of Commons on 29 July. Newfoundland was much discussed, but the debate was dominated more by the High Commission Territories than by any other part of the Empire. Several speakers – Pethick-Lawrence, Creech Jones, Pickthorn, Riley and Fletcher – stressed the supreme importance of the transfer issue, its status as a long-term first-class problem which highlighted the direct collision between two diametrically opposed policies, imperial and South African, towards the treatment of Africans. Kenneth Pickthorn* ascribed to the Territories an importance which could scarcely be exaggerated: they were strategic areas in upholding trusteeship and the moral values of the Empire, and so, he declared, it was essential that 'faith should be kept and should be evidently seen to be kept, with the inhabitants of these Territories'. In reply, MacDonald first denied charges of neglect and stagnation, outlining the 'active and comprehensive' development programme which had been started. Then he dismissed the allegation that Britain had not wholeheartedly implemented the 1935 agreement. The government had done its duty and abided by the pledges 'without any qualification at all'. He could not however feel that it would be proper for him to interpret the word 'consultation', since this might either contract or expand the pledge. The government, he explained, was not contemplating any new policy, merely further implementation of the existing agreed policy. The matter, he reminded his hearers in a flagging conclusion (though they hardly needed the reminder) was not simple: the Territories were not regarded as 'pawns in some game' between the two governments and they had to consider very seriously indeed the interests of the populations, both European and African.[74]

* M.P. for Cambridge University and author of two volumes on *Early Tudor Government*.

Some months later MacDonald suggested that the Union should prepare a document estimating what would happen upon transfer. Hertzog agreed this would serve a useful purpose, and himself suggested the establishment of a joint advisory committee of Union and British officials to deal with improvement schemes and accelerate the rate of progress. (While rejecting most of Hertzog's ideas, MacDonald found this one acceptable). Presumably Hertzog decided nothing was now likely to be gained if information regarding the good intentions of the Union were left to be conveyed by British officials. He also appeared to think that propaganda for transfer was now far less important than measures which might remedy the 'deplorable misunderstanding in England as to Union native policy'. He indulged in a certain amount of further grumbling about its' being 'merely playing with words' to suggest that the 1935 policy had been fully implemented by Britain. MacDonald thought it important to avoid as far as possible a purely theoretical discussion as to exactly how far the officers in the Territories could properly go in 'assisting to obtain the goodwill of the natives towards the idea of transfer' and instead to concentrate on considering practical action, which should be possible once the Union produced its memorandum.[75]

Further progress awaited the production of this document. Hertzog however seemed to forget all about it, and work upon it started slowly. Eventually a draft appeared on Clark's desk in February 1938. From this it appeared that an undertaking would be given to observe the substance of the Schedule's safeguards and to guarantee the maintenance of existing educational, medical, agricultural and social services. The Memorandum did not impress either the high commissioner or the Dominions Office.

The South African government had rather bungled its chance. The draft did not make enough of the essential dependence of the Territories on Union markets which only transfer could permanently secure. For political reasons the Union government felt unable to abolish the weight restrictions on cattle, which was the one really spectacular piece of co-operation open to them. They overstated their case by ignoring the important efforts Britain had made, and in the face of these actual works and financial contributions they could hold out only vague promises. They should have tried more definitely to outbid Britain, though perhaps this was not easy to do in the light of the facts. The Colonial Development Fund had not only paid £170,000 for combating soil erosion in Basutoland, £273,000 for improvement of water supplies, roads and bridges in Bechuanaland, and £113,000 for general purposes in Swaziland; but also made grants-in-aid in the past ten years of £402,000 for Bechuanaland and £326,000 for Swaziland.[76]

After a considerable amount of informal discussion as to the form this Memorandum should take, the final version was ready by August 1939 but showed little improvement. It concentrated on the negative side, enumerating the existing privileges which might be forfeited if transfer were unduly postponed. It was not an imposing production. It was never published owing to the outbreak of war.[77]

To return to the chronological narrative. At a cabinet meeting on 16 March 1938 (preparatory to a Commons announcement on 29 March) MacDonald argued that the preparation of Union documents on the estimated effect of transfer would be 'very useful for clearing the air, as there was much confusion both in South Africa and here as to what would be the position'. A Joint Statement would restate British pledges and announce the terms of an agreed future policy. Documents would be available to chiefs for study, and resident commissioners would make it clear that they were not commending or opposing South African proposals. The cabinet showed considerable interest in the problems involved, and the atmosphere was to some extent critical of MacDonald's handling. (Beyond recording the *colonial* secretary's opinion that one Union document was purely propagandist, the minutes provide no details. Perhaps it was noted that a joint committee would bring more Union officials onto the scene, men who might be a better agency for the fulfilment of Hertzog's attempts to establish his government's goodwill.) MacDonald conceded that the matter was not without difficulties, but his defence was the existence of a strong demand, even from persons who were opposed to the transfer, for the publication of these documents. 'We were pledged', he reminded his colleagues, under the Hertzog–Thomas agreement, to which he paid tribute, 'not to discourage the natives, but we had given no undertaking to urge them to accept the policy of transfer'.[78]

The Joint Statement was issued towards the end of March 1938. It announced the setting up of a joint committee to study openings for co-operation and to consider matters of mutual concern, such as animal diseases and the marketing of produce. More important, the Statement announced that the Union would prepare memoranda setting forth the terms which they would propose for transfer, in order to clarify the whole position, for the benefit of the populations concerned, in a form more complete and convenient than the Schedule. The Statement also reaffirmed Britain's recognition that section 151 of the South Africa Act referring to transfer of the High Commission Territories had a 'meaning and an intention' which she did not seek to minimise.[79]

The Joint Statement met with a mixed reception in the Union, chiefly because it did not even approximately define the period within which transfer might come about. It was on the whole welcomed as a constructive anodyne by the British conservative press.[80] It was however criticised by the Labour Opposition because there was no provision for African representation on the joint committee. African opinion itself was uneasy. Sobhuza thought the reference to a 'meaning and an intention' too emphatic and it made him apprehensive.[81] The resident commissioner of Basutoland had to reassure the chiefs in council that the joint committee had nothing whatever to do with transfer, and as he was made chairman of it, his word carried some authority. He added that the publication of South African terms 'will not affect the question of transfer in any way, they will bring that no nearer', and any discussion of the terms when issued would not constitute the consultation Africans had been promised long ago. The resident commissioner's explanation was replied to briefly by Bolokoe Potsane: 'I thank you, Sir. It is because when we think of the Union we think of a lion'.[82]

Some members of Hertzog's circle had unofficially suggested in Whitehall in 1937 that Sobhuza was not averse to coming under the Union and if given the slightest British encouragement might even apply for it. Whilst maintaining a proper scepticism as to the significance of 'these obviously inspired statements', the Dominions Office asked Clark to investigate any possible foundation for thinking that the attitude of the Swazi might differ in some way from that of the other Africans. If Sobhuza did indeed regard the matter mainly from the standpoint of the terms he could get, he alone of the leaders of the three Territories might be prepared to consider transfer on terms. The South Africans seemed disposed for the time being to concentrate on Swaziland alone. It was rumoured that Sobhuza would ask for a special concession which would formally bring under his allegiance the large number of Swazi hitherto outside the borders of Swaziland.[83] When the high commissioner talked with him at the end of December 1937 Sobhuza was if anything more cautious than previously, possibly because of the presence of two councillors: 'he would be glad to consider any terms but that if his people were to be influenced the terms would have to be very good indeed'. He asked whether there would be any objection to his inviting a Union official to come to Swaziland to expound the terms and answer questions. Somewhat surprised, Clark gave him a non-committal reply. 'While he was anxious, he [Sobhuza] did not at any time in our talk take up a *non possumus* attitude about transfer'.[84]

Presumably Sobhuza wondered whether he might produce better terms by taking the initiative and approaching the Union direct about an early transfer. Probably he had no enthusiasm for the Union, but was anxious lest worse befall if he stayed out too long. He knew perfectly well however that his people did not see it so. By February 1938, therefore, Sobhuza's attitude seemed definitely to have hardened against transfer, and he spoke with a hostility to it which contrasted with the more or less open mind indicated in private talks. The change was thought to reflect his fuller realisation of the strength of opposition among his councillors.[85] Perhaps in any case he realised that Hertzog would be unwilling to lower his dignity by offering 'bribes to natives' in the shape of a really good offer. By December 1938 however he was moving in the opposite direction again, and was prepared to consider an offer of transfer on certain conditions. 'When a young man comes to woo a girl he first places his gifts before her': if the offer was attractive (i.e. additional land for the native areas and guarantee of the preservation of the status of the tribe and of native institutions, etc.) he personally would be prepared to consider it, provided he was advised to do so by the British government; there would however have to be a very definite guarantee that in the event of South Africa's becoming a republic, Swaziland would have the right to revert to the protection of Great Britain. Malcolm MacDonald commented that this was 'interesting and important'.[86] Its significance was evidently not lost upon Smuts, as we shall see in the next chapter. In August 1939 Sobhuza asked Clark if the Swazi should in their own interests acquiesce in transfer or continue to oppose it. Taken aback, Clark said he could not possibly advise him in such a matter. Clark believed Sobhuza to have a firm grasp of the various aspects of the transfer issue, realising that there were two sides to the question, but even if Sobhuza decided to acquiesce, Clark did not think him strong enough to carry it against the strenuous opposition of other Swazi.[87] With so much of its land in European hands already, Swaziland had less to lose by transfer than the other two Territories, and this might explain Sobhuza's attitude. But it was an argument which could be used in two ways.

7 The High Commission Territories, IV: The Failure of Smuts, 1939–48

HERTZOG's government fell at the outbreak of the Second World War on the issue of South Africa's neutrality. Smuts broke with the Nationalists, formed a government on 5 September 1939 and declared war. Col. Deneys Reitz, the new minister for native affairs (and deputy prime minister 1939–42), agreed with the high commissioner that on account of the war the question of transfer should be allowed to remain in abeyance and consequently that the Memorandum on its effect should not be published. In England, Anthony Eden shortly after taking office as Dominions secretary (3 September 1939 to 10 May 1940) minuted 'It is clear that here is a "sleeping dog" which we are fortunate to be able to let lie'. His complacent misjudgement was to be rudely shattered.

For Smuts dropped a bombshell of the first magnitude. Accustomed to the shuffling unrealities of the Hertzog regime, the British were forced to sit up with a nasty jerk. The first intimations came when Clark thought quite casually that he had better ascertain whether Smuts agreed with the decisions Clark had taken with Reitz. Smuts appeared to do so. Then Clark happened, to quote his own report:

> without any special intent, to speak of 'abeyance for the duration of war', but Smuts at once substituted 'abeyance for the present'. Later on he said war might present a convenient opportunity for putting transfer through. He was speaking in a light vein but no doubt feels it desirable to avoid committing himself in case an opportunity should arise for making a deal.

Clark was surprised, but did not yet take Smuts particularly seriously.[1] With rather more perception, and without Clark's evidence, Tshekedi Kgama guessed that Smuts might try seriously to use the war to achieve transfer. Tshekedi offered Tswana co-operation in the British war effort, even mentioning a readiness to help if necessary in putting down an Afrikaner rebellion in South Africa![2]

In the middle of October 1939 Smuts indicated that he wished the question of transfer to be raised with the Dominions secretary in London. Smuts said quite unashamedly that during the war the British House of Commons would probably take less interest in the question and it should be easier to put through the transfer at any rate of Swaziland or possibly of Swaziland and the Bechuanaland Protectorate. Clark immediately suggested that Smuts was mistaken about this: M.P.s interested in the Territories would more probably draw an uncomfortable contrast 'between our chivalrous attitude toward small nations in Europe and somewhat high-handed procedure apparently contemplated in respect of no doubt smaller nations in South Africa'.[3]

The fact that in October 1939 it was Smuts and not Hertzog who was prime minister for the first time in fifteen years gave an entirely different and more serious complexion to the overture for two reasons. The first was that Hertzog had been ageing and it had been increasingly difficult to take him really seriously. The second was that Smuts was *persona gratissima* in Britain, indeed idolised by the Establishment for his palpably great qualities, and he had brought South Africa into the war.

Hertzog had a massive determination which his critics called sheer stubbornness. 'Hertzog has a one-track mind', wrote Sir William Clark, 'and when he has his mind on a particular objective he is blind to the consequences in other directions'. He was excessively sensitive about his management of the transfer issue, especially when it became bedevilled by his own indiscretions. Clark cursed the vagaries of his mentality: 'the old gentleman can be infernally obstinate when he gets an idea or grievance into his head. The trouble is that whatever one settles with him the said idea or grievance is always apt to bob

up again'. This happened with the *aide mémoire*.* Hertzog
disputed the interpretation of this until the end of 1937 and
then agreed to differ, but a year later he returned again, briefly,
to one of the points at issue. If Smuts became thoroughly restless
at this perpetual wrangling British ministers chafed even more.
Hertzog was much too inclined to represent transfer as urgent,
as a burning issue. An exceedingly talkative person, he was also
prone to overstate the unanimity of Union demand for transfer.
And yet at the same time he fluctuated between a sense of
urgent grievance and long periods of idle quiescence. The
British government thus saw him as unreasonable in manner
and unrealistic in comprehension; he was also, at the age of 73,
found dithering in action. With increasing infirmity his
attention to public affairs was correspondingly intermittent,
with long absences on his farm, where official files were not
welcome. Hence the curious delays in the preparation of
memoranda between October 1937 and August 1939. Always
slow to take a point in conversation, at one moment in this
period Clark found him 'very confused . . . his memory was at
its haziest'. In any case, Hertzog's qualities had never been of
the type which produces efficiency and despatch in the discharge
of business. His leadership was the outcome rather of forceful
personality and resolute tenacity in the pursuit of a few
political ideas. His government, in Clark's opinion, was a
dilatory and indifferent one.[4]

Smuts, on the other hand, was regarded at one and the
same time as more reasonable and sympathetic and as infinitely
more astute and capable. Throughout the discussions in which
he had occasionally taken part in the Fusion government he
appreciated British difficulties much more clearly than Hertzog
did. The situation always seemed to improve after talks with
him. Smuts repeatedly returned to the suave argument that
every effort must be made to prevent the Territories' becoming a source of ill-feeling between the two goverments, as
transfer seemed to him the only issue left which could possibly

---

* Clark had to remind Hertzog in February 1937 that Hertzog had earlier concurred in MacDonald's statement that no time had been fixed for transfer: 'He
turned rather red', looked worried and 'badly deflated', as if he had forgotten the
whole episode in his muddled transaction of business. (DO. 35/900/Y.6/12).

have that effect. It was a plausible approach. Thus, Sir William Clark warned, when Smuts really decided to put his mind to the question:

It will be a more formidable affair than when General Hertzog was in charge. I do not know whether he has the same personal feeling about it as General Hertzog, who regarded our hesitancy as a slur upon South Africa's rule as embodied in himself, but he certainly wants to get the question disposed of. He has more than once said to me that he considers it the only dangerous rock of offence still remaining between our two peoples, and apart from that, he is doubtless human enough to wish to wipe General Hertzog's eye by succeeding where his brother General had failed – and in an affair which the latter had made peculiarly his own. How far he will carry things if he does take the question up is another matter. When he has once made up his mind, General Smuts can be very determined and ruthless, though I can hardly believe that he would wish to go so far as to risk a serious breach with our Government on this question.

Clark added a penetrating insight into Smuts' character:

But it is always possible that he may go farther than he intends, because, despite his outlook and culture being so much wider than that of most of his countrymen, he is never-theless too much of an Afrikaner of the old school altogether to appreciate that the British Government and Parliament will insist on taking their obligations to our natives seriously, even though the result may be prejudicial to the relations between two white peoples of the Commonwealth.[5]

The British in 1939, however, refused to be overawed or brow-beaten by Smuts, who, for his part, certainly knew when to retreat decently. But he was disappointed at the stony reception accorded his overture.

Smuts' government was prepared to offer generous terms to Swaziland, including purchase of land for enlargement of Swazi reserves, and re-consideration of the possibilities of a through-railway and the reduction of native taxation. The South African government wished to have permission to negotiate on this basis with Sobhuza. These terms were obviously a big improvement on anything previously hinted at, and Clark commented that when the Union got down to details, if 'they feel able to make as generous an offer as they fore-shadow at present, it is one which Swazis would have to con-sider most seriously and might one hopes accept'.[6] Smuts had further conversations with his colleagues, and in briefing Col. Reitz to negotiate in London said that while he was in general agreement with a policy of concentrating on Swaziland, Reitz must also raise the question of transferring Basutoland and Bechuanaland. Smuts hoped that if the British government were faced with the demand for the transfer of all three Ter-ritories she might find it easier to convince the British public that one must be transferred as a compromise solution.[7]

To ask for three in order to obtain one was a foolish tactic. Smuts did not understand that to the Dominions Office it was not a matter of bargaining but of honouring pledges. Moreover, on the larger issue, it is difficult to see how he could have failed to realise that Africans would regard any attempt to put them under an alien government as the antithesis of the principles for which Britain had taken up arms in Europe. The British govern-ment was unquestionably displeased at the behaviour of Smuts. Eden decided to send a rather stiff reply, thinking it better to be tough at the outset and make the British position absolutely clear. He telegraphed (18 October 1939): 'It has come as an unpleasant surprise to me that General Smuts wishes to raise question of transfer again at this moment'. Of course he would be ready to discuss the matter with Reitz as requested, but

it would certainly be wrong to assume that Parliament would be indifferent to the matter if there was any suggestion of trying to make use of the present preoccupation of public opinion with the conduct of the war to force through transfer of any of the Territories, if there should be strong opposition from the native inhabitants . . . we could not contemplate

making any prior bargain for the transfer of Swaziland alone
as a compromise solution as he seems to suggest.

If there was to be any action, Eden continued, it should be to
pursue the policy already determined, that is to say the publication of the Memorandum, though of course it could not be
guaranteed either that even the most favourable terms might
not leave a large body of Swazi opinion strongly opposed
or that the issue of the Union Memorandum might not provoke
demonstrations against transfer in all three Territories. Hence
Britain could not welcome publication, since Eden was naturally anxious while 'our activities must be so largely devoted to
matters connected with the war' to avoid the administrative
difficulties in the Territories which might result.[8]

Col. Reitz went to London as South Africa's representative
to discuss with delegates from all the Dominions plans for the
joint conduct of the war. The kindly tenth Duke of Devonshire (parliamentary under-secretary for the Dominions 1936–
1940) was his host. As Chatsworth was serving as an evacuation
school for Manchester girls, Reitz stayed in a small cottage a
mile or two away from the ancestral seat. Apart from his other
business, Reitz had long discussion about the Territories with
Eden on 23 October and Devonshire on the following day.[9]
From these Eden gathered that there was to be no proposal
after all with regard to Basutoland and Bechuanaland, 'as
neither of these would be an asset to the Union'. Smuts did not
treat the issue as immediate, Reitz said, but he (Reitz) was
quite sure that when the war was over the demand would
become insistent, and he therefore hoped some arrangement
could be arrived at between them straightaway. Would Britain
agree to transfer Swaziland if Sobhuza were satisfied with the
offer of territory which the Union was prepared to make? Eden
was new to his office, but having received cabinet approval of
his telegram of 18 October and being well briefed by his officials
he had no hesitation in saying:

it would be a grave mistake to underrate the public interest
in this matter at the present time. Nothing could make a
worse impression than if we were to appear to hand over these
Territories in time of war when we were fighting for the

interests of small nations. . . . I could give him no kind of assurance.

With Devonshire, Reitz said he fully realised that Bechuanaland and Basutoland must wait for a long time, probably for a generation, but he thought 'that Sobhuza could be got round'. Devonshire tentatively suggested there might be some exchange of officials: if this were possible, he felt it would be a valuable first step. Devonshire's account of the interview proceeds thus:

> While I thought transfer should be our ultimate policy, I did not regard it as a practical possibility at present and that our policy should be rather to produce conditions which made transfer possible: he would always find us very willing to co-operate with him in this policy, but this did not mean we could bring pressure to bear on Sobhuza.

Reitz seemed to accept this adherence to established policy quite calmly. Towards the end of this conversation he seemed to become much less insistent, even accommodating. His final position was as follows:

> if some sort of move could be made in the next ten years he thought his Government would be satisfied; they quite realised that these Territories were a liability and not an asset to whoever administered them and they did not want them for themselves in the least but only because of the political difficulties which their existence created: he wished most heartily that the paragraph about them in the Act had never been written.

Devonshire got the impression that Reitz had been instructed to 'fly a kite but not to press matters or to embarrass us if we found difficulties in making a move'. Even so, it is to be wondered whether Smuts would have endorsed what Reitz had so cheerfully said. The Dominions Office felt happier about the situation after Reitz's departure than it had before his arrival. There seemed no need directly to discourage him from pursuing the matter.[10] No more was heard of it for the remainder of 1939, or during the next three years.

Why did Smuts take this extraordinary action so soon after the outbreak of war? As in 1914, he lost no time in searching out ways of turning the war to South Africa's advantage, and his overture suggests he attached a high degree of importance to transfer. The ostensible excuse was that he believed Hertzog would move for transfer from the Opposition front bench. This, Clark thought, was hardly an impressive bogey after Hertzog's fifteen years of official discussion which had never led him to such an extremity from the government front bench, and it could have been repulsed with the argument that this was a question which ought not to be decided amid the exigencies of war. More probably the explanation is that Smuts allowed himself to be dazzled by the prospective political advantages of obtaining one of the Territories speedily in contrast to the failure and general mismanagement of the whole business by Hertzog, especially since the latter had made it so much his personal concern. Smuts seems to have thought the British House of Commons would be more reluctant than usual to oppose the wishes of a Dominion standing by Britain in war, especially a Dominion doing so only after having squashed its neutralists, and he did not want to lose the opportunity. There was however a more fundamental political explanation which Clark telegraphed to London:

> He is afraid of secessionist movement gaining strength through combination of Malanite and Hertzogite forces and if war lasted three or four years he himself might not for long be able to combat it. . . . He regards United Kingdom attitude on the question of transfer of High Commission Territories as one thing left which can be represented as an infringement of Union's sovereignty and which will therefore afford secessionists dangerously useful ammunition. For himself he said . . . he would prefer to evade transfer issue during the war by arguing that it could not properly be handled under war conditions, etc.; his only reason for pressing it was to get out of the way a factor which could be dangerous to the constitution of the Union in the future. . . . A complicating factor will be that if Republicanism comes increasingly to the front as seems probable at the present time the reluctance of our natives to be transferred will be correspondingly increased.[11]

Eden appreciated Smuts' political problems, but regarded African opinion as the governing factor in the situation (as Margery Perham had realised before him). Meanwhile he did nothing to discourage Smuts from making as attractive an offer as possible to Sobhuza.[12] Smuts did not bother.

The position at the end of 1939 was ambiguous. Britain had pledged herself to co-operate with the Union. The implied intention was to enable transfer to be carried through with African goodwill. Yet in practice administration stood aloof from all attempts to forward transfer. Indeed, reforms in African administration were rather working against it. Systematising the powers of native authorities, courts and treasuries, and preparing them for the introduction of Indirect Rule, took place in Bechuanaland from 1934, Basutoland from 1939 and Swaziland in 1944. Following Lord Hailey's advice, from 1941 this distinctive native policy was gradually but definitely expanded in accordance with the general practice in other imperial dependencies. No public statement, written or otherwise, was made about this process. Though it might have reassured Africans, in relations with the Union it would at best have been an embarrassment and at worst have added to Nationalist animus against Britain.[13] Transfer could hardly be considered until the changes were brought to fruition.

The one fixed point to which all longer-term considerations always came back was the necessity of securing African acquiescence — a fact which the Union government showed inadequate signs of facing realistically. But was this acquiescence to be total or partial? Transfer was repeatedly postponed in a mushy undefined hope that African assent might eventually be given. Futhermore, it was never clear what 'consultation' with Africans meant. When challenged, the invariable government reply was equivocal ' "consultation" means consultation'. Consultation became a stumbling block, but no one seemed to know precisely what it entailed. If it meant that Britain would be guided by the views of Africans then it was tantamount to consent; if it meant merely that inquiry would be made without any commitment as a result, then it was empty verbiage.[14]

The problem of transfer was one of those in which the British found it easier to enumerate the various conflicting complexities than to propound any definite conclusions. They were in a dilemma between on the one hand the moral obligations to parliament and the Africans, and on the other an expediency which made it desirable to avoid a 'breach of faith' with expectant South Africa and to bring to an end what was at one and the same time a source of friction between two Commonwealth governments (a friction endangering South Africa's Commonwealth role, especially in war), and a drain on the British exchequer. The question was: on which horn of the dilemma would Britain choose to be impaled? By the thirties it was in reality not so much the long-standing pledges which prevented any pressure being brought to bear on Africans to accept transfer, as the fact that Britain seriously doubted whether Africans would be happier under Union than they were outside it. The South African regime was recognised to be governed in the last resort by popular feeling and colour prejudice. The alleged historical claim of the Union to Swaziland might make it more difficult to refuse, but it did not make it easier to concede, the transfer of that country.

Perhaps the one decisive position Britain could have taken in 1939 was to declare the opposition of the Africans to be an effective and final barrier to transfer. But she could not use this reply, both on account of declarations to the contrary made in 1909, and because, as J. H. Thomas said, in words quoted above, whatever the future in this part of the world, Britain felt she could achieve nothing without the goodwill of South Africa.* Thus an unqualified negative appeared to be a non-starter. They were therefore back to the familiar problem of making some sort of gesture to conciliate the white South Africans, a gesture which would have enough substance to achieve its object, without having so much as to cause trouble with the Africans or appear to commit Britain beyond her pledges. Granted that a purely negative attitude was impossible, there had to be a degree of collaboration with the Union.

* See above, p. 20 and p. 131.

If Britain was in a dilemma, so was the Union. Expediency in many ways favoured letting things go on as they were — letting the United Kingdom shoulder the expense while the Union reaped the fruits of informal control: the use of British African labour, securely segregated by the general desire of the Sotho, Tswana and Swazi to remain under the aegis of Britain, and the avoidance of the cost and possible friction involved in administering reluctant tribes. The economic advantages of transfer would not be many. The administrative burdens would be heavy. The initial bribes would have to be substantial. But historical and geographical logic pulled another way, and the political and sentimental aspects were paramount. South African pride and prestige demanded that she should continue to insist on transfer. The Union argued that the state of affairs was anachronistic, anomalous in principle, and an affront in practice, tending to give rise to supposedly serious administrative difficulties, and orginally tolerated only on the understanding that it would shortly be regularised by transfer.

Was there a way out? Sir William Clark, retiring as high commissioner early in 1940, in his final summing up, signed in his customary violet ink, was not at all sure that there was, unless it be for Swaziland to accept a spectacular offer from Smuts. Union prestige would than be assuaged, Britain would he relieved of the Territory which was in some ways the most difficult to handle satisfactorily because of the European population. He brought forward again the 'test case' theory: transfer Swaziland and it would be a catalytic object lesson to all concerned, and might, whichever way it worked out, contribute to a final solution of the entire question, either by making possible a confident transfer of the other Territories with African approval or by the Union government's drawing back and deciding not to press its claims further.[15]*

* After the 1940 coalition between Hertzog and Malan, Clark added a 'Further Note': 'It could scarcely be argued that the meaning and intention of Section 151 of the South Africa Act would hold good if South Africa becomes a foreign country; and in view of the formal adoption of the republican principle by this much more comprehensive official opposition, objectors to transfer seem entitled to contend, despite the provisos to the formula, that secession is at least a possibility and that transfer should be regarded as out of the question until the trend of politics in South Africa can be more clearly discerned'.

The Dominions Office felt that if faced with the political necessity of appeasing the Union, action confined to Swaziland would be 'a convenient solution', *provided* transfer could be effected with the goodwill of the Swazi. The proviso was all-important. Meanwhile, they insisted that nothing should be done to encourage Smuts' expectations. Nor should Britain show herself forthcoming in any way. They recognised that it would be better to deal with Smuts, 'who might be relied on to take a reasonable and statesmanlike view', rather than a Nationalist government. The latter would however have one advantage. It would be easier to say 'no' to it.[16]

Lord Harlech (formerly Sir William Ormsby Gore, under-secretary of state for the Colonies, 1922–24 and 1924–29, and secretary of state 1936–38) became high commissioner in May 1941 and held the post for the next three years. He favoured an early all-round settlement and a 'long-range deal' while Smuts was still in power. In this deal, Swaziland would be transferred, the boundaries of the Bechuanaland Protectorate would be 'rectified', while Basutoland would be totally untouched. He would gladly have let Smuts have Swaziland, because British rule was unpopular there, and subject to obstruction; and because it was too small (and its frontiers too artificial) to make an efficient unit of administration without a railway and mining development; he therefore feared it would always be a source of confusion and trouble. If the Nationalists came to power, he expected Swaziland to become the first bone of contention. And so he would prefer to cede it to Smuts rather than see the issue drift inexorably into a real conflict. To be tied for ever to the legal wording of the Act of Union without making any adjustment after the passage of more than thirty years he considered the 'negation of humanity, justice and commonsense'.[17]

The Dominions Office did not think Lord Harlech quite realised just how delicate the British position was as a result of the pledges. At all events officials expected trouble immediately the war was over. There could be no question of seeking to upset the *status quo* until negotiations were forced upon Britain by the Union. The first step would then be for the Union to try to make an offer acceptable to the Swazi. This would, they thought, in future be more difficult after the British grant of £190,000 to purchase back more land for the Swazi nation. In theory the 1935 policy of co-operation between Britain and the Union still held the field, but this they understood as no more than a paper formula.[18] Lip-service could be paid to it, but it could never reconcile divergent attitudes.

After the end of 1939 the whole question was genuinely in abeyance for the duration of the war. In 1943 Smuts showed no disposition to raise the issue, agreeing that it should definitely be suspended. Agitation for the acquistion of the three High Commission Territories was gradually dying, and he did not wish to see it revive. Britain he knew was anxious to damp the matter down, if only because this was a means of preventing the Rhodesian amalgamation issue flaring up again.[19] Smuts for his own part realised that the end of the war could bring widespread administrative and territorial changes in Africa. Posing as an 'African apostle', determined to promote 'African interests' and development to the north in the interests of all races (in accordance with his own haughtily paternalistic ideas, as opposed, he thought, to other people's subordination, rejection or exploitation of the Africans), he envisaged the possibility of some vast federal structure rivalling the United States of America. If he could induce Britain to link up some of her 'fragments' in east and central Africa, a new large state to the north might be coaxed into partnership with South Africa. In such a scheme, the High Commission Territories were relatively small and unimportant, and he was perhaps genuinely concerned not to let them develop into a bone of contention. Thus, unlike his Nationalist opponents, he did not find the transfer question an urgent one. If transfer materialised, it should do so as part of larger changes. Britain was known to be contemplating the establishment of a Southern African Regional Council, and he might have been content with the inclusion of the Territories in that.[20]

In 1945 Smuts said that the states to the north need not fear being swallowed up: annexation was obsolete. His current ideas for the north were limited, initially at any rate, to a big southern African conference system which would concern itself chiefly with economic affairs throughout Africa south of the equator, and perhaps further north. This kind of collaboration he found 'one of the most salutary prospects before us'.[21]

His Nationalist opponents were sceptical. They wanted more concrete objectives. From 1943 they began through press and parliament to use the High Commission Territories as a stick with which to beat both Smuts and the British government. Smuts dealt with this by two pronouncements in March and April 1944. In the first, on 17 March, he hinted that acceptance of a post-war request for transfer would be a way in which Britain could express her gratitude for 'African' participation in the war. It would reduce the anomalies of the African situation: people in Africa (white people, presumably) were entitled to get some good out of the struggle.[22] In the second statement, to the Senate, he implied that the matter had not been forgotten, but since it was not urgent and since it would cause a certain amount of difficulty on both sides, it was a question which they could safely leave until after the war, and 'then tackle and solve'.[23]

This statement gave rise on 24 May 1944 to a Question in the British House of Commons. In reply the government stuck to its pledges about consultation.[24]

Smuts was in London early in July 1945. He did not raise the matter. Perhaps this was because an election was pending and the existing British government could not be sure of continued tenure. Smuts made no further statements until 1 February 1946, when, in the briefest possible reply to a Question in the Union House of Assembly, he simply said there had been no further development since his statement on 3 April 1944.[25] The matter was however debated on 21 March 1946. Smuts reminded parliament that the question had made 'fairly good headway' before the outbreak of war, but that in the last years of the war it was not possible to deal any further with the problem; it would be resumed again 'at the right time'. Though there were certain difficulties, he did not foresee any insurmountable objections. The High Commission Territories were 'an indivisible part of South Africa' and the object and purpose of his government was to get them under their administrative control. There would be no necessity for quarrels or misunderstandings. 'At the right time', he added, 'if I am there, I shall tackle the matter and try to dispose of it'.[26] Hardly an intimation of immediate action. South-West Africa was probably begining to preoccupy him instead.

Smuts, it is plain, had hopes of a post-war informal expansion to the north, but no territorial ambitions there. These were confined to the High Commission Territories, whose inhabitants his United Party accepted as 'natural' (though not equal) South Africans, along with all other inhabitants of the Union. This view was not shared by the Nationalists (with their narrowing definition of true South Africans as Afrikaners only), but Smuts' aim in respect of the Territories was identical. His main difference from the Nationalists, though it was considerable, was one of timing. For he no longer seemed so concerned to achieve transfer himself. Smuts could wait a bit. The Nationalists could not. Other more pro-British South African politicians and officials urged on Britain the wisdom of transfer to a United Party government. But the renewed and obvious Nationalist interest in the Territories, especially from 1946, could only have the effect of inducing further caution in the attitude of the British government. Nationalists were expecting these enclaves to pose constitutional difficulties when they came to try to establish a republic.

In 1946 almost everybody was expecting Smuts to open negotiations, and the organs of public opinion in Britain, in the Union and in the Territories got to work. A noteworthy memorandum reached the Dominions Office in April 1946. It was an unqualified declaration of opposition to transfer by a group of fourteen distingushed Africans in the Union. These included Professor D. D. T. Jabavu, Professor Z. K. Matthews and Dr A. B. Xuma, president of the African National Congress. Eight of them sat upon the Natives Representative Council. In fact, the signatories included most of the politically influential members of the African intelligentsia.[27]

In Britain too, the House of Commons was keenly alive to the issue. Kenneth Pickthorn, and even the Anti-Slavery and

Aborigines Protection Society, started making representations again.[28] Attlee's victorious Labour government was kept on its toes by the radical socialist-Christian element among its supporters. From the prime minister's answer to a Question by Tom Driberg on 24 January 1946 it appeared that the government had received no representations from Smuts and would not be likely to welcome any.[29]

In the aftermath of the Second World War, indeed, British official feeling hardened quickly and conclusively against the transfer even of Swaziland. Sir Evelyn Baring (high commissioner, October 1944 to October 1951) had decided by April 1945[30] that despite the increasing strategic imperial importance of South Africa, 'we should never sacrifice the true interests of Africans to a desire to remain friendly with a United Party Government at Pretoria'. (If this was so, how much the more, it may be presumed, would Britain be unwilling to sacrifice them to a Nationalist government after 1948). But, Sir Evelyn added, if there was to be retention, the position would be impossible to defend unless there was proper development in agricultural, health and educational services. If the High Commission Territories fell below the new modern standards of good administration this could only exacerbate feeling in South Africa.

An official in the Dominions Office noted in March 1946: if African feelings were respected, transfer had become 'nothing but a Nationalist pipe-dream'.[31]

The documents for 1948 are not yet available to historians. It does not however seem a particularly daring speculation to suggest that when Smuts lost the election of 1948 to the reunited Afrikaner National Party under Dr Malan, South Africa finally lost her vestigial chance of a negotiated transfer of any of the Territories. In winning the election, the Nationalists ensured the defeat of South African expansion.

It is all too easy to conclude, as Lord Hailey does, that British reaction to South African claims 'revealed a measure of hesitancy, and at times even of evasion, which must have appeared unworthy of a great nation'.[32] As far as the period to 1948 is concerned, certain principles were consistently applied, and not yet to a point where they had lost their validity. Playing for time was one of them, and patiently seeking a means of side-stepping an intractable problem is inherently neither ignoble nor irrational. Far from it, since it is in human history the way in which most fundamental problems are overcome. Nor did any British spokesman ever say anything publicly to contradict the principle that Britain was anxious not to stand in the way of transfer, or contest that in the long run, pending a better future, it was the inevitable, perhaps ideal, solution. There was nothing particulaly iniquitous in such a view for most of the period: at any rate it was shared by the missionaries of the Paris Evangelical Society in Basutoland and no one questions their independence and integrity.[33] As to the hope that a majority of white South Africans might one day accept Africans as human beings, is hope unworthy of a great nation? And Britain stuck doggedly to her pledges, both to the Africans and to the House of Commons. Unless African goodwill could be obtained, no scheme would ever be laid before the House of Commons, if only because adverse parliamentary criticism would in turn merely confirm African doubts. For this was a question which cut right across party lines. Transfer would be opposed by a considerable section of Liberal and Labour opinion (which was subject to influence from missionaries and others), strongly resenting any arbitrary treatment of Africans. On the other hand, there was still a considerable body of true-blue Tories who were not so sympathetic to the Africans, but disliked the idea of hauling down the Union Jack anywhere, especially where a government might some day seek to establish a republic outside the Commonwealth. It would obviously have been intensely difficult for any British government to carry through a proposal which united both the left wing and the right wing against it.

It has also frequently been charged that so prolonged a postponement of transfer was not in the interests of the Territories themselves. Did Africans suffer as a result of British policy? There are of course causes of economic depression other than neglect. However, undoubtedly development was ignored until the late twenties, because it was feared improvements would only lead to an earlier South African formal demand for take-over. The chiefs had no wish to stimulate Afrikaner covetousness in this way. The only benefit the Africans got in those years from British policy – but it was an immense one and at the time they regarded it as such – was being kept out of the clutches of the Union and so enabled to maintain their self-respect and prized sense of identity under their own chiefs and in accordance with their own cherished customs. Besides this, what material benefits could the Union have given to them as opposed to the white settlers within their countries? Outside the mining sector, South Africa even in the 1930s was a relatively poor country. When Deneys Reitz became minister of agriculture in April 1934 he found it a troublesome post. With the Depression, everything had become rotten; and then there were drought and locusts. 'Tobacco-planters, cattle-breeders and dairy farmers demanded the impossible. It was like a law-suit in hell . . . '[34] Even allowing for a little exaggeration, was this a favourable environment for the promotion of African interests? The fact that African reserves inside the Union had so little spent upon them, and were subject to so many restrictions (such as the cattle embargo in the Transkei) does not suggest that without a change of heart the immediate economic benefits of transfer would have been large. And then the big strides forward which were made in the Territories in the late thirties must not be forgotten. Pim's recommendations on soil erosion and water supply were implemented, and the Territories presented a quite different aspect at the end of the first post-Pim quinquennium. The Dominions Office was always incensed thereafter if anyone said the Territories were stagnating; to them this was rank heresy. If anything held development back the fault did not, they believed, lie with a lack of policy direction by Britain, but with the hampering effect of South Africa's constant pressure for transfer and attempts to influence British policy meanwhile.[35] The Colonial Development and Welfare Act of 1940 converted from loans to free grants sums amounting to £563,000 lent to Swaziland. The same Fund set aside £190,000 to purchase back land for Swazi use. An American expert in 1944 thought Basutoland was coping with the problems of soil conservation better than the Union was.[36] In short, as Professor Hancock noted, the tension over transfer produced creative results: 'It has stimulated the British Administration to formulate and carry through an active policy. It has challenged the South African administration to emulate that policy'. An arid political controversy had begun to transform itself into an experiment in economic statesmanship.[37]

The Territories moreover already enjoyed the benefits of Union without its disadvantages, a fact which South African opinion was quick to point out irritably. Their postal, customs and transport services were all run from the Union; South African banks, insurance companies, building societies and other capital enterprises operated in each of them – though it might be argued this was not an unmixed blessing; Union general law was common to all three and they had the same currency. These were useful benefits, obtained without the price of being caught legally in a segregated society which, as was clearly understood by everyone outside it, was based on dominance and repression designed to isolate the non-European majority while extracting from it the maximum use of its labour.[38]

Although in 1908–10 local African pressures against inclusion in the Union were hardly of central importance to imperial decisions,* they subsequently became so prominent a feature of the problem, that there is a sense in which the Africans saved themselves, acting on the principle of the Sotho chief who said 'You must object all the time so that it will be known that you have been objecting', and not keep quiet until transfer took place.[39] Africans saw to it that their hostility – as much to the general native policy of the Union as to the specific issue of transfer – was seen to grow steadily. Most African men had worked in the Union. Many of their relatives lived there. Thus they knew their own minds well enough. There was not really any significant difference between the peoples of the

* *Pace* Alan Booth; see his article 'Lord Selborne and the British Protectorates [*sic*] 1908–10', *Journal of African History*, x (1969) 133–48.

three Territories in this respect, except that it was widely believed that feeling was most deeprooted and best articulated among the Sotho. For them, the adoption of a separate South African national flag in 1928 had been a critical landmark: they viewed it as a blow to British prestige and as a standing danger to their enclave across the Caledon River which continued to fly only the Union Jack.[40]

The Duke of Devonshire visited South Africa in the middle of 1939 and was thoroughly impressed with the strength and unanimity of the chiefs' views. Tshekedi told him his people would sooner die of thirst than live under the Afrikaners. Devonshire was considerably moved by an old chief who said, 'Our prayer is that our Mother may keep her baby on her back and that she will not drop the blanket for a stranger to pick up'. Sobhuza told him that his people could not see (as he did) the advantages of joining the Union under suitable conditions:

> The Boer was to them a landgrabber, a man with a *sjambok* in his hand and, moreover, many of his people, who were not criminals, had suffered under the pass laws and the 'pick up' of the Johannesburg police and, though quite innocent, found it hard to earn money in the mines without both 'knowing gaol and being robbed by the police'.[41]

Hertzog's government itself was largely to blame for this increasingly more unfavourable African temper. The continuing failure of South African expansion was implicit in the adoption of a new national flag, in the elimination of the old Cape franchise in 1936 and in the proliferating stigma of segregation. These things were widely known among Africans, and the more intelligent chiefs were also fully aware of the trend among Malanites towards a more uncompromising antinative policy. Tshekedi Kgama submitted to the British government a memorandum of 27 foolscap pages in June 1938. Union native policy was the crux of his fear of transfer. He subjected the policy to detailed and devastating analysis. The Dominions Office found his memorandum 'well written and well documented . . . a formidable indictment of Union native policy . . . altogether it is a striking document . . . '.[42] The case against transfer was also fortified by the spread of republican propaganda, and nobody could say that Malan's reunited National Party would not oust Smuts in a post-war election. The chiefs, as a generation before at the time of the Afrikaner rebellion in 1914, were genuinely shocked by Hertzog's passionate advocacy of neutrality in 1939. The Tswana chiefs wanted to move a formal resolution to that effect. Though forbidden to do this, they insisted on at least voicing their disgust: 'and these are the people to whom you talk of handing us over!'

No longer could the isolated example of a minor chief in favour of a transfer be produced. British administrative changes had led to a more satisfactory relationship with chiefs, and the Tswana chiefs in particular appreciated the greater responsibilities which were entrusted to them and which they would not have enjoyed under the Union.[43]

The continual frustration by the Colonial and Dominions Offices of South African informal overtures in the half century after the passing of the Act of Union is a notable tribute to twentieth-century imperial trusteeship, exercised at the expense of imperial political advantage. Britain risked the hostility of whites in South Africa whose loyalty hung in the balance, a loyalty much to be desired before 1948 on grounds of general Commonwealth policy. No comparable advantage could be expected from the goodwill of small African communities enmeshed in the South African structure. Britain's resistance to Union demands was played from a position of steadily decreasing strength. She could so easily have bought the favour of the South African government, which economic and strategic interests seriously required, by relinquishing the High Commission Territories, which of themselves were a drain rather than an asset and in no sense valuable as showpieces of Empire. In so far as the continuing failure of South Africa to achieve a formal extension of her boundaries cannot be explained simply by the folly of the South Africans themselves, it may be ascribed to policies upheld by the British government. Running parallel (though over a shorter period) to this example of trusteeship, was the frustration of the attempts of the Southern and Northern Rhodesian settlers to achieve complete amalgamation.[44]

8 Epilogue: 1948–68

WITH the fall of Smuts from power in 1948 – and great was
the fall thereof – the failure of South Africa's formal expansion
into the High Commission Territories was final in the sense
that no British government thereafter would lift a finger to
further it. In Britain Labour gave way to Conservative in
1951, but it made no difference. Agreement about the transfer
question, declared prime minister Winston Churchill, was
so widespread that there was no point in debating it in parliament.[1] Despite appearances, which were carefully nurtured,
British policy was not simply stagnating on the issue. Continued refusal to transfer the Territories had a more positive
dimension. More than pure procrastination, it was in a sense
congruent with a reassertion of the imperial factor in East and
Central Africa from 1945. In a world becoming increasingly
uncomfortable for Britain, Dr Malan was more of a bogeyman
than Dr Nkrumah.

Paradoxically it was Smuts who seemed to have been stagnating most. Even before his fall from power, his enthusiasm
for an expansion policy showed signs of wilting. The more
obvious objectives – Rhodesia, the South-West, the High Commission Territories – were not abandoned, but the famous expo-
nent of holistic philosophy seemed prepared patiently to abide
the day of their realisation. He was quick to see that the possibilities of informal expansion in the north held out better prospects
of returns, without the recriminations which formal extension of
boundaries might engender; and by the 1960s his Nationalist
opponents would have agreed with him.

The dream of a Greater South Africa however did not die in

1948. But as far as territorial acquisition was concerned, his successors were writing the coda rather than elaborating the theme.

How did matters stand in 1948? Mozambique was unreservedly accepted as a useful neighbour, and all ambitions in that direction were dead. To the north, although Smuts long ago tacitly had to accept the fact that his youthful vision, inherited from Rhodes, of a *single* state from Simonstown to the Sudan was finally shattered,[2] he continued to console himself with the thought that the Rhodesian settlement of 1923 was no more than a setback to his plans. To the end of his life he regarded the ultimate incorporation of Rhodesia as inevitable, but saw no point in hurrying it – Rhodesia would enter the Union in its own good time. During the Second World War Smuts held discussions on a merger, taking as his starting-point the fact that Rhodesian soldiers fought together with the Springboks in the Union Defence Force under his own overall command. Mutual regard was good and South African terms were attractive.[3] Hofmeyr visited the country. Rhodesia was feeling her financial straits and looking for a solution, but once again the question of prestige dragged out and finally vitiated the negotiations, as it is so often apt to do in the affairs of states. When Smuts' government was ousted from office, the project died a natural death as far as South Africa was concerned, and Rhodesia turned its back upon a Union evolving towards a secessionist republic. Or so it seemed then. By its Unilateral Declaration of Independence in 1965 Rhodesia drew closer to South African attitudes to African majorities. Social, business, family and sporting ties had remained strong. Rhodesia took part in the Currie Cup championships. Individual white Rhodesians, of whom the most notable was Colin Bland, played in South African test cricket teams as well, and, it has been observed, 'for cricket and rugby union, Rhodesia and South Africa become one and the same'.[4] Trade seldom follows the flag, but, who knows, there is an outside chance that the flag may follow the ball. In the dark matter of the future of Rhodesia, however, it would be inexcusable if this remark were merely flippant. But is it? Questions of political identification are clearly not irrelevant to the composition of sports teams, at least not in southern Africa.*

Smuts' final exertion in expansion was devoted to South-West Africa rather than the High Commission Territories. This reflected a fairly general view in South Africa that the incorporation of the South-West was an object of far greater importance than the transfer of the Territories. Raising the one precluded raising the other. While the future of the South-West was in the balance, it was not in Smuts' interest to tackle the Territories.

In May 1946 the Windhoek Legislative Assembly unanimously asked for the incorporation of South-West Africa. Six months later, Smuts appeared before the Trusteeship Committee of the newly formed United Nations, and asked for permission to incorporate the country. His case was presented as follows: the South-West was already firmly integrated into the Union in administrative practice; uncertainty about status was retarding the South-West's development; and its inhabitants were overwhelmingly in favour. After long and bitter debate, his request was rejected. South Africa then refused the United Nations' invitations to place the South-West under the new trusteeship system, although Smuts kept the door open for negotiation by continuing formally to adminster the territory as before under the Mandate, sending annual reports to the Trusteeship Committee. This was despite pressure from Malan not to do so.[5]

When Dr D. F. Malan came to power in June 1948 his Nationalist government ceased reporting to the United Nations, maintaining that South Africa was no longer legally bound by the Mandate System created by an organisation (the old League of Nations) now defunct. Whereupon Tshekedi Kgama, who, fearing the implications for Bechuanaland, had kept a close watch on the situation for several years, at once mobilised a campaign against the incorporation of South-West Africa.[6]

---

* Mr A. G. Barlow, an M. P. since before Union, declared in 1954: 'the Rhodesians come from the loins of South Africa. They are only South Africans living north of the Limpopo, and as the days and the years go by we will be joined together'. (HAD. 85/3930, 13 Apr 54.)

In 1949, Dr Malan agreed to have the matter referred to the International Court of Justice for an opinion. This was given in 1950, but it in no way offered a means of settling the dispute. Meanwhile Malan enacted the South-West Africa Affairs Amendment Act in 1949, which provided for representation of its European community in the Union Parliament. To all intents and purposes it became a fifth province of the Union. It henceforth shared the Union's elections (and its referendum on the republic) as well as its economy; it had neither separate flag, nor passports nor representation abroad. And yet it was not subject to taxation by the Union Parliament. Thus it enjoyed representation without taxation, a not unenviable circumstance. Moreover, the 70,000 whites, despite their solid and gratifying support of the National Party, retained a distinct outlook (to say nothing of the German language). And since South Africa's rule was not internationally recognised, a doubt about South-West Africa's status remained.[7] Even after the administration of native affairs there was transferred to the Union minister for native affairs in 1954, it could not be described as fully incorporated, although it certainly was not independent. Unequivocal incorporation was impossible granted the strength of world opinion and South Africa's continuing desire to remain a member of the United Nations. National Party supporters in the South-West in 1954 urged the German-speaking population to look forward to the day when there would be a single republic south of the Limpopo and Kunene rivers, a state in which they would clear Africans off the lands in 'white' areas, when the Group Areas Act had been extended to their territory; they claimed that the Mandate was dead and gone, and that they had become one people with the Union as far as the outer world was concerned. Malan's reply was brusque: all good Nationalists, he said, had known this for a long while.[8] Years later, reacting against such a view, all good internationalists in the world preferred to regard South-West Africa as Namibia.

The question of the High Commission Territories had of course also been exercising Dr Malan and his supporters, who were restive about it. As prime minister in London for the first

time in 1949, he followed the time-honoured ritual of his predecessors, and in a preliminary canter tentatively raised the
question of transfer with Mr Bevin and Mr Noel-Baker and
expressed impatience at British inaction despite numerous
attempts made over a period of forty years by every South
African government. Then in February 1950 the Labour
government's secretary for Commonwealth Relations, Mr P. C.
Gordon Walker, visited the Territories, and in Cape Town on
9 February Malan publicly addressed him much more definitely and with good-humoured frankness. If delay was 'due
to the fact that we are not trusted with the protection and promotion of Native interests . . . we have every reason to feel
wronged and aggrieved' – the Union, he claimed, had never
encroached one inch on African reserves, but added to them at
great cost, and in measures for establishing self-government
and for the general uplifting of the inhabitants of reserves he
confidently invited comparison with any other native administration in southern Africa. But apart from the question of
'grievous mistrust' there was the Commonwealth aspect, a
point expounded perhaps a trifle whimsically: 'It affects our
equal status and place among the other members of the
Commonwealth as well as our self-respect as a nation'. Within
her embrace and even within her borders she had to harbour
territories entirely dependent on her economically and largely
on her also for their defence, but which were governed by
another country. Such a condition would not, he claimed, for
a 'single moment be tolerated in their case, either by Canada
or Australia or New Zealand, not to speak of India or Pakistan
or Ceylon or Britain herself'.[9]

Malan in fact as prime minister did extremely little to
advance matters. This was almost certainly because as a result
of his initial informal soundings he saw clearly that it was futile
to proceed as his predecessors had done: not one step of progress
could be made that way: all South Africa's trouble had been in
vain, and it looked as if she might well be in the same position in
a hundred years' time. Always the British politicians shrugged
their shoulders, said the moment was inopportune and
sheltered behind the shield of 'parliamentry outcry'. Yet what

alternative procedure could be devised? At one time it began to look as if Malan would try to make capital out of deadlock and seek to quarrel about the question of transfer as part of his propaganda in favour of a republican secession from the Commonwealth. In September 1951 he warned the new Conservative government in Britain that he would if necessary make the question an issue at the South African election of 1953. He did not in fact do so, despite the reaffirmation by prime minister Churchill on 22 November 1951 of the time-honoured pledges about consulting parliament and the inhabitants. In reply to a Question by Mr Driberg, Churchill made it perfectly clear that Britain would not initiate any change in so well-established a situation.[10] The only immediate outcome of the 1951 interchange was an agreement to publish a selection of correspondence down to 1939.* This publication horrified Africans in the Territories. They were shocked to discover how intense discussions had been, and their protests showed a fresh upsurge.

At various times Malan repeated his vague threat to treat the inhabitants of the Territories as foreigners. After the Central African Federation was set up in 1953 he castigated the inconsistency of Britain's pushing millions of protesting Africans into it while simultaneously maintaining in effect that Africans further south could veto a transfer.[11] From the British angle there was of course no inconsistency at all, since the main (though largely unspoken) motive behind the Federation was anti-South African, and its object the counterbalancing of Afrikanerdom. If Rhodesia would not perform her longed-planned function of a counterpoise within the Union she might be made to do so from without. Thus British policies on the Federation and the High Commission Territories were but different aspects of the same historic objective: the containment of the Afrikaners. The creation of the Central African Federation nevertheless heightened African fears in the Terri-

* The main difference between these two official publications (London and Pretoria 1952) is that the South African one included expressions of public opinion made in 1934–35, especially those of Tshekedi Kgama, and the British one (Cmd. 8707) did not.

tories. The Basutoland National Council, noting that six million Africans had been put under European settler rule, wondered what was to stop Britain from transferring a mere 600,000 Sotho.[12]

The Basutoland National Council was meanwhile waging battle against British-born South African officials in various branches of Basutoland's administration. Resolutions of protest had been passed in 1949 and a petition presented. An uproar was caused in 1956 with the appointment of a South African-born resident commissioner, Mr A. G. T. Chaplin, who, despite dire warnings of non-co-operation from the chiefs, nevertheless served out his term. The paramount chieftainess petitioned the secretary of state for his removal, but the petition was not accepted. A reply in March 1958 reminded the Sotho that 'good relations and co-operation in practical matters between Basuto and the Union of South Africa are important to the welfare and progress of the Basuto Nation'. Some councillors grumbled that South Africa herself did not intend to live in good relations, and anyway all South African-born officials regarded them as animals and not as human beings: 'we all the time find ourselves humiliated'. However, despite evidence of unofficial seepage of colour-bar attitudes into Basutoland, the reply was accepted by the Council by a majority of 51 to 4.[13] There seems no reason to suppose that British approval of the appointment of these officials had a sinister intention: there was nothing new about it, and the continuation of such appointments was, perhaps, a sop to South Africa, part of the familiar search for a safe conciliatory gesture to the Union.

Towards the end of his premiership, which had not been notable for action over the Territories, Malan notified the British government early in 1954 that he was going to introduce a motion in the House of Assembly recommending a resumption of negotiations at the stage reached in 1939. In the long and unpleasant debate on the motion in April, Malan spoke of Britain's clinging to the Territories as though her life depended upon it; British administration was he said an 'intolerable idea . . . in conflict with South Africa's national right . . . [and] self-respect'. Britain, he observed, had eliminated her

jurisdiction over 700 million people. She had no longer any say
in the affairs of India or Ceylon for example, but in the case of
South Africa was unwilling to do the same. He had little to say
about the positive reasons for wanting transfer. Illegal immigrants entered the Union via Swaziland from Lourenço
Marques. An extra harbour with a railway through Swaziland
was blocked by British presence: 'that is the shortest route and it
will be able to serve the greatest development'. Basutoland
was 'a hotbed of Communism' and they could do nothing about
it. The motion was passed by 75 votes to 31.

On 13 April 1954, Winston Churchill advanced slightly but
significantly beyond the standard reply to a parliamentary
Question (this time put by Mr Sorensen). While reiterating the
well-known public pledges, he hoped that the Union would not
'needlessly press an issue on which we could not fall in with
their views without failing in our trust'; 'there could be no
question of Her Majesty's Government agreeing at the present
time to the transfer'. His statement gave great satisfaction to
the House of Commons, even though he declined to be drawn
into the 'legal subtleties' and 'deep constitutional implications'
involved in the question of whether consultation meant consent.
He thought it probable that things would be settled in a more
friendly manner than would appear on the surface at that
moment. For the first time ever on this issue, a British government was thanked and congratulated by its parliamentary opponents on its reply to questioning.[14]

The statement was not received so favourably outside
parliament. Tshekedi once more published a restrained pamphlet, in which he described this latest pronouncement as still
in effect the policy of procrastination. He conceded however
that it provided another breathing space, which he hoped
would be used to consider how consultation with the Africans
should be made and to prepare them for the responsible task of
stating their case. He added: 'We are confused, and at times
frustrated, when we try to puzzle out what policy the British
government intends to pursue'. This observation was taken up
by Margery Perham in her foreword to Tshekedi's pamphlet.
'Dense mist', she wrote, obscured the future of the Territories.

She saw no need any longer for Britain to remain static in an entrenched position, and thought it was high time the government faced the issue with more courage and resolution, and with less caution.[15]

Mr J. S. Strydom, 'the Lion of the North' (i.e. northern Transvaal), succeeded Malan as prime minister in December 1954. The ritual Afrikaner stance naturally required him to assume Malan's moral obligation to secure transfer. While in London in July 1956 for the Commonwealth Prime Ministers' Conference, Strydom found opportunity to remind the British government of South Africa's desires. The British government, once again through the medium of an answer to a Question in parliament (put to the prime minister, Anthony Eden, by Mr Fenner Brockway), re-stated its pledges, as well as its refusal to be drawn as to the meaning of 'consultation'.[16] (As Africans had been consulted about, but did not consent to, the Central African Federation, this was hardly surprising.)

By this stage, even *The Round Table* had for several years opposed transfer, accepting Miss Perham's estimate that it would have serious repercussions throughout British Africa and in the international sphere also. With deep regret, it realised that 'the new Krugerism' was not to be trusted.[17]

Added substance was given to this feeling by the report of the Union's Tomlinson Commission, which, rather casually in its text and explicitly in its maps, included all the High Commission Territories among its proposed 'consolidated Bantu Areas', or Bantustans as they became called. This 'Commission for the Socio-Economic Development of the Bantu Areas within the Union of South Africa' was appointed in 1951 under the chairmanship of Professor F. R. Tomlinson. It was asked to make an exhaustive enquiry and to propose a comprehensive 'scheme of rehabilitation'. This took the Commission four years, to the autumn of 1954. The Commission collected oral evidence from 322 Europeans and 106 Africans. It received 250 memoranda. Its original research data occupied 69 volumes. It cost the Union taxpayer £56,750. Its report ran to 3,755 pages in typescript, together with 598 tables and an atlas of more than 60 large-scale maps. To print 10,000 copies of this report in one language alone would have cost more than £22,000. Only a summary therefore was published, while a number of roneoed copies of the original report were made available for reference in the Union.[18] The *Summary of the Report* itself is not exactly a small production. There are 211 pages of double-column text on large quarto paper, with all the maps appended, although reduced to fit the quarto format.[19]

A report of such magnitude, embodying much fundamental research, could be publicised as an achievement in which Afrikaners could take pride, as one of the most comprehensive and thorough reports on 'development' yet to appear in the world.[20] At least they could claim to have produced some sort of general blueprint for the Africans' future (and one applicable to the High Commission Territories), while Britain had not. Britain had ceased to contemplate transfer, but, although busy with economic and railway planning, she had not yet begun to think of independence.

Although the Tomlinson Commission did not apparently make any detailed study of the High Commission Territories, or assess their potentialities, it regarded them as 'artificially excluded' from the Union in 1910, and it claimed to follow the land legislators of 1913 and 1936 in relating them to the larger Bantu heartlands, or 'geographical cultural-historical complexes', which bound together the Africans within the Union and in its vicinity. It stated that the High Commission Territories should be incorporated (*sic*) as soon as possible. It proposed a goal of 'separate development' in which the Africans would develop in independent homelands '*alongside of* not in *opposition to*' Europeans. This separation would have to be effected 'within the framework of the consolidated Bantu Areas of the Union, those of South-West Africa and the High Commission Territories'. Calculating that the future maximum extent of the Bantu Areas in the Union would be fixed at 13·7 per cent, this proportion would be completely altered if the High Commission Territories ('which are essentially Bantu Areas') were included. 'Greater South Africa' (the Commisonsis' term)

would then cover some 766,000 square miles (excluding the
South-West), of which (allowing for European settlement in
Swaziland), 45 per cent would belong to the Africans. Thus on
this basis, seven 'national homes' could be systematically
expanded, with the least possible transgression of ethnic bonds,
'around historico-logical centres' or 'power stations', namely:
Tswanaland, Vendaland, Pediland, Swaziland, Zululand,
Xhosaland (i.e. the Transkei) and Sotholand. In each, the
Africans themselves would exercise administrative functions to
an ever-increasing extent. In this way, the problem of the existing scattered 110 African areas, together with the 154 'black
spots', which formed no foundation for the growth of an
independent community, could be overcome. The professed
aim was to turn this programme into reality by a broad frontal
attack on human and social problems as well as economic ones.
The entire pattern envisaged was one directed towards 'the
complete development of the human being and the soil'. The
scheme would derive its driving power from the prospects of
political expression which it supposedly offered the Africans.
The first ten years of such a large-scale and sustained programme of development could be expected to cost £104 million.
But, the Commission hinted darkly, unless this challenge was
taken up, 'as an act of faith', South Africa must face the
consequences of integration of black and white in a common
society.[21]

On the surface, the proposals of the Commission had a
potentially exciting plausibility, and gave a much-needed
positive aspect to apartheid. South African Liberals however,
such as that remarkable person Margaret Ballinger, had no
difficulty in penetrating the façade and offering some devastating criticisms of the horrors implicit in it.[22]

Dr H. F. Verwoerd (at the time minister for native affairs)
initially denied that the inclusion of the High Commission
Territories was a basic requirement for the success of this new
policy, though he claimed that it would be in the interests of
the inhabitants of the Territories themselves to join in. There
was room for a sceptical reception of these remarks.

Some South Africans who rejected the (in practice) dismal

science of Bantustans turned to the 'felicific calculus' of federation. The search for panaceas went on, and in trying to think out a middle way between universal suffrage and Bantustan ghettoes, between violence and stagnation, the idea of an enlarged Southern African Federation was inevitably canvassed once more.[23] Some, like Heaton Nicholls, continued to expound in effect Smuts' well-worn 'African Confederacy of South and Central States'.[24]*

Quite how far the Tomlinson Report might have provoked the British government to re-formulate its policy for the High Commission Territories is difficult to say. In 1955 a very short report on the Territories' economic development and social services was issued as Command Paper 9580. But it was not until after the Suez Crisis of 1956 had been lived down and perhaps learned from, and after disillusionment with the Central African Federation had begun to grip Whitehall that, as part of a wider process of decolonisation, Britain from 1959 began belatedly to grasp for a more tangible positive political assertion of her remaining responsibilities in southern Africa.[25] Since apartheid, the National Party and even Bantustans had obviously come to stay, Britain openly committed herself to bringing the Territories into the orbit of her general colonial policy and guiding them towards self-government.[26]

A natural term in discussions came with the departure of South Africa from the Commonwealth in 1961. The transfer issue fizzled out with a whimper; the bang had been in 1948. The British deemed the South Africa Act legally to have lapsed, and clearly the 'meaning and intention' contemplated by the Schedule – transfer of administration from one of the British

* 'The Federal Panacea' is an extremely tenacious delusion. Men continue to propound it even when they are aware of its enormous difficulties. Leo Marquard (vice-president of the South African Liberal Party), for example, is fully aware that federations must not contain imbalance between the component units, and so he would subdivide the Republic into eleven units and then add the three former High Commission Territories and Namibia. This hardly seems more realistic than Heaton Nicholls's earlier conception of a confederation embracing South Africa, the (former) Central African Federation, Belgian Congo, French Congo, Tanganyika, Kenya, Angola and Mozambique, some of whom would be accepted as 'black states', while the federation as a whole would be in opposition to 'United Black Africa'.

sovereign's Dominions to another – no longer held good in
theory when South Africa became a foreign country, and it was
in practice impossible to put it into operation. Dr Verwoerd,
being a practical man, abandoned the idea of acquisition as a
hopeless objective, and later candidly dismissed the possibility
of incorporation as incompatible with the British policy of
granting independence to African territories, and no longer an
active part of his policy.

The alternative would have been forcible seizure, which
would have made nonsense of the Bantustan policy, since,
as Tomlinson had stressed, African co-operation was a prerequisite for its success.[27] But this did not mean that South Africa
ceased to have any interest in maintaining some form of looser
control over the Territories. Indeed, to all the familiar reasons
were added several fresh ones. Future economic growth might
depend increasingly on water supplies from Basutoland and the
Portuguese territories. A particularly pertinent point had its
origin, as Lord Hailey put it, 'in the measure to which the
Nationalist Party has accustomed itself to look to the expansion
of the criminal law as a bulwark for defence of its political
philosophy':[28] South Africa resented the refuge which the
Territories might afford to politically suspect persons. Outposts
of Pan-African hostility to the Republic and potential bases for
subversive operations would be 'a source of instability throughout South Africa'. Again, Mr F. C. Erasmus (minister of
defence) was concerned at the gaps they caused in the advance
system of radar control which protected the Rand.[29] Bechuanaland was an especial source of anxiety.

In a statement on 3 September 1963 prime minister Verwoerd
requested that the three High Commission Territories should
be given the opportunity to develop as Bantustans under
Republican guidance rather than under British protection. In
seeking thus to become their guardian and their guide, he said
South Africa had no ambitions over the Territories but if she
were to become their protector instead of Britain she could lead
them more effectively and more quickly to independence and
economic prosperity. The reaction to this statement was
strongly hostile, so much so that he subsequently denied any

suggestion of annexation or take-over. It seems he completely
failed to understand the extent of the world-wide opposition
which the apartheid policy evoked. The Nationalists were
always ready to criticise British administration while resenting
any outside criticism of their own governance of Africans. In
thus challenging Britain, Verwoerd showed however a perhaps surprising flexibility and pragmatism. From 1955 South
African policy has emphasised the necessity for co-existence
with the new states of Africa and this speech was only temporarily out of line. Formal expansion having failed, and an era of
decolonisation having begun all over Africa, the 'good neighbour' policy of informally extending commercial relations to
the north once more came into favour. With proprietary
and prudential interest it euphemistically emphasised a 'co-
prosperity' area of all Africa south of the Congo (except,
possibly, a recalcitrant Zambia) within which South Africa
would have the key role of an undoubtedly senior partner,
determined to assert its power. Mr B. J. Vorster declared in
February 1967 that 'South Africa was on the threshold of
moving out into the world'; thus taking up Pirow's programme of thirty years before.[30]*

In 1962 British stewardship of the three High Commission
Territories was adversely criticised by the United Nations
General Assembly, despite the fact that she had held on through
multiple troubles that might well have caused another trustee
to throw in the towel – through South African protest, through
'medicine murders' in Basutoland, through the perpetual if
hesitant Swazi attempt to play off Boer and Briton and preserve
its own *imperium in imperio*; and through the wretched contro-
versies in Bechuanaland which surrounded Tshekedi's regency
and the marriage of his nephew Seretse Kgama. Moreover,
from 1955 Britain increased the amount of her economic aid,
and from 1959 tried to sort out the intractable problem of
suitable constitutions for these unusual Territories.[31] Time and
time again senior British civil servants in the Territories were
heard to say: 'We have no other interest here but to seek an
honourable discharge'.[32]

* See above, p. 39.

This was eventually sought through the grants of independence to Botswana and Lesotho in 1966 and to Swaziland in 1968. During the 1960s the Union's 'colonies' became transformed into the Republic's 'neighbours'.[33] Within the decade, then, all parties to the High Commission Territories' problem achieved, perhaps not without surprise to themselves, some of their historic objectives. For South Africa, a Republic; for Britain, disengagement without too much dishonour; for Lesotho, Botswana and Swaziland, a chance (however slender) to live their own lives in their own way.

References

Abbreviations

CAB. Cabinet papers, minutes and conclusions ⎫ Public
CO.   Colonial Office   ⎬ Record (London)
DO.   Dominions Office   ⎭ Office
HAD. Union of South Africa, House of Assembly Debates (Cape Town)
HGP. Viscount [Herbert] Gladstone Papers (British Museum, Add. Mss.)
LGA. Lesotho Government Archives (Maseru)
LHP. Lewis Harcourt Papers (Stanton Harcourt, Oxford)
PD/C. British Parliamentary Debates, 5th Series, House of Commons
PD/L. British Parliamentary Debates, 5th Series, House of Lords
SBP. Sydney Buxton Papers (Newtimber Place, Hassocks, Sussex)

Also: H/C   high commissioner
        S/S   secretary of state
        memo memorandum
        tel. telegram

References inside brackets give alternative locations for the same document. The originals are normally cited first, but where Confidential Print provides a *significantly more convenient* location (e.g. for a group of related documents otherwise scattered), this is given preference.

All books published in the U.K. except where otherwise indicated.

NOTES TO CHAPTER 1 (pp. 1–22)

1. J. C. Smuts, *War-Time Speeches* (1917) 88.
2. HGP. 46007/174, Botha to Gladstone 7 Nov 13.
3. J. H. Hofmeyr, *South Africa* (1931) 211.
4. PD/L. 2/767, Crewe, 27 Jul 09.
5. Harcourt, memo on 'Suggested re-organisation of the Colonial Office', Apr 1911 (LHP.). Northern Rhodesia was only remotely expected to enter the Union, and only contingently upon the entry of Southern Rhodesia.
6. *The Round Table*, XLII (1951) 93; HAD. 85/3784–5, 12 Apr 54; C. Arden-Clarke, *Optima* (Johannesburg, 1958) VIII, 163, 'The problem of the High Commission Territories'.
7. W. M. Macmillan, *Bantu, Boer and Briton: the Making of the South African Nativ Problem* (rev. ed. 1963) 73; J. D. Omer-Cooper, *The Zulu Aftermath* (1966) 176; J. A. I. Agar-Hamilton, 'The South African Protectorates' (*Journal of the African Society*, XXIX (1929) 12–26); *The Oxford History of South Africa* (2 vols: 1969, 1971, ed. M. Wilson & L. Thompson), I, 391–446, ch. by Thompson.

8. *Southern Africa in Transition* (ed. J. A. Davis & J. K. Baker 1966) ch. by D. V. Cowen, 93.

9. H. Kuper, *An African Aristocracy; Rank among the Swazi* (1961) 19–31; C. C. Watts, *Dawn in Swaziland* (1922) 14–42; D. Reitz, *No Outspan* (1943) 88–9.

10. CO. 879/25/330, memo by H/C Sir Hercules Robinson 9 Oct 86; CAB. 37/32/44, memo by S/S Ripon 23 Nov 92; see also CO. 879/42/485, memo by G. Bower 1 Feb 95.

11. N. G. Garson, *The Swaziland Question and a Road to the Sea 1887–95* (Archives Year Book for South African History, [Cape Town] 1957, II/2, 350).

12. CAB. 37/36/15, 'The Swazi Crisis', memo by Ripon 18 May 94; CO. 879/41/476, Ripon to H/C Sir H. B. Loch 19 Oct 94, & 42/483, memo by Ripon 25 Sept 94; see also R. E. Robinson & J. Gallagher, *Africa and the Victorians* (1961) 414.

13. Garson, 391, 407, 418.

14. R. Hyam, *Elgin and Churchill at the Colonial Office 1905–08* (1968) 263–4, 284.

15. *Ibid.* 381–7; CO. 417/546/24698; CO. 879/81/729/21, Milner to S/S 18 Jan 04.

16. CO. 417/712/16242, 'The Swazi Case' (1924) by Sobhuza II. CO. 417/456/ 13884 gives CO. opinion.

17. Omer-Cooper, 99–113; V. Ellenberger, *A Century of Mission Work in Basutoland 1833–1933* (Morija, 1938) 169; W. P. Morrell, *British Colonial Policy in the Mid-Victorian Age* (1969) 152–71.

18. J. Widdicombe, *Fourteen Years in Basutoland* [1891] 134.

19. C. W. de Kiewiet, *Imperial Factor in South Africa [1872–85]* (1937) 304; CO. 879/20/264, Derby 14 Jun 83.

20. D. M. Schreuder, *Gladstone and Kruger: Liberal Government and 'Home Rule' 1880–85* (1969) 342–3.

21. A. Sillery, *The Bechuanaland Protectorate* (1952) 120–1; H. M. Hole, *Passing of the Black Kings* (1932) 147: J. Mockford, *Khama, King of the Bamangwato* (1931) 180.

22. Schreuder, 393.

23. Robinson & Gallagher, 202–09; E. T. Stokes & R. Brown (eds.), *The Zambesian Past: studies in Central African history* (1966) 262, in ch. by Stokes.

24. Schreuder, 257–9; *Oxford History of South Africa*, II, 267–78, in ch. by Thompson.

25. Robinson & Gallagher, ch. vii.

26. W. R. Louis, *Great Britain and Germany's Lost Colonies 1914–19* (1967) 18.

27. CO. 291/123/15508; Elgin Papers (Broomhall, Fife), S/S Elgin to Botha 4 May 07 (draft).

28. Elgin Papers, Elgin to H/C Selborne 5 Jul 07 (copy).

29. B. Williams (ed.), *The Selborne Memorandum* (1925) 14, 140–5.

30. CO. 417/458/19782 & 463/16130.

31. Asquith Papers (Bodleian Library), 46, Asquith to S/S Crewe [n.d./1908] (copy).

32. CO. 417/459/29929, 21 Jul 08.

33. CO. 417/482/16895 & 516/7384, (the quotation is from a minute by H. C. M. Lambert, 16 Mar 12.)

34. Asquith Papers 9/95.

35. W. K. Hancock & J. van der Poel (eds.), *Selections from the Smuts Papers* (1966), II, 307.

36. L. M. Thompson, *The Unification of South Africa 1902–10* (1960) 269–79 for discussion in the Convention.

37. *Selections from the Smuts Papers*, II, 442.

38. CO. 417/458/19782, CO. memo 25 Jan 09; CAB. 37/94/110, Crewe to Selborne 1 & 12 Aug 08.

39. PD/C. 9/1649, statement by Col. Seely 19 Aug 09; PD/L. 2/870, Crewe

3 Aug 09; see also E. Baring, 'Problem of the High Commission Territories' (*International Affairs*, XXVIII (1952) 185.

40. W. K. Hancock, *Survey of British Commonwealth Affairs*, II 'Problems of Economic Policy 1918–39', Pt 2 (1942) 131.

41. R. Hyam, 'African interests and the South Africa Act 1908–10', *Historical Journal*, XIII (1970) 85–105.

42. J. W. Mackail & G. Wyndham, *Life and Letters of George Wyndham*, II, [n.d.] 15.

43. C. Headlam (ed.), *The Milner Papers: South Africa 1897–1905* (1931–3), I, 144 & II, 35.

44. CO. 417/434/16276; Hyam *Elgin and Churchill*, 287–8.

45. CO. 417/466/23023.

46. R. Jenkins, *Asquith* (1964) 192–3.

47. F. V. Engelenburg, *General Louis Botha* (1969) 185.

48. N. G. Garson, *Louis Botha or John X. Merriman: the choice of South Africa's first prime minister* (London University Institute of Commonwealth Studies Paper 12, 1969).

49. Miss Perham in M. Perham and L. Curtis, *The Protectorates of South Africa: the question of their transfer to the Union* (1935) 117.

50. Earl Buxton, *General Botha* (1924) 79, 331; T. R. H. Davenport, *The Afrikaner Bond* (Cape Town, 1966) 251.

NOTES TO CHAPTER 2 (pp. 23–46)

1. J. C. Smuts, *Africa and some world problems* [1929 speeches] (1930) 37–69.

2. Smuts, address on East Africa, Mar 1918 (*Geographical Journal* vol. 51, 129–49).

3. Hofmeyr, *South Africa* chs. x & xiv.

4. *Selections from the Smuts Papers*, IV, 19–20: letter from G. C. Olivier, 18 Nov 18.

5. Elgin Papers, W. S. Churchill to Elgin 16 Oct 06.

6. Louis, *Great Britain & Germany's Lost Colonies*, 33.

7. HGP. 46008/57.

8. W. R. Louis & P. Gifford (eds.), *Britain and Germany in Africa* (Yale, 1967) ch. by G. Smith, 276.

9. Engelenburg, *General Louis Botha*, 215, 291.

10. *Selections from the Smuts Papers*, III, 198.

11. *Britain and Germany in Africa*, ch. by M. W. Swanson, 634.

12. D. Reitz, *Trekking On* (1933) 67.

13. SBP. *or* LHP.: H/C Buxton to S/S Harcourt 24 Sep & 2 Dec 14; reply 17 Jan 15.

14. Harcourt to Buxton 27 Mar & 17 May 15.

15. Buxton to Harcourt 28 Apr & 15 May 15.

16. SBP, Buxton to S/S Bonar Law 11 Aug 15.

17. *Selections from the Smuts Papers*, III, 310, 374–5.

18. SBP, Bonar Law to Buxton 9 Nov. 15.

19. SBP, Buxton to S/S W. H. Long 1 Feb 17. Buxton did not see how 'national self-determination' could be applied to the 'mainly European' South-West (W. R. Louis, 'The South West Africa origins of the "Sacred Trust" 1914–19', *African Affairs*, 66 (1963) 26).

20. Louis, *Great Britain & Germany's Lost Colonies*, 73–4, 83–4, 107.

21. SBP, note by Buxton 10 Aug 15.

22. SBP, to S/S Milner 10 Jul 19.

23. J. Meintjes, *General Louis Botha* (1970) 272.

24. Ruth First, *South West Africa* (1963) 106–09.

25. Hofmeyr, 188.
26. *Selections from the Smuts Papers*, III, 284 (Botha to Smuts 25 May 15), 541, 609 (Botha to Smuts 26 Feb 18)
27. Louis, 7, 108, 159.
28. Engelenburg, 325.
29. Reitz, *No Outspan*, 64; G. Heaton Nicholls, *South Africa in my time* (1961) 146–7.
30. CO. 537/1208 (i.e. 33605/1921, Secret), Mozambique Convention.
31. E. A. Walker, *A history of Southern Africa* (3rd ed. 1957), 615.
32. W. K. Hancock, *Smuts*, II, *The fields of force 1919–50* (1968) 223.
33. F. S. Crafford, *Jan Smuts: a biography* (2nd ed. 1946), 118.
34. J. C. Smuts, *Greater South Africa; plans for a better world: speeches* (Johannesburg 1940), published in England simply as *Plans for a better world: speeches* (1942) 243–54.
35. L. E. Neame, *General Hertzog* (1930) 269–70.
36. Walker, 593–4, 615.
37. Hancock, *Smuts*, II, 218.
38. Crafford, 241.
39. Neame, 270. The 'Black Manifesto' charges were still being recalled in 1940 (by N. J. van der Merwe): see M. Roberts & A. E. G. Trollip, *The South African Opposition 1939–45* (1947) 41.
40. Smuts, *Africa & some world problems*, 37–69; Crafford, 225.
41. Hofmeyr, 263.
42. C. M. van den Heever, *General J. B. M. Hertzog* (Johannesburg 1946), 169, 276.
43. Hancock, *Survey of British Commonwealth Affairs*, II (2) 91.
44. O. Pirow, 'How far is the Union interested in the continent of Africa?' *Journal of the Royal African Society*, CXLIV (1937) 317–20.
45. CO. 417/513/28347.
46. James Bryce Papers (Bodleian Library), Merriman to Bryce 26 Dec 15, 17 Dec 16, 23 Mar & 2 Oct 17, 14 May & 28 Sep 18, 22 Dec 20.
47. Bryce Papers, J. G. Kotzé to Bryce 20 Sep 19; *Selections from the Smuts Papers*, III, 410 Smuts to Merriman 27 Oct 16.
48. Buxton, *General Botha*, 34, 177, 279–81; SBP, Buxton to S/S 1 Jun 15.
49. SBP. 26 Apr 20
50. CO. 537/1203 (i.e. 6957/1921, Secret) S/S to Smuts, tel. 11 Feb 21.
51. DO. 9/3/D. 11043, H/C to S/S 1 Oct 26.
52. DO. 35/393/224, Clark to E. J. Harding (DO.) 25 May 35.
53. van den Heever, 206–7
54. M. Wilson & L. M. Thompson (eds.), *The Oxford History of South Africa*, II *1870–1966* (1971), ch. by D. Hobart Houghton, 31.
55. Cmd. 4714, *Summary of the proceedings of the Imperial Economic Conference at Ottawa 1932* (H.M.S.O.) 14–15.
56. Hofmeyr, 221.
57. DO. 117/120 (i.e. D. 11424/1928 Secret), B. E. H. Clifford to DO. 17 Oct 28, & 149 (i.e. D. 6538/1929) Clifford to E. J. Harding 15 Apr 29; Bede Clifford *Proconsul: being incidents in the life of . . .* (1964) 159.
58. Thompson, *Unification of South Africa*, 278–9.

NOTES TO CHAPTER 3 (pp. 47–71)

1. J. P. R. Wallis, *One Man's Hand: the story of Sir Charles Coghlan and the liberation of Southern Rhodesia* (1950) 93, 102, 107, 118, 155; L. H. Gann, *A history of Southern*

Rhodesia: early days to 1934 (1965) 231–50; C. Palley, *The Constitutional History and Law of Southern Rhodesia 1888–1965* (1966), ch. 10, 'Constitutional changes from 1899–1923'; J. D. Fage, *The Achievement of Self-Government in Southern Rhodesia 1898–1923* (unpublished Cambridge University Ph.D. thesis, 1949).

3. CO. 417/499/34759, H/C to S/S 9 Oct 11; HGP. 46002/251–2.
4. HGP. 46007/172–5, Botha to H/C Gladstone 7 Nov 13.
5. HGP. 45999/142–3, Harcourt to Gladstone 17 May 13.
6. HGP. 46000/212, Harcourt to Gladstone 20 Aug 13; LHP. 2, J. Anderson (CO.) 21 May 13.
7. CO. 417/511/17710, minute by H. C. M. Lambert (CO.) 18 Jun 12, & 524/24038, 18 Jul 13.
8. CO. 417/526/41619, Gladstone to S/S 13 Nov 13.
9. CO. 417/616/7749, minutes by Milner 22 Apr 19, & 15145. Lambert (17 Feb 19) A.
10. SBP, Milner to Buxton 8 Apr 19.
11. SBP, Buxton to Milner 10 May 19.
12. SBP, 26 Apr 20.
13. CO. 417/637/24803, draft memo by Lambert, & 33095.
14. CO. 417/620/45008, Buxton to S/S 13 Jul 19.
15. *Ibid.* minute 6 Aug 19.
16. CO. 417/637/24803.
17. CO. 417/622/64964; Wallis 159.
18. CO. 417/637/23894 & 24803.
19. CO. 417/638/33095.
20. CO. 879/120/41929, H/C to S/S 6 Aug 20; CO. 417/657/4054.
21. SBP, S/S Churchill to Buxton 26 Feb 21.
22. SBP, Buxton to Milner 30 Apr 21 (copy).
23. PD/C. 144/2385–7, 21 Jul 21.
24. CO. 417/660/24526, 29337.
25. SBP, Buxton to Smuts 17 Apr 21 (copy).
26. CO. 537/1183 (i.e. 24860/1921 Secret), Smuts to Churchill 11 May 21, reply 19 May, minute by Lambert 12 May; SBP. Lambert to Buxton 3 Apr 21. The Rhodesian election in April 1920 led Milner to promise responsible government not later than 31 Oct 24.
27. CO. 537/1184 (i.e. 50699/1921 Secret).
28. SBP, Smuts to Buxton 22 Mar 21.
29. CO. 537/1182, Churchill to H/C 26 Apr 21; SBP, Buxton to Smuts 17 Apr 21.
30. CO. 417/661/31825 & 662/58428.
31. CO. 417/664/52736.
32. CAB. 23/27/28.
33. Wallis, 184–93.
34. CO. 417/679/29571, H. J. Stanley to J. Masterton-Smith (permanent under-secretary, CO. 1921–4) 19 May 22.
35. Hancock, *Smuts*, II, 154.
36. SBP, W. H. Long to Buxton 14 Apr 17.
37. T. Wilson (ed.), *The political diaries of C. P. Scott 1911–28* (1970) 306.
38. Hancock, II, 151–4.
39. *Ibid.*, Smuts to M. C. Gillett 31 Jul 22.
40. CO. 417/681/44403, 52199.
41. CO. 417/682/53041.
42. CO. 417/682/53041.
43. L. H. Gann & M. Gelfand, *Huggins of Rhodesia* (1964) 60.

44. CO. 417/663/50518, *The Star* (Johannesburg) 6 Sep 21 & 682/59531, Stanley
    to Masterton-Smith 7 Nov 22. The triangle of forces – Britain, the settlers
    and the Company – and the reasons for the 'Unconsummated Union' are
    admirably dissected by M. L. Chanock, *British Policy in Central Africa 1908–26*
    (unpublished Cambridge University Ph.D. thesis, 1968). See also M. A. G.
    Davies, *Incorporation in Union of South Africa or Self-Government?: Southern
    Rhodesia's Choice 1922* (University of South Africa, Communication C.58,
    Pretoria, 1965) 36–56.
45. Wallis, 180–9.
46. CO. 417/682/59531.
47. Wallis, 186.
48. Stanley, *loc cit.*
49. Wallis, 180.
50. PD/L. 54/1020–5.
51. R. E. Robinson, *The Trust in British Central African Policy 1889–1939* (unpub-
    lished Cambridge University Ph.D. thesis 1950).
52. CO. 417/680/40540; DO. 116/5/4.

NOTES TO CHAPTER 4 (pp. 72–100)

1. CO. 417/459/29921; Elgin Papers, Selborne to Elgin 24 May 07.
2. CO. 417/594/5833 & 608/7737.
3. HAD. 23/2757 (du Plessis, 25 Apr 34) & see also HAD. 27/5926, Mr Grobler
   on soil erosion, 11 Jun 36; DO. 35/1172/Y.701/17 & Y.708/7.
4. HAD. 56/4000–01, 21 Mar 46.
5. L. Marquard, *The peoples and policies of South Africa* (2nd ed., Cape Town,
   1960) 230.
6. HAD. 27/5924 *ff.*, 11 Jun 36; see also HAD. 85/3804–23, 12 Apr 54, speech
   by Dr T. E. Dönges.
7. CO. 417/459/29921, Selborne to Crewe 27 Jul 08.
8. DO. 35/393/207, 224; J. E. Spence, *Lesotho: the politics of independence* (1968)
   24–5; HAD. 85/3960–1, 13 Apr 54.
9. DO. 35/901/Y.6/58, H/C Clark to E. G. Machtig (DO.) 24 Jul 37; DO.
   35/900/Y.6/17 & 901/Y.6/86.
10. Lord Hailey, *The Republic of South Africa and the High Commission Territories*
    (1963) 51.
11. L. Marquard, *A Federation of Southern Africa* (1971) 42.
12. DO. 35/1172/Y.706, minute by H. M. Tait 29 Nov 43 (Tait was in touch with
    the High Commission Territories from 1912 when he entered the CO. until
    1949 when he retired from the Commonwealth Relations Office.)
13. For example: HAD. 48/3359, 3407, 3490, 17 Mar 44 (Smuts and the minister
    for mines), HAD. 56/3982, 21 Mar 46 (Malan).
14. Reitz, *No Outspan*, 229.
15. *Oxford History of South Africa*, II, 477, ch. by J. E. Spence.
16. CO. 417/482/16895, Kgama's Petition.
17. LGA.: S. 3/20/1/2 & 3 (1908, 1909, 1910).
18. CO. 417/546/7029.
19. CO. 417/566/52148, meeting of chiefs with resident commissioner Mr. D. Honey
    26 Aug 15; see also 526/41583 & 529/40557.
20. CO. 417/625/40002, Petition 19 Apr 19.
21. LGA.: S.3/20/1/11, 12, 14 (1919–22), 48 (1955) & 50 (1958); see also Arden-
    Clarke, *Optima*, VIII, 170.

22. CO. 417/624/47175, Petitions of 12 May 19.
23. CO. 417/624/58631.
24. CO. 417/502/15689, Botha to H/C 21 Apr 11; see also 13342.
25. HGP. 45997/144, Gladstone to Harcourt 12 Apr 11; 45999/39-42, 16 Nov 12.
26. CO. 417/502/13342, minute by Harcourt 7 Jun 11.
27. *Selections from the Smuts Papers*, III, 37; for Harcourt's firm character see R. Furse, *Aucuparius: recollections of a recruiting officer* (1962) 30.
28. HGP, 45999/39-42.
29. CO. 417/529/6255.
30. CO. 417/476/23097 & 511/16179; LHP. 2, minutes by H. W. Just & J. Anderson on Gladstone to Harcourt 12, 19 & 30 Mar 13.
31. LHP. 2, minutes by Just & Anderson on Gladstone to Harcourt 12 Mar & 10 Jun 13; CO. 417/523/13330 (minute by Lambert 24 Apr 13) & 524/28556 & 528/4471.
32. CO. 417/523/13330, S/S to H/C 2 May 13 (DO. 116/1/6-7).
33. HGP. 46000/210, Harcourt to Gladstone 20 Aug 13.
34. CO. 417/524/28556; HGP. 45997/186-9 & 46118/187.
35. HGP. 45999/47, Gladstone to Harcourt 23 Nov 12.
36. HGP. 45999/191-2, draft memo 30 May 13.
37. CO. 417/525/37150, S/S to H/C 24 Nov 13.
38. CO. 417/526/41572.
39. HGP. 45999/183 & 46006/162 & 46007/27.
40. Buxton, *General Botha*, 215; *Mildred Buxton: a memoir based on her letters* (ed. M. Cropper & W. Barnes [1966]) 70-8.
41. SBP, Buxton to Selborne 3 Jan 25; LHP, Harcourt to Buxton, tel. 21 May 15.
42. CO. 417/634/47514, Botha to Milner 2 Jul 19.
43. CO. 417/625/43018, H/C to S/S tel. 21 Jul 19 & S/S to H/C, tel. 21 Aug 19.
44. *Ibid.* 53446, H/C to S/S tel. 13 Sep 19, minute by Lambert 23 Sep.
45. SBP, H. J. Stanley to Buxton 14 Aug 19.
46. SBP, note by Buxton on talks with Smuts 4 & 12 Sept 19.
47. *Ibid.* 12 Sep.
48. CO. 417/648/47159, H/C to S/S 1 Sep 20, memo by Buxton 24 Aug 20.
49. *Ibid.* Smuts to Buxton 24 Aug 20.
50. CO. 417/666/19519.
51. CO. 417/685/52705.
52. CO. 417/594/6436, report on visit to Swaziland, Sep 1917; A. C. G. Best, *The Swaziland Railway* (East Lansing, 1966) ch. iv, 54-86 & map of railway proposals 1902-24 (p. 58).
53. CO. 417/684/4887, Smuts to H/C 5 Jan 22 & 9120.
54. CO. 417/685/52079, H/C to S/S tel. 18 Oct 22.
55. CO. 417/685/56311, Smuts to H/C, tel. 24 Oct 22.
56. T. J. D. Fair, G. Murdoch & H. M. Jones, *Development in Swaziland* (Johannesburg 1969) 28.
57. CO. 417/684/30892 & 685/49651.
58. CO. 417/697/4551, statement by S/S, 31 Jan 23.
59. *Ibid.* 16786, Honey to H/C 6 Mar 23.
60. CO. 417/697/53707.
61. CO. 417/712/5813.
62. CO. 417/708/36977 & 43587.
63. DO. 35/902/Y.6/155, H/C Clark to H. F. Batterbee (DO.) 4 Feb 38; DO. 35/1172/Y.708/7 (1943).

64. DO. 35/1172/Y.701/1/2, H/C Harlech to S/S 8 Jun 43. Harlech thought Miss Perham too sympathetic to Sobhuza and hoped that she would be told so, perhaps by Lord Hailey (*ibid.* & Y.708/7).

NOTES TO CHAPTER 5 (pp. 101–24)

1. Buxton, *General Botha*, 124–5; *Mildred Buxton: a memoir*, 124.
2. *Sydney Olivier: letters & selected writings* (ed. M. Olivier, 1948) 164.
3. CO. 417/488/19648.
4. Reitz, *No Outspan*, 145.
5. Reitz, 135.
6. M. E. Sara, *The Rt. Hon. the Earl of Athlone* (1941) 176, 188–206; 217; Heaton Nicholls, *South Africa in my time*, 173–91.
7. CO. 417/707/3310 & 714/22776.
8. O. Pirow, *James Barry Munnik Hertzog* (Cape Town, n.d.) 203–4.
9. DO. 35/4/6093; I. Edwards, *Protectorates or Native Reserves?* (Africa Bureau pamphlet [1956]) is very helpful on the constitutional aspects of the Territories' problem.
10. CO. 417/709/54256, H/C Athlone to S/S 29 Oct 24 (DO. 116/1/25 and Cmd. 8707 – *Basutoland, the Bechuanaland Protectorate and Swaziland: history of discussions with the Union of South Africa 1909–39. Correspondence, extracts from parliamentary reports and other documents*, H.M.S.O. 1952 [Accounts and Papers, vol. xxiii] p. 15).
11. CO. 417/709/55124, Athlone to S/S 7 Nov 24 (DO. 116/1/33–4).
12. CO. 417/709/58648, S/S Amery to H/C 17 Dec 24.
13. CO. 417/705/60080, H/C to S/S 22 Dec 24.
14. CO. 417/709/55124, to S/S 7 Nov 24.
15. *Ibid.* 54256 (DO. 116/1/31).
16. CO. 417/713/5351, H/C to S/S tel. 3 Feb 25 (DO. 116/1/44).
17. CO. 417/705/60080, S/S to H/C tel. 19 Jan 25.
18. CO. 417/713/8828, H/C to S/S 6 Feb 25 & 714/39794.
19. CO. 417/709/55124, minute by Tait 1 Dec 24; see also 713/17129.
20. CO. 417 /709/58648, minute 17 Dec 24.
21. CO. 417/714/39794, S/S to H/C 4 Dec 25.
22. *Ibid.*
23. DO. 9/1/D. 3716, H/C to S/S 18 Mar 26.
24. DO. 9/1/D. 8682 (DO. 116/1/100) 4 Aug 26.
25. DO. 9/2/D. 8885, Hertzog to H/C 6 Apr 26 (DO. 116/1/105 & Cmd. 8707/18–20).
26. DO. 116/1/109–13 & Cmd. 8707/29–36, H/C to Hertzog 14 Jul 26.
27. DO. 116/1/114–15, H/C Athlone to Hertzog 20 Jul 26.
28. DO. 9/2/D. 9120, H/C to S/S 30 Jul 26.
29. *Ibid.* Hertzog to H/C 13 Aug 26 (DO. 116/1/119) & 14 Sep, DO. 9/3/D.10476.
30. DO. 9/3/D. 11020, H/C to S/S 1 Oct 26 & D. 11543, H/C to S/S 15 Oct 26.
31. DO. 9/1/D. 3716, minute 14 Apr 26.
32. DO. 9/3/D. 10742, Clifford to C. T. Davis (DO.) 21 Sept 26.
33. DO. 9/3/D. 11543, S/S to H/C 18 Feb 27 & DO. 9/4/D. 1829, minute by Davis 9 Feb 26.
34. DO. 9/6/D. 5772.
35. DO. 9/1/D. 3717 & DO. 9/4/D. 2508, letters from Clifford to Davis 18 & 26 Mar 26.
36. DO. 9/8/D. 8984, S/S Amery to Davis 15 Aug 27 (from Salisbury, Rhodesia).

37. L. S. Amery, *My Political Life*, II, *1914–29* (1953) 415.
38. Cmd. 8707/36–8, note by Amery on his discussion with Hertzog 6 Sep 27.
39. DO. 9/8/D.10967, C. G. Whiskard (DO.), notes on Amery's meeting with Hertzog 6 Sep 27.
40. DO. 9/8/D. 10918, Amery to prime minister S. Baldwin 24 Sep 27 (copy, extract) & DO. 35/901/Y.6/51, quoting Amery to H/C 16 Nov 26.
41. DO. 9/8/D. 10918.
42. DO. 9/8/D. 10867, memo 5 Oct 27.
43. D. 10967.
44. DO. 9/7/D. 10867 & 10443.
45. DO. 9/7/D. 10443, Amery to Billy [W. A. Edgecumbe, his private secretary] 24 Sep 27 (from Cape Town).
46. DO. 9/8/D. 10918 & D. 10867, Amery to Davis 24 Sep 27 & to prime minister 4 Oct. 27
47. DO. 9/12/D. 3818, minute by Amery 18 Apr 28 & Churchill to Amery 3 May 28; see also D. 1925.
48. T. Jones, *Whitehall Diary* (ed. K. Middlemas), II, *1926–30* (1969) 171, 180.
49. DO. 9/10/D. 6068 & 12/D. 506, Amery to Sir A. Bailey 24 Sep 27.
50. DO. 9/12/D. 10967, minute of 6 Nov 28.
51. DO. 9/6/D. 7528 & 14/D. 1827, note by Amery 11 Feb 29.
52. DO. 117/120 (i.e. 11244/1928 Secret), minute by Tait 24 Jan 29.
53. DO. 9/15/D. 11562 S/S to H/C tel. 28 Sep 29.
54. DO. 116/5/10991/19, DO. memo Jul 1932, p. 3.
55. Hofmeyr, *South Africa*, 196.
56. J. A. I. Agar-Hamilton 'The South African Protectorates' (*Journal of the African Society*, XXIX (1929) 26.

NOTES TO CHAPTER 6 (pp. 125–62)

1. CO. 417/714/27178.
2. Pim Report on *Financial and Economic situation of Swaziland* (1932) Cmd. 4114, p. 76.
3. DO. 116/5/204–08, H/C Stanley to S/S, 13 & 27 Jul 32, reports on visit to Swaziland.
4. DO. 35/392/45, 57, 75 & D.O. 35/900/Y.6/19.
5. DO. 35/392/45, H/C 9 Nov 32.
6. Reitz, *No Outspan*, 84–5; Furse, *Aucuparius: recollections of a recruiting officer*, 135.
7. J. H. Thomas, cab. memo 10 Nov 33 DO. 35/392/75; comment by Amery in *My Political Life*, III, 113.
8. DO. 35/392/27, 30, 40.
9. Reitz, 236.
10. DO. 35/392/48, H/C Stanley to Harding 16 May 33.
11. DO. 35/392/62 & DO. 35/393/192, statement to deputation headed by Selborne 15 Nov 34.
12. DO. 35/393/287, note by R. R. Sedgwick (DO.) 4 Jan 36.
13. DO. 35/393/207, minute by Tait 24 Jan 35.
14. DO. 35/904/Y. 6/356 & 358.
15. DO. 35/393/192.
16. DO. 35/393/207, Stanley to Whiskard 4 Jan 35.
17. DO. 35/393/192, speech 6 Nov 34.
18. DO. 35/393/202, Harding to W. Clark 19 Dec 34.

19. DO. 35/392/19, 9 Dec 31.
20. DO. 9/8/D. 9500.
21. DO. 9/3/D. 11545.
22. DO. 9/7/10430, Amery to H.U. Moffat 24 Sep 27.
23. DO. 117/120 (i.e. D. 11424/1929 Secret), minute by Amery 3 Feb 29; Hancock *Survey of British Commonwealth Affairs*, II(2) 139–40.
24. DO. 117/149 (i.e. D. 6358/1929 Secret), Clifford to Harding 15 Apr 29.
25. DO. 116/5/10991/75, Hertzog to S/S Thomas 1 Oct 33 (see also Cmd. 8707/44).
26. DO. 116/5/10991/40, Hertzog to S/S 30 Nov 32 (Cmd. 8707/38).
27. DO. 116/5/10991/62, Smuts to S/S 28 Jul 33 (Cmd. 8707/39–41).
28. Hailey, *The Republic of South Africa and the High Commission Territories*, 64–65.
29. CAB. 23/77/62, meeting of 15 Nov 33 & 79/31, of 31 Jul 34.
30. DO. 35/392/75, S/S to Hertzog 27 Nov 33 (Cmd. 8707/45).
31. DO. 35/392/108, Hertzog to S/S 25 Apr 34 (DO. 116/6/1–2 & Cmd. 8707/46–9).
32. Hailey, 68–9; see also A. Pim in *International Affairs*, XIII (1934) 674.
33. Cmd. 8707/49–53.
34. DO. 35/393/108, 145.
35. DO. 35/392/41; *Round Table*, XLII (1951) 93.
36. SBP, J. Harris to Buxton 27 May 34.
37. The Pim Reports: Cmd. 4114 (H.M.S.O. 1932) *Financial and economic situation of Swaziland;* 4368 (1933) *Financial and economic position of the Bechuanaland Protectorate;* and 4907 (1935) *Financial and economic position of Basutoland*. In the Union brief reports on the Territories were made by M. L. (née Hodgson) & W. G. Ballinger, *Indirect Rule in Southern Africa (No. 1): Basutoland* (Lovedale 1931) and *Britain in Southern Africa (No. 2): The Bechuanaland Protectorate* (Lovedale 1932).
38. PD/L. 88/1122–30 and 90/466–94.
39. *The Round Table*, XXIV (1934) no. 96, 785–802, 'The Protectorates and the Union'; XXV (1935) no. 98, 318–23, 'The South African Protectorates'; also XXV, 746–53, 'Reform in the Protectorates'.
40. M. Perham, *Colonial Sequence*, I, *1930–49* (1967), 119–30; for DO. opinion see DO. 35/392/62, Harding to H/C Clark 17 May 35.
41. DO. 35/393/234.
42. Walker, *A history of Southern Africa*, 661.
43. M. Benson, *Tshekedi Khama* (1960) 252 and ch. 9 generally. See also: *Dictionary of National Biography*, *1951–60* (1971), 995–7.
44. For this and other evidence of press reaction see *Negotiations regarding the transfer to the Union of South Africa of the government of Basutoland, the Bechuanaland Protectorate and Swaziland* (Government Printer Pretoria, 1952, 11–13)
45. DO. 116/6/23–33, H/C to S/S 2, 11 & 30 Mar 35 (DO. 35/393/213, 220, 227); for Hertzog's statement, 25 Apr 34: HAD. 23/2759–62.
46. DO. 116/6/35–6 (Cmd. 8707/57–8).
47. Cmd. 8707/53; printed separately as Cmd. 4948 (H.M.S.O. 1935).
48. Cmd. 8707/58.
49. Perham, I, 138 & *Round Table*, XXV (1935) 746.
50. DO. 35/394/302, Clark to Harding 27 Feb 36; Heaton Nicholls, *South Africa in my time*, 327–30.
51. DO. 116/6/43–4, H/C to S/S 1 Jul & 25 Oct 35 (DO. 35/393/262, 276).
52. DO. 116/6/49–50, H/C to Harding 15 Nov 35 (DO. 35/398/281).
53. DO. 116/6/57, reply by S/S 2 Dec 35 (DO. 35/393/278).
54. HAD. 26/2297, 22 Apr 36.
55. HAD. 27/5918–41, 11 Jun 36.

56. DO. 35/394/383, minute by Harding 29 Sep 36.
57. DO. 116/6/91, 15 Jun 36 (DO. 35/393/337).
58. On the whole episode see DO. 116/6/75–104, especially telegrams from H/C 16 & 17 Jun 36 (DO. 35/393/345, 348) & S/S to H/C tel. 29 Jun 36 (*ibid*. 350).
59. Cmd. 8707/80–5, Hertzog 29 Dec 37.
60. Cmd. 8707/59 & 63, H/C's *aide mémoire* to South African minister for native affairs 1 Jul 35; J. E. Spence, 'British policy towards the High Commission Territories', *Journal of Modern African Studies*, II (2) (1964) 240; see also I. Edwards, *Protectorates or Native Reserves?* (Africa Bureau pamphlet [1956] 14.
61. *Negotiations regarding the transfer* . . . (Pretoria, 1952) 12.
62. DO. 35/903/Y.6/215; DO. 35/393/215, H/C Clark to S/S 11 Mar 35.
63. G. Blaxland, *J. H. Thomas: a life for unity* (1964) 262–85.
64. DO. 35/900/Y.6/17, note by S/S 3 Jun 37.
65. *Ibid.*
66. DO. 116/6/66–8 (DO. 35/393/302).
67. Hailey, 81–2; DO. 116 /7/20 (DO. 35/901/Y.6/92).
68. DO. 35/903/Y.6/324, cab. memo by MacDonald 23 Jul 37 (CP(37)197); see also Y.6/254, DO. meeting, 23 Jun 38; Hancock, *Survey*, II (2) 133.
69. DO. 35/900/Y.6/19, 7 Jun 37.
70. PD/L. 105/425–66.
71. DO. 116/7/1 & 2 (DO. 35/900/Y.6/18 & 21).
72. CAB. 23/88/29, 7 Jul 37 & 89/32, 28 Jul 37.
73. PD/C. 326/737–42, 1050–53, 1996–7, 2890.
74. *Ibid.* 3359–3436, 27 Jul 37.
75. DO. 116/7/25, S/S to H/C tel. 3 Dec 27 (DO. 35/901/Y.6/97).
76. DO. 116/7/7/50 & 81.
77. Cmd. 8707/100*ff* gives the text.
78. DO. 35/903/Y.6/324 for memo 11 Feb 38; CAB. 23/93/14.
79. Cmd. 8707/89.
80. *Round Table*, XXVIII (1938) 629.
81. DO. 116/7/59.
82. LGA.: S. 3/20/1/30, 19–21 Nov 38.
83. DO. 116/7/3 & 12, S/S to H/C 2 & 30 Jul 37.
84. DO. 116/7/37, H/C to S/S tel. 31 Dec 37 (DO. 35/901/Y.6/128).
85. DO. 116/7/40, H/C to S/S tel. 3 Feb 38.
86. DO. 35/903/Y.6/311 & 317, memo by MacDonald 14 Jan 39.
87. DO. 35/903/Y. 6/351, 26 Aug 39.

NOTES TO CHAPTER 7 (pp. 163–83)

1. DO. 35/903/Y.6/349, minute by S/S Eden 2 Oct 39; DO. 116/7/90, H/C to S/S 19 Sep 39.
2. Benson, *Tshekedi Khama*, 145.
3. DO. 35/903/Y.6/349 & 352, tel. H/C to S/S 12 Oct 39 (DO. 116/7/91).
4. DO. 35/902/Y.6/238 & 904/Y.6/356; DO. 116/7/36, 45 & 50.
5. DO. 116/7/96, notes by Clark, Jan 1940.
6. DO. 116/7/92 (12 Oct 39).
7. DO. 116/7/93 (12 Oct 39).
8. DO. 116/7/94; DO. 35/903/Y.6/352 including memo by Eden 19 Oct 39; CAB. 65/1/54, 20 Oct 39.
9. Reitz, *No Outspan*, 244, 249.

10. DO. 35/904/Y.6/356 & 358; CAB. 65/1/54.
11. DO. 35/903/Y.6/354, H/C to S/S 20 Oct 39 & 904/Y.6/356.
12. DO. 35/903/Y.6/352, cab. memo by Eden (W. P. [G.] [39] 43) 19 Oct 39; Perham & Curtis, *The Protectorates of South Africa*, ch. by Perham 'Curtis Reviewed' 96.
13. DO. 35/904/Y.8/59 & DO. 35/905/Y. 8/64, minutes Jun & Aug 1942.
14. C. R. Rey, *The Future of the British High Commission Territories in South Africa* (South Africa House pamphlet, London 1961), 6; PD/C. 326/3410.
15. DO. 35/904/Y.6/361 (DO. 116/7/96) Jan. 1940.
16. DO. 35/905/Y.8/69, minute by Machtig 27 Nov 42; DO. 35/1172/Y.706, minutes by Tait 29 Nov & C. W. Dixon 30 Nov 43.
17. DO. 35/1172 /Y.706, H/C Harlech to S/S, 1 Nov 43 & 17 Jan 44.
18. Minutes by Tait: DO. 35/905/Y. 8/64, 23 Jun 42 & DO. 35/1172/Y.706, 29 Nov 43 & 28 Sep 45.
19. DO.35/1172/Y.706, S/S Cranborne to Harlech 13 Dec 43.
20. *Ibid.* Y.706, Harlech to Machtig 2 Apr 44 and related minutes.
21. HAD. 56/3491, 20 Mar 46.
22. HAD. 56/3417.
23. DO. 35/1172/Y.706/10.
24. PD/C. 400/750-1.
25. HAD. 55/831.
26. HAD. 56/4026; DO. 35/1172/Y.706/7 & 10.
27. DO. 35/1172/Y. 706/11.
28. *Ibid.* Y.706/1, 4 & 5.
29. PD/C. 418/298-9.
30. DO. 35/1172/Y. 706/7, H/C Sir E. Baring to S/S 2 Apr 45.
31. DO. 35/1172/Y. 706/10, minute by Coulborn 5 Mar 46.
32. Hailey, *The Republic of South Africa and the High Commission Territories*, 98, 104.
33. Ellenberger, *A century of mission work in Basutoland*, 284-5.
34. Reitz, 186.
35. DO. 35/905/Y.8/64 & 68.
36. DO. 35/1172/Y.701/1/10, H/C Baring's report 21 Dec 44.
37. Hancock, *Survey of British Commonwealth Affairs*, II (2) 134, 145.
38. DO. 35/392/19, 41 & 904/Y.6/356.
39. LGA: S.3/20/1/46 (1953).
40. Ellenberger, 373.
41. DO. 35/903/Y.6/349, 352: minutes by Devonshire 29 Sep & 16 Oct 39.
42. DO. 35/903/Y.6/278, 283.
43. DO. 116/7/96, notes by Clark, Jan 1940.
44. R. E. Robinson, *The Trust in British Central African Policy* (Cambridge Ph.D. thesis 1950).

NOTES TO CHAPTER 8 (pp. 184-98)

1. PD/C. 526/968, 13 Apr 54.
2. *The Oxford History of South Africa*, II, ch. by J. E. Spence, 492.
3. J. C. Smuts, jnr, *Jan Christian Smuts* (1952), 266-7, 344.
4. C. Fortune, *M.C.C. in South Africa 1964-65* (1965) 13 (I owe this reference to Mr G. W. Martin).
5. Walker, *A history of Southern Africa*, 759; Marquard, *The peoples and policies of South Africa*, 220-25.

6. Benson, *Tshekedi Khama*, ch. 13.

7. Marquard, *A Federation of Southern Africa*, 46–48, 58.

8. Walker, 910.

9. N. Mansergh (ed.), *Documents and speeches on British Commonwealth Affairs 1931–52* (1953), II, 928–9. British missionary concern is indicated in R. P. Orchard, *The High Commission Territories* [1952] pamphlet, legal in R. C. Fitzgerald, 'South Africa and the High Commission Territories' (*World Affairs*, n.s. IV, 1950, 306–20).

10. HAD. 85/3776 (12 Apr 54) & 3964–5 (13 Apr); PD/C. 494/559–60.

11. Walker, 853.

12. LGA.: S. 3/20/1/46 (1953).

13. LGA.: S. 3/20/1/50 (1958).

14. HAD. 85/3769–3971: 12, 13 & 14 Apr 54 – for Malan's opening and closing speeches see 3769–84, 3959–71; PD/C. 526/966–8.

15. Tshekedi Khama, *Bechuanaland and South Africa* (African Bureau pamphlet, 1955, with a foreword by M. Perham).

16. PD/C. 556/195.

17. *Round Table*, XL (1950) 121–6, XLI (1951) 224–5, XLII (1951) 90–4 & (1952) 141–51; Perham, *Colonial Sequence*, I, 327.

18. HAD. 87/715–16, 8 Feb 55 & 99/4000.

19. *Summary of the Report of the Commission for the Socio-Economic development of the Bantu Areas within the Union of South Africa* (Government Printer Pretoria, U.G. 61/1955).

20. HAD. 91/5360.

21. See *Summary of the Report* . . . especially 105, 180–3, 207–11.

22. HAD. 91/5366–76, 14 May 56.

23. Marquard, *A Federation of Southern Africa*. Note particularly 34, 70, 135–9.

24. G. Heaton Nicholls, *South Africa in my time*, 478–81. The author was Smuts' wartime choice for the post of the Union's high commissioner in London.

25. Benson, 285; Cmd. 9580 (H.M.S.O. 1955), 19 pp.

26. *Southern Africa in transition* (ed. Davis & Baker), ch. by D. V. Cowen, 91.

27. *Summary of the Report* . . . 210.

28. Hailey, *The Republic of South Africa and the High Commission Territories*, 107–8; Marquard, *A Federation*, 48, 59.

29. E. S. Munger, *Bechuanaland: Pan-African Outpost or Bantu Homeland?* (1965), *passim*; P. Giniewski, *Bantustans: a trek towards the future* (Cape Town, 1961) 180; Marquard, *A Federation*, 55.

30. Spence, *Lesotho: Politics of independence*, 75–8; *Round Table*, LIV (1963) 105–6; see also D. Austin, 'White Power?' (*Journal of Commonwealth Political Studies*, VI (1968) 95–106) for some interesting speculations.

31. J. Halpern, *South Africa's Hostages: Basutoland, Bechuanaland and Swaziland* (1965) gives a detailed account of all these matters.

32. Cowen in *Southern Africa in transition*, 91.

33. Marquard, *The peoples and policies of South Africa*: in the 1960 edition, ch. 10 on South-West Africa and the High Commission Territories is headed 'The Union's "Colonies" '; in the 1969 edition it has been renamed 'The Republic's Neighbours'.

Bibliographical Note on Sources (1908–48)

THE basic sources are the South African High Commission original correspondence, and the Colonial and Dominions Offices papers preserved in the Public Record Office in London: CO. 417/422–716 (1906–25), of which I have used the 110 most relevant volumes of files, together with DO. 9/1–15 (1926–29), DO. 35/392–4 (1932–36), DO. 35/900–905 (1937–42) and DO. 35/1172/Y.706 (1943–46); Supplementary Secret correspondence is to be found in CO. 537/1182, 1183, 1184, 1203, 1204 and 1208, and DO.117/120, 147 and 172. Dominions Office Confidential Print provides a useful check: see DO.116/1, and 3–7 (these six volumes in turn formed the basis for the digest of material published as Cmd. 8707, *Basutoland, the Bechuanaland Protectorate and Swaziland: a history of discussions with the Union of South Africa, 1909–39*, H.M.S.O. 1952). References will be found in CAB. 23 (Public Record Office) to about half a dozen relevant British Cabinet discussions, one on Southern Rhodesia in 1921 and the rest on the High Commission Territories between 1933 and 1939 (see also CAB. 65 for 1939). From 1932 onwards the British *Parliamentary Debates* and the Union of South Africa *House of Assembly Debates* provide a record of parliamentary Questions, statements and discussions of the problem. As to unofficial and private sources, the published *Selections from the Smuts Papers* (four volumes to 1919, ed. W. K. Hancock and J. van der Poel) are occasionally illuminating. There are three important interlocking unpublished collections of the private papers of key office-holders: high commissioners Viscount Gladstone (British Museum Add. Mss) and Earl Buxton (at Newtimber Place, Hassocks) and secretary of state Lewis Harcourt (at Stanton Harcourt); and I gratefully acknowledge the permission and co-operation of Mrs John Clay and Viscount Harcourt in respect of my use of the latter two. I have also drawn marginally on the contents of the Asquith Papers (Bodleian Library), the Bryce–Merriman Correspondence (Bryce Papers, Bodleian Library) and the 9th Earl of Elgin Papers (at Broomhall, Fife).

In comparison with the materials available in Britain, the sources in southern Africa are much less accessible. I spent a fruitful time in the pleasant atmosphere of the Lesotho Government Archives at Maseru, in particular reading the *Proceedings of the Basutoland National Council 1908–58* (S.3/20/1/1–50). It was not possible to consult the government archives of Swaziland at the time when I was in Mbabane (December 1969). The Republic of South Africa continues to operate a 50-year rule, and in any case, as far as this study is concerned, most of the relevant official material found its way to England in one form or another.

Index